THE INSTITUTE OF ECONOMICS
INVESTIGATIONS IN INTERNATIONAL
COMMERCIAL POLICIES

THE TARIFF ON WOOL

THE MACMILLAN COMPANY
NEW YORK · BOSTON · CHICAGO · DALLAS
ATLANTA · SAN FRANCISCO

MACMILLAN & CO., Limited
LONDON · BOMBAY · CALCUTTA
MELBOURNE

THE MACMILLAN CO. OF CANADA, Ltd.
TORONTO

THE INSTITUTE OF ECONOMICS

The Carnegie Corporation of New York in establishing the Institute of Economics declared that "in committing to the Trustees the administration of the endowment of the Institute of Economics, over which the Corporation will have no control whatsoever, it has in mind a single purpose—namely, that the Institute shall be conducted with the sole object of ascertaining the facts about current economic problems and of interpreting these facts for the people of the United States in the most simple and understandable form. The Institute shall be administered by its Trustees without regard to the special interests of any group in the body politic, whether political, social or economic." In order that the Council and Staff of the Institute may enjoy the freedom which is conceded as essential to scientific progress, the Trustees of the Institute have adopted the following resolution: "The primary function of the trustees is not to express their views upon the scientific investigations conducted by the Institute, but only to make it possible for such scientific work to be done under the most favorable auspices."

SHEEP ON SUMMER RANGE IN GALLATIN NATIONAL FOREST, MONTANA

Photo by K. D. Swan

THE TARIFF ON WOOL

BY

MARK A. SMITH

WITH THE AID OF THE COUNCIL AND STAFF
OF THE INSTITUTE OF ECONOMICS

New York

THE MACMILLAN COMPANY

1926

11589

Printed in the United States of America by
J. J. LITTLE AND IVES COMPANY, NEW YORK

AUTHOR'S ACKNOWLEDGMENTS

The author desires to make grateful acknowledgment of the assistance given him by Director Harold G. Moulton, Dr. Thomas Walker Page, and Dr. Edwin G. Nourse, of the Institute of Economics. The members of the Tariff Division of the Institute, Mr. Philip G. Wright, Mr. Lynn R. Edminster, and Miss Evelina P. Kean, read the manuscript and offered much constructive criticism. Mr. Sheldon B. Akers aided greatly in the collection of statistical material.

Professor Arthur H. Cole of Harvard University and Dr. Louis G. Connor, of Washington, D. C., both gave generously of their time to consider the entire study in detail and made suggestions of the greatest value. Dr. Connor prepared the statistical tables on pages 140 and 167. Mr. W. A. Graham Clark, Chief of the Textile Division of the U. S. Tariff Commission, and Mr. G. M. Youngman, Special Expert of the Commission, read portions of the text, and gave the author the benefit of their intimate acquaintance with the wool trade and industry. It is needless to add that none of these helpful critics should be held responsible for any of the conclusions.

Washington, D. C.,   MARK A. SMITH.
    November, 1925.

DIRECTOR'S PREFACE

To the people of the United States international commercial policies constitute, at the present time, a subject of unusual interest. Within the last decade an entirely new set of economic relationships between this country and the rest of the world has been created. Certain old questions have reappeared in new aspects and with changed implications. The tariff, as the most important expression of trade policy of this country, deserves renewed attention and a fresh examination. Consequently, the Institute of Economics has undertaken an analysis of the entire American system of customs duties.

Before attempting any broad generalizations regarding the wisdom of American tariff policy as a whole, the Institute will first present a series of special investigations dealing with the relation of the tariff to particular lines of production in the United States. The tariff is not a single problem to be solved by the application of any one general formula. With reference to each particular industry it affords a variety of concrete questions of public policy. There has been an abundance of abstract theorizing in the United States about the principles of protection and free trade and there has been no dearth of statistical data submitted by interested parties. But unfortunately, there has been very little effort toward dispassionate investigation of the concrete effects of tariff legislation from the point of view of the public welfare.

The studies of special commodities, together with more general discussions which are now in preparation and which will be based largely on the evidence adduced in the commodity studies, are designed to meet this need. The purpose of each commodity study is primarily to clarify the reader's mind with respect to the actual relation of the tariff to the industry in question. Pertinent facts are brought out relating to the character, importance, and geographical distribution of the industry. Answers are made to the questions: What has been its tariff history? What is the present situation with respect to the burdens and benefits of the tariff? What would be the probable effects upon the industry and upon the public of a change in the rate? Finally, in the light of all the evidence available a conclusion is arrived at as to what ought to be done.

In all matters except the conclusion the study need make no reference to general tariff policy. Each specific case can be studied simply on its own merits. In some cases even the conclusion may be arrived at without giving consideration to general principles of tariff policy. The facts may point so clearly to the futility or to the ill effects of a duty that its removal appears desirable from any point of view. In other cases, however, some balancing of conflicting national policies cannot be escaped. The study will show that the duty has certain definite effects. It may bring a pecuniary benefit to some interests and a pecuniary burden to others. It may be indicative of a trend towards national self-sufficiency and insularity on the one hand or towards increasing international interdependence on the other. It may promote a diversity of industries but at considerable economic cost.

Under such conditions individual appraisal of these several ends must influence the conclusion. For example, suppose the study shows a pecuniary gain to one class purchased at the expense of a greater pecuniary loss to another. A person may be convinced that good national policy calls for the assistance of the benefited class even at that cost. Suppose that the study shows that the duty will greatly expand an important domestic industry, but at the cost of diverting labor and capital from channels in which they might be more effectively employed. To some minds such expansion may seem well worth the cost. Suppose that the study shows that the removal of the duty will cause considerable disturbance to an existing business adjustment and considerable loss to the laborers and investors concerned. Some persons will nevertheless feel that the ultimate public good justifies the incidental disturbance and loss. The conclusion in each study represents the opinion of the Institute arrived at by men of quite different points of view after thorough discussion both of the evidence adduced in the specific case and of the ends sought. It therefore should carry some weight. It cannot be expected, however, that all readers will accept this opinion. But if the study has put before the reader all the pertinent facts in the case and the reasons on which the findings are based, and has thereby so clarified the whole situation in his mind as to enable him to form an intelligent judgment of his own, it will have amply justified itself.

The present study of the duties on wool is one of several dealing with agricultural commodities. This particular aspect of the tariff is not only economically important, but it also serves to illustrate the diversity of considerations that must be weighed before appraising our general customs policy. The first agricultural commodity study was "Sugar in Relation to the Tariff." Other investigations will deal with the tariff in relation to cattle raising, cotton growing, wheat farming, and the production of animal and vegetable oils. These separate studies are to be followed by a volume devoted to a general discussion of the effect of the tariff on American agriculture. The reader will find the conclusions of the present study on pages 287-94.

H. G. MOULTON,
Washington, D. C., *Director*.
January, 1926.

CONTENTS

CHAPTER III

PART II. HISTORY OF THE WOOL DUTIES IN THE UNITED STATES

CHAPTER IV

CHAPTER V

CHAPTER VI

PART III. THE PRESENT PROBLEM

CHAPTER VII

CHAPTER VIII

CHAPTER IX

CHAPTER X

CHAPTER XI

CHAPTER XII

APPENDICES

APPENDIX A.

APPENDIX B.

APPENDIX C.

APPENDIX D.

INTRODUCTION

Wool has been the subject of more protracted and bitter controversy than any other commodity which has been given tariff protection in the United States. There are several reasons why it has been the "bloody angle" of the tariff battles. It is an article of common use, the raw material for one of the largest manufacturing industries. Also, it has been for many years imported in large quantities because the domestic supply has not been great enough for our needs. These facts in themselves might suffice to make it important, but in addition the wool schedule of the tariff has occupied a conspicuous place ever since the Civil War as a typical instance of adjustment between the duty on a raw material and that on the products made from it. It has furnished, therefore, many a bone of contention between wool growers and manufacturers as well as between both groups of producers and the consuming public. It deserves additional attention at present because changes have recently been taking place in the methods of sheep husbandry and in the conditions under which it operates. Moreover, the increase in the rate of duty on wool in the Tariff Act of 1922 makes it an especially noteworthy subject.

I. THE PRESENT SITUATION

The most striking fact in connection with the history of the sheep industry in the United States is that the production of wool has not increased in the past forty years. During the twenty years following the Civil War, the sheep industry grew rapidly in the Rocky Mountain and Inter-Mountain states, while the decline in the Eastern and Middle Western states was correspondingly fast. The domestic wool clip amounted to about 300,000,000 pounds in 1883, and the yearly output since that time has averaged about the same, although it has fallen considerably below that total since 1920. The ratio of imports to domestic production, on the other hand, has greatly increased. Before the European war, the imports of competing wool were about one-half as large as domestic production, while in six of the ten years since 1914 they have been greater than the home-grown output.

Australia has enormously augmented its output in the period during which the American production has been stationary. Argentina also greatly increased its output until a few years ago, and it is from these sources that the wool manufacturers of this country now obtain most of their foreign supply. The decline of wool growing in the United States naturally gives rise to an inquiry regarding the net effect of the past tariff policy toward wool and the ultimate consequences of the recent increase in the duty.

The significance of the facts for the consumers of the country is important, but in seeking the origin of the present situation the subject should be treated first from the point of view of those interested in sheep raising. The nature of the industry has been changing, and even in the "range" territory of the Far West increasing reliance has been placed on lamb production as a source of profit to the flock owner. In that section, where the industry is still mainly conducted on a large scale and the flocks are grazed over wide areas which have very sparse vegetation, more than half of the gross returns come from the sale of mutton and lamb. The tendency toward development of meat production as the more important part of the sheep industry is not confined to this country, however, but has been exhibited in Argentina and, to a less marked extent, in Australia. In New Zealand the industry has long been characterized by its dependence on the exportation of frozen mutton. This trend toward mutton production has caused a change in the kind of wool grown. Both in this country and abroad there has been a lessening production of the fine Merino wools necessary in the manufacture of high grade cloths.

The westward shift of the sheep industry in this country, with a check to its expansion because of the disappearance of the frontier, the present tendency toward greater dependence on mutton production, the increasing reliance of American manufacturers on imported wool, and the changes in nature and amount of foreign production of wool, are all significant in a study of the position of the industry with reference to the tariff.

II. QUESTIONS WHICH THIS STUDY MUST ANSWER

The purpose of this study is to assemble and analyze relevant information with the object of determining whether the policy of protecting the wool-growing industry of the United States is wise and expedient. In a word, an effort will be made to decide whether the wool duties materially help the sheep owners and also whether they burden the consumers of woolen goods. If the interests of these groups are found to be opposed, an attempt will be made to strike a balance which shall represent the predominant interest of the whole country. To bring the complex problem to a focus the following questions are proposed, all of which this study must answer:

1. Can the American sheep industry hold its present position without tariff aid?
2. If the American sheep industry, or a part of it, as now organized and conducted, cannot compete with the sheep industry of foreign countries, what is the nature of the disadvantage of domestic producers?

3. Can the disadvantages of the range and farm branches of the domestic industry, respectively, or of the unfavorably situated domestic producers, be measured by any exact criterion?
4. Is there any scientific method for the determination of a correct rate of duty?
5. What would be the effect on sheep husbandry in the United States of different rates of duty on wool?
6. Is it possible to measure the burden imposed on consumers by a duty, and, if so, how great is it?
7. Should changes be made in the wool schedule irrespective of any change in the duty?
8. What is the desirable public policy in regard to a duty on wool?

Part I will treat in detail conditions in the American range wool-growing industry and in the farm sheep industry. The situation in competing countries will also be studied. Part II will give the background of the present tariff law. The early history of the wool duties will be related briefly, and the experience with free wool in 1913 and with wool control during the war will be described. Then, after appraising the "Emergency Tariff" of 1921, we shall turn to an analysis of the provisions of the Act of 1922. Part III will discuss the present problem and evaluate the various proposed bases for a duty. Conclusions will be formed as to the effects of a wool duty on American sheep husbandry and on the consumers of wool goods. Finally, the desirable public policy in regard to a wool duty will be considered.

PART I

THE SHEEP INDUSTRY IN THE UNITED STATES AND FOREIGN COUNTRIES

THE TARIFF ON WOOL

CHAPTER I

THE RANGE WOOL GROWING INDUSTRY

Sheep-raising is carried on as an independent enterprise in the United States chiefly in the great expanse of territory between the Pacific Coast and Rocky Mountains, and on the plains directly east of the mountains. Here are found areas useful for little else but stock-raising. Flocks of sheep graze the semi-desert lands in winter, while in summer they may be found in the forest reserves, often far up toward the timber-line. In studying the wool-growing industry of this country in its relation to the tariff, attention should first be turned toward sheep husbandry in the Far West.[1]

Although sheep had been kept in New Mexico from the time of the early Spanish occupation, the first encouragement to the extension of the industry in the western states came from the opening of mines, when flocks of sheep were needed to produce mutton for the growing population. In 1870 the

[1] This includes the following states: Montana, Wyoming, Idaho, Colorado, Utah, Nevada, Arizona, New Mexico, Texas, California, Washington, and Oregon.

Westward Movement of Sheep Raising in the United States

I. Leading Sheep Raising States in 1840

Leading Group

Second Group

Third Group

States Classified by Total Number of Sheep

II. Leading Sheep Raising States in 1860

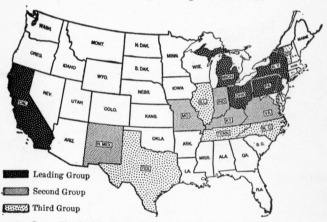

Leading Group

Second Group

Third Group

States Classified by Total Number of Sheep

4

III. Leading Sheep Raising States in 1880

- ▨ Leading Group
- ▨ Second Group
- ▨ Third Group

States Classified by Total Number of Sheep

IV. Leading Sheep Raising States in 1900

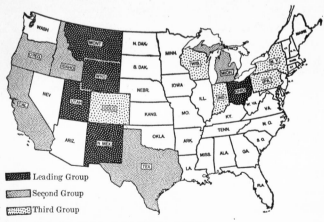

- ▨ Leading Group
- ▨ Second Group
- ▨ Third Group

States Classified by Total Number of Sheep

Pacific Coast states had more sheep than the Rocky Mountain states and Texas, but by 1880 the distribution was about equal between them. The year 1884 marks the growth of the sheep industry in the Far West to the point of predominance in the country. In that year the number of sheep in the region

V. Leading Sheep Raising States in 1920

Leading Group
Second Group
Third Group

States Classified by Total Number of Sheep

first became greater than the number in all other sections. The improvement of the transportation facilities made it possible to undertake wool growing there on a commercial scale.

The territory which now comprises the Rocky Mountain and Inter-Mountain states was largely unsettled public domain until after the Civil War. The Homestead Act, passed in 1862, was gradually extended to include the territories of the Far West. Settlement continued to increase until in the years between 1890 and 1910 it reached tremendous volume. There is now very little land which remains unoccupied on which crops can be grown. Much land has been irrigated, and dry farming, widely attempted, has been very successful in some sections. Improvements in method and more judicious use of natural resources may greatly increase the amount of such cultivation. However, stock-raising still is the leading industry throughout large areas. (See, on pp. 4-6, charts illustrating the westward trend of the sheep industry in the United States.)

I. IMPORTANCE OF THE SHEEP INDUSTRY IN THE FAR WEST

Before we consider the management of the sheep industry, in its technical details, it is important to comprehend the broader implications of the existence of the industry and its connection with other parts of the general economic organization of the country.

The wool-growing industry of the Far West has important and far-reaching relations with other forms of economic activity. It is the chief economic reliance of large areas in that part of the country; in fact, it is almost the only industry in counties of some Rocky Mountain and Inter-Mountain states. The assessed valuation of the sheep is sometimes as great as the value of all other property, and the number runs, in localities, to many thousands per head of population. But even where this industry does not thus dominate the whole economic organization, it is an important part of the structure. It is connected in many ways with other forms of enterprise. The banks are prepared to finance the sheepmen with loans, and an important part of the bank profit is secured from such business. Manufacturers of supplies, both in the West and East, have an important market in the range sheep country. Sheep dip, paint for branding, ear tags, sheep shears, camp equipment, and other commodities are demanded in large quantities by the owners of flocks. The local dealers in merchandise—both of a general character and the special sorts used by sheepmen—depend for their prosperity upon the state of the wool and lamb markets. Arrangements in the business of transportation are predicated upon the average quantity of wool and number of sheep and lambs to be transported to Eastern markets, and a decrease means a diminution in freight revenue of the railroads furnishing such service.

Agriculture and other kinds of live-stock raising —especially cattle-raising—are partly competitive with sheep-raising and partly supplemental to it. In places, sheep and cattle can be run together to good advantage, but there are many regions where the feed is too sparse for anything but sheep or goats. The development of irrigated ranching means a limitation of the range in some places, but in others it merely adds to the possibilities of the region without restricting the range area. The problem is therefore one of combining enterprises in the most effective way.

The sheep industry has also afforded the basis for economic development along other lines in the Far West. It is obvious that development in that section has only been possible by the investment of outside capital or by the accumulation of capital in some of the basic industries. Together with its mineral, oil and timber resources, the live-stock industry has afforded a chance for profits which have been used in the construction of cities, in irrigation projects, and in many other ways.

Important interstate commercial relations have been created by the development of the sheep industry in the Far West. The great wool market of the country is Boston, which has come to that position of prominence by virtue of its proximity to wool manufacturing centers and by other advantages given by an early start in the business. New York and Philadelphia are also important markets, and the erection of wool-warehouses in Chicago and Columbus in recent years has given an impetus to the business in those cities. Wool buyers go out from the great wool markets each year and purchase most of the western clip which is shipped eastward to be sorted, graded, and sold to the manufacturers. In consequence, individual wool growers have established relations with wool merchants which in many instances have continued over a long period of years with satisfaction to both. One feature of the relationship has been an extension of credit to growers by dealers and their financial associates. The sectional division of labor and interchange of goods is similar to that existing between different political sovereignties in other parts of the world.

Sheep and lamb production, and consumption of the meat products also give rise to a limited territorial division of labor, although this phase of the industry is important to Middle Western and Eastern farmers. The sheep and lambs raised on the western ranges are shipped to Denver, Omaha, Kansas City, Jersey City and Chicago, the last-named being the greatest slaughtering center. Particularly in that city have extensive facilities been created for preparing the products for market, and for distributing them to the eastern centers of population which consume by far the greater proportion of lamb and mutton. This development also has brought about established relations between the producers, commission men, packers, wholesalers and retailers.

II. DISTINCTIVE CHARACTERISTICS OF THE RANGE INDUSTRY

Before analyzing the situation in the range area of the United States we must speak in general terms about certain features of sheep raising. Sheep husbandry on the "range plan" exhibits certain general characteristics, in whatever country it is carried on, which distinguish it from the farm system.

The range plan is adopted where there is an abundance of unenclosed grazing—usually in new countries where there is great deal of free or very cheap land. The flocks can roam at will over great uninhabited areas. If the vegetation is abundant, large numbers of sheep may be kept. Even if vegetation is very light, there is still such a great area of grazing land that the flocks of one owner frequently are counted in tens of thousands. Such a method of sheep raising constitutes a distinctly pastoral economy. It was the type found in Argentina and Australia in the early years of their development, when they were more sparsely populated than at present.

The paddock system, now widely adopted in both those countries, is a modification of the range system under which the sheep are run in enclosures. It reduces the labor required in tending flocks and permits more economical utilization of the feed. The sheep do not traverse the country in close herds as under the open range system, and in consequence less grass is trodden down. The fences are frequently made proof against wild animals and serve to reduce the losses on that score. Considerable capital is necessary to embark upon such an enterprise, and thus we find the paddock system only in those localities where economic conditions are not expected to change rapidly.

While the paddock system permits somewhat

more systematic use of the natural resources than the open range, the farm carries this utilization beyond the paddock. With the incoming of settlers the soil is more intensively cultivated; and tillage, for special crops, with a gradual development of more diversified farming, becomes the rule. This does not always reduce the number of sheep, as the farmer has surplus field crops which he can feed them. He has sheds and barns where they can be sheltered from the winter storms. The danger from wild animals is less in a more populous region. As the individual flock becomes smaller, the supervision which the owner gives to it may be closer even though it may be but an incident in the conduct of his farm. The sheep are not away in the mountains or out on the plains in the care of a herder for months at a time. They are in pastures close to the farmstead, and in the intervals of farm work the owner can give them his personal attention.

III. ADAPTATION OF BREEDS TO SYSTEMS OF HUSBANDRY

These different methods of sheep husbandry call for different types of sheep. The leading varieties of improved sheep are the Merinos, the English sheep, and crosses of these two breeds.

The Merinos, or sheep having a strong infusion of Merino blood, are best adapted to range conditions. Under the range system wool is usually the product of major importance and Merino wool is finer than

any other. Furthermore, Merino sheep not only are
hardy but also they have the herding instinct which
makes them peculiarly suitable for the type of husbandry which is conducted on an unfenced pasture
or range. These sheep originated in Spain, and it
was not until the time of the Napoleonic wars that
they were secured in considerable numbers by breeders of other countries. In the United States, Australia, Argentina, Uruguay, and South Africa, they
have been kept under range conditions with great
success. Many variations in type have been produced by breeding. The Vermont Merino was developed from sheep imported into this country in
the early years of the nineteenth century. Many of
this variety, which has a particularly heavy and
greasy fleece, were exported to Australia, but it was
found eventually that they were not adapted to the
heat and droughts of that country.[2] The Rambouillet and Wanganella are varieties of Merino; the
former was developed in France and the latter in
Australia. The Delaine of the Ohio region is still
another type of Merino. These variations of the
original breed all keep the essential characteristics
of their prototype. They are small-bodied sheep,
and not so good for mutton production as the
English sheep.

The English breeds are best adapted to the farm.
They have coarser wool than the Merino but are
good mutton producers. There are two distinct

[2] U. S. Tariff Commission, *The Wool Growing Industry,* p. 438.

types, the "Longwools" and the "Downs" or short wools. The latter are shorter-legged and more square-bodied. The Lincolns, Cotswolds, and Leicesters are the leading long-wool breeds, while the Hampshires, Oxfords, Shropshires, and Southdowns are the leading varieties of Down sheep. Great care in breeding has been taken by the English shepherds to adapt the sheep to their particular environment. The sheep of Great Britain have become, as a consequence, well suited to the soil and climate of their habitat as well as to the prevailing methods of husbandry, and they have been profitable for sheep raisers in other countries affording similar natural conditions and using similar methods. The English sheep are better adapted to a moist climate than the Merino, which thrive well in arid regions. A point of superiority of the English breeds for meat production is that the lambs mature early. This is especially true of certain types, like the Hampshires. The lack of herding instinct does not affect the availability of the English breeds for use on farms or for other types of sheep-raising where enclosures are used.

The cross between the Merino and any one of several of the English breeds may be used on either the range or the farm. The crossbreds have been introduced in an effort to combine the best qualities of the English and Merino breeds. With the growth in demand for mutton and lamb the production of meat can not be neglected by sheep raisers—even by those who own the fine-wool flocks. The English breeds, which are preëminently the mutton sheep, are not adapted to the conditions found in the countries which have open ranges, like Australia and western United States. The crossbred, however, has a fairly large frame, giving a good mutton conformation; the lamb matures fairly early; the wool retains strong Merino characteristics (unless the Merino blood has become much diluted); and the sheep retains the herding quality and much of the hardiness of the Merino. When these desired results are obtained the crossbred is an ideal "dual purpose" sheep. The crossbreds, however, do not breed true to type nor retain the combination of characteristics. An infusion of pure blood at least once in two or three generations is necessary in order to produce satisfactory results.

Various kinds of crossbreds are popular in different localities. For example, in those parts of Australia where there is rich feed, crosses between Longwools and Merinos and between Downs and Merinos are common. The Romney-Marsh, a Longwool, is the favorite English breed for crossing with the Merino in New Zealand, a country where crossbreds are kept almost to the exclusion of other breeds. In South America the Lincoln has been one of the leading English breeds used for crossing with the Merino. In the range section of the United States the Lincoln, Cotswold, and Hampshire are much used for that purpose.

IV. PRESENT ORGANIZATION OF THE WESTERN SHEEP INDUSTRY

The problem of organization in the sheep industry of the Far West is principally one of adaptation of breeds and methods of flock management to the change in system caused by the reduction of the range area. The industry now suffers the disadvantage of being in a transition stage. It no longer holds as important a place in the economic organization of the West as it did formerly, and the position which it is to hold as the result of irrigated ranching, dry farming, and the growth of population, is yet to be determined. We find many types of sheep husbandry now represented in the region which was formerly the home of the range industry.

Formerly, the sheep were run in bands of 3000 to 5000 head, each band in charge of a herder. When there was only one band in the outfit, the owner frequently acted as camp tender, while in larger outfits there was but one camp tender for two or three bands. It was usually unnecessary for the sheepmen to own land, as there was an abundance of feed on the open range. The sheep, camp equipment, and sufficient funds to provide for current expenses were all the investment required.

As the range became more crowded it was found necessary to provide hay and grain for winter feed; and the flock owners began to acquire title to land in order to insure control of their range. In some places it is now the usual practice to have special warehouses in which to store feed for emergencies. With the change in methods of operation has come the necessity for dipping vats, wells, and water tanks. Sheds to protect the sheep in stormy weather on the northern ranges are also sometimes built. In some regions, notably in Washington, Oregon, and Montana, the real estate investment is greater than the value of the sheep.

The curtailment of the range has made necessary a reduction in the total number of sheep "run" and also in the size of the bands. In the southern part of the range country, bands now usually number 800 to 1,000 ewes, with their lambs, while on the northern ranges, the bands number 1,000 to 1,200—a striking reduction from the number formerly run in one band. The number of men required to look after the sheep has increased; and because the number of herders is greater it is sometimes necessary to have a camp tender with each band.

The most important alteration in method has been the change from Merino to crossbred. Under the new conditions which came about with closer settlement, it is not profitable to keep sheep for the wool clip alone. The market for lamb and mutton has grown, and the crossbreds produce a much larger lamb than the Merino. The Rambouillet which has long been popular is now frequently bred to long wool rams of the Lincoln, Cotswold, Leicester, or Romney types. The departure from the Merino type involved some loss of the herding instinct and of the hardiness necessary to stand severe range conditions. In regions where irrigated ranching has changed the operations so that they more closely resemble those of the Middle Western farm, the Down breeds, such as the Hampshire, are much in favor.

Although lambs of the first cross can be herded very well, flock masters have often followed the practice of selling them instead of using any of them for replacement. When this is done the old Merino ewes are replaced with others of the same breed. It is not always possible to follow this method, and when crossbreds are mated together the flocks become very irregular in fleece and other characteristics. The price of fine wool has been so high for most of the time since the war that the use of Merino rams with crossbred ewes has been common. The ideal which the breeders seek, however, is the best dual-purpose sheep.

V. LOCAL VARIATIONS IN SYSTEM

While the sheep industry of the various sections of the Far West exhibits some common characteristics, there are many local variations which should be given consideration before any judgment is formed as to its future. The general trend throughout the range states is toward private ownership of land, increase of capital investment, decrease in the size of flocks, dependence on mutton and lamb production, and combination of sheep-raising with general ranching operations. It is apparent that sheep husbandry in the Far West is in a stage of transition. It is tending to become more and more like the farm sheep industry of the Middle West and the East.

The "central range area," comprising the semi-desert region of southwestern Wyoming, western Utah, southern Idaho, southeastern Oregon, and Nevada, includes large areas available for winter grazing.[3] The sheep are kept on these deserts four to six months, while summer grazing for two or three months is obtained in the mountains. The remainder of the year is spent en route between winter and summer ranges.

Most of the sheep owners of this region own or lease part of their range. Sometimes they own only isolated quarter-sections or plots on which water is found, but frequently they have large tracts of spring and fall range where their sheds, warehouses, and vats are located. Part of the land is used for the production of winter feed, when enough water is found for irrigation. Considerable investment in camp equipment is required. The herders and camp tenders make their headquarters in the old-fashioned camp wagon when they are on the deserts in the winter time; but in the summer time, when the sheep are in the mountains, a tent is used instead of a wagon. Saddle horses, burros, and a wagon or

[3] U. S. Tariff Commission, *The Wool Growing Industry*, p. 180.

auto truck for hauling supplies, are also necessary parts of the outfit.

A large proportion of the sheep in this region are crossbreds of the Merino-Longwool type, and the production of lambs for feeding or slaughter is considered about as important as the production of wool. The methods of management, as compared with those of an earlier period, show more dependence on raised feeds, less spring and fall grazing, much greater capital investment, and more outlay for supervision.

The contrast between the methods which have just been described and those of the Idaho region is striking. This section represents a distinct transition to more settled conditions. There is very little winter range in Idaho, except in the southern and southwestern sections. Summer range is found in the mountains, however, and many flock masters own irrigated farms and ranches where they raise winter feed. In the fall the sheep are turned into the fields to eat the stubble or crop refuse. This method of management promotes the production of early lambs for market, due to protection and good feed in winter and early spring; and the Idaho section has become noted for its development of this branch of the business. Ewes of the Rambouillet-Longwool cross are used, and rams of the Down breeds—particularly the Hampshire—a combination which gives an early maturing lamb of large frame. A large investment in feed and in sheds for winter care is necessary, but the high cost of production is more than offset by the large lamb crop and by the high price received for early lambs.

In the Pacific Northwest there is very little open range left.[4] Most of the land has been homesteaded or has been purchased in large tracts for wheat-growing. There is considerable summer range, and the system of management is similar to that described for the Idaho region. Mutton and lamb are more important than wool; early lambs are raised from Rambouillet ewes bred to Hampshire rams. Precautions must always be taken in the Northwest against the blizzards, which cause heavy losses. Winter feeding has, however, tended to reduce the hazards, and thus to make the business less speculative.

In the eastern "high plains area," which includes the greater part of Montana, Wyoming and Colorado, sheep-raising has decreased rapidly in late years.[5] The number of homesteads has increased very fast, especially in Montana and Colorado, and most of the sheep owners now operate on owned or leased land. Here the co-operative running of sheep is practiced extensively, especially in Montana. Ranchers often own from 200 to 1,000 head—less than enough to run as a separate band. In the summer several men co-operate and keep their sheep as one band in the forest reserve. In the valley of the Yellowstone River in southern Montana, this

[4] U. S. Tariff Commission, *The Wool Growing Industry,* p. 185.
[5] *Ibid.,* p. 186.

method of management is common. Many Montana sheepmen lease lands on Indian reservations; but competition for range has become keen and grazing fees have been raised to a high point.

In the prairie section of Colorado there are now very few sheep. In the vicinity of Denver there are flocks of registered sheep which are usually kept on the home place all the year; but the owners frequently also have bands of grade ewes which are kept in the mountains in the summer.

In the different parts of California, conditions in the sheep raising industry are diverse. The old range plan of management has, however, practically disappeared. In the northern part of the state there is considerable forest reserve and much privately owned timber land which can be leased for summer range, and here the method of management is not essentially different from that described for the central range area. In many parts of the state irrigated ranches are found, and the plan followed is like that of Idaho or Montana. Many California ranches carry purebred flocks.

In Arizona and New Mexico lamb production has not been as successful as in the northern states of the range area. The Merino blood is consequently predominant there, but, even in these states, the flock owners depend on lamb and mutton production for a substantial part of their returns. Winter range on the desert and summer range in the forest reserve is found, but the ranges are becoming more and more restricted. About a third of the sheep in Arizona are shipped back and forth by rail between winter and summer ranges—a condition indicative of restricted range. The capital investment is increased by the meager water supply in the Southwest. Wells and reservoirs must be built, often at considerable expense.

In Texas, there is practically no free range left. The plan of running sheep within wolf-proof fences has been quite generally adopted, as it conserves the feed, protects the sheep, and reduces the cost of supervision. Cattle and goat raising are frequently combined with sheep husbandry, and the majority of owners have not more than 1,000 sheep each.

VI. DIFFICULTIES OF THE INDUSTRY

One of the principal problems which confronts the Western rancher is the choice between sheep raising and other lines of production. Incident to, or allied with, this problem is the question of the best combination of sheep raising with agriculture. Other forms of activity are following hard upon the heels of the sheep industry.

The trend toward diversified agriculture in the Western states is shown by a comparison of crop statistics of 1924 with those of 1913. Although prices of farm products were not particularly good in 1924,[6] the acreage and output of many leading

[6] Index number of prices of farm products in 1924 was 134 (base = 1913). Index number of prices of manufactured commodities

crops were higher than in 1913 and the number of farm animals was greater, with the exception of sheep. The decline in number of sheep is the more noteworthy because, contrary to the tendency of prices in the case of most other animals and of crops, the average price per head was $7.87 in 1924 as against $3.94 in 1913.[7]

There was an increase both in acreage and in output of hay in the 12 western states.[8] The number of acres increased from 8,092,000 in 1913 to 10,-230,000 in 1924, and the number of tons from 16,052,000 to 20,024,000. The price of hay increased from $10.33 per ton to $14.67 per ton (Dec. 1 prices: preliminary estimate). This is significant when considered in connection with the increase in the number of cattle in the Far West from 14,602,000 in 1913 to 17,647,000 in 1924, in spite of a fall in the average value per head in those states from $32 to $30.

An increase in the price of wheat, from 1913 to 1924, was accompanied by a large increase in acreage. Winter wheat brought $.76 per bushel in those states in the earlier year and $1.28 per bushel in 1924. The acreage harvested increased from 4,165,000 to 6,288,000. The price of spring wheat was $.72 per bushel and $1.24 per bushel in the two

150. (base = 1913). U. S. Department of Agriculture, *Yearbook*, 1924, pp. 1176-80.

[7] U. S. Department of Agriculture, *Yearbook*, 1924, p. 931.

[8] California, Oregon, Washington, Idaho, Nevada, Utah, Colorado, Montana, Wyoming, Arizona, New Mexico, and Texas.

years, and the acreage harvested increased from 2,293,000 in 1913 to 4,888,000 in 1924.

The acreage in corn remained about the same. It was 7,502,000 acres in 1913 and 7,441,000 acres in 1924. The product, however, declined from 177,-110,000 bushels in 1913 to 156,458,000 bushels in 1922 and to 122,373,000 bushels in 1924. The acreage, however, is more significant as it denotes the change in the use of land, while the output is affected by climatic conditions. The acreage in oats increased from 3,378,000 in 1913 to 3,446,000 in 1924 and the price from $.42 per bushel to $.58 per bushel.

The period from 1913 to 1924 was marked by a tremendous increase in the use of automobiles and tractors, yet the number of mules increased and the number of horses fell off but slightly. The number of swine increased from 4,661,000 to 4,877,-000, attendant upon a slight rise in price ($9.79 per head in 1924 as against $9.20 per head in 1913, farm price).[9]

These figures illustrate the change which is taking place throughout that region. Irrigated ranches and dry farms are bringing more acreage under cultivation, and are raising more fodder for a larger number of cattle and hogs. Farmers have put a large acreage into wheat in spite of the agricultural depression and the slack demand for wheat in foreign countries. More mules and about the same

[9] U. S. Department of Agriculture, *Yearbooks,* 1913 to 1924.

number of horses are used for the farm work in
spite of the increase of automobiles and tractors.
But although the price per head of sheep was
higher than in 1913, the number of sheep in these
states decreased from 30,439,000 in 1913 to 25,007,-
000 in 1924.[10]

*A second problem is found in the financial diffi-
culties of the western wool growers.* These spring
largely from the increased investment in land and
equipment which has become necessary both for
the reasons given above and owing to the great
rise in the price of feed and all kinds of material
used in sheep husbandry. The financial situation
is, therefore, a symptom, not a cause, of the wool
growers' troubles.

In the regions in which the greater part of the
land must be owned by the sheep raiser, the borrowed capital employed in the sheep business is
often 75 or 80 per cent of the whole. Most sheep
owners carry a mortgage on land and equipment,
and sometimes also on the sheep. They also carry
short-term loans—60 or 90 days, or in some cases 6
months—which are used for operating expenses.
The sources of credit are varied. Often the wool
merchant with whom the grower deals makes an
advance on the clip before it is sheared. Loans are

[10] Even if allowance were made for the fact that the estimate
for 1913 was based on the 1910 Census, in which lambs were included, while the 1924 estimate was based on the 1920 Census, in
which lambs were not included, the number of sheep in 1924
would probably be lower than in 1913.

also made by live-stock dealers on the lamb crop before it is marketed. These advances are secured by mortgages on the wool or lambs. Short-term loans made by the local banks are usually secured by chattel mortgages. The great degree of reliance placed on these loans for current expenses is a weakness in the method of management of the industry. Efforts have been made to bring about the use of acceptances in financing the wool grower, but the practice has not gained ground rapidly. It is less satisfactory to the sheepmen than consignment of the wool to dealers, because there is no termination to consignment except the date of sale, while the acceptance falls due at a particular date.

Financial assistance is not one of the most pressing needs of the Western wool grower. The Federal Reserve System, the Federal Farm Loan Board, the local banks and live-stock loan companies, and the new system of Intermediate Credit afford the means of covering most legitimate needs. The extent to which current expenses are met by heavy borrowing indicates that the conditions are not now as favorable for the Western wool grower as formerly. The heavy mortgages on land and equipment cause a severe drain on the resources of the sheep owners, and the fact that the business is largely conducted on credit points to the probable elimination of some of those who are yet struggling to maintain a foothold in it.

Other problems arise in the marketing of wool and lambs. Wool is sold in the United States at private sale, not at public auctions as in London and Australia. There is no future trading in wool because of the almost endless variation in shrinkage, grade, and condition of the various clips. The wool of the Western ranges is sold in one of five different ways. The first is sale by a contract with the wool dealer before the wool is shorn; such a sale usually takes place in seasons when there is a rising market and dealers are optimistic. The second is by consignment to firms of wool dealers for sale at the most favorable price which they can obtain and is usual in years when buyers are hesitant. Advance of part of the price is commonly made to the grower at the time of the consignment. The third method, the one most often followed, is sale at the shearing shed to the representative of a firm of wool dealers. This has the advantage to the grower of giving him the proceeds of the sale at once, and it is often favored by the buyer because it gives him opportunity to make a speculative gain by the exercise of good judgment. The fourth method is sale by co-operative associations of wool growers. These associations accept wool on consignment from individual growers, frequently grade it at warehouses which they own or lease in marketing centers, and pro-rate to the grower costs which constitute only a small fee for their services. Fifth, sale is sometimes made through wool pools organized by the growers to give them added bargaining power in trading with wool firms. Pooled lots of wool are often sold by "sealed bid" auctions. This method of sale is more popular in Texas than any other part of the range country, because the clips of that section are small.

Consistency in using a definite method of sale would promote the growers' interests. The practice of shifting from one form of sale to the other has been inimical to their best interests. They are apt to sell at the shed when there is an active market, and the dealer reaps the benefit of the rise in price; while in dull years they consign and gain nothing by waiting.

More co-operative action would help the growers. Co-operation in the sale of wool has been quite successful in the Middle West and East where the individual clips are small, and it is probable that the decrease in the size of individual outfits in the Far West will tend to promote co-operation in that section also.

Adoption of a better system of grading wool at the shearing shed would benefit the grower. The growers' ignorance of the grade of their wool and of market conditions is a disadvantage in dealing with the wool buyers. Officials of state and national associations and representatives of government departments have constantly urged better methods of grading and marketing wool and more joint action, but the educational work has taken effect slowly.

Experiments have been made, in the United States, with wool-classing as it is conducted in Australia. It has been argued that, since many American mills have become accustomed to wools classified in this way, American growers could get a better price and more successfully meet Australian competition if their product were similarly prepared. The weight of opinion, however, seems still to favor marketing wool in a few main grades, leaving it to the mills to classify it more minutely according to their particular needs. Grading at the shearing point, however, has the effect of teaching the growers the true grade of their own wool, which few of them know accurately. Therefore, even though the Australian system does not prove to be adapted to American conditions, it is probable that more grading will be done at the points of origin, and that this will help the grower to market his wool more advantageously, and to increase his net returns.

The wool firms perform valuable functions in classifying wool, grading it, and offering a good selection to the mills. They also frequently help to finance both the grower and the mill; very often the mill does not pay for the wool until the finished product is sold. The dealers also assume the risk of a falling market and bear the financial burden of carrying large stocks for considerable periods. These functions must be assumed by the growers when they act co-operatively or by commission firms which act for them. The dealers' contribution to the marketing of wool is so important that it is hardly possible that co-operative action will entirely supersede it, but such action may improve the position of the wool growers by giving them an alternative method of disposing of their product. Improved marketing methods might easily raise the net return to the growers as much as would a duty of several cents per pound on wool.

The principal remedy for lamb marketing difficulties lies in breeding for an earlier or later lamb. The chief trouble is the glut of the market, which takes place in the fall from September 1 to December 1. Distribution of shipments through earlier months would prevent the break in price which often comes at the height of the season and causes loss to the Western shippers. "Feeder" lambs— those which are to be fattened at the feed yards or on farms—come on the market at about the time when the supply of other lambs is greatest. Their presence in the market helps to depress the price of lambs for slaughter. If, therefore, the sheep raisers can adopt some method by which they can sell at an earlier or a later date, they can enhance their profits.

The most serious problem of range sheep husbandry grows out of the land system. The fundamental cause of trouble lies in the reduction of available free range. Sheep raising on vast uninhabited tracts of semi-desert country is a very different thing from sheep raising in a country interspersed with irrigated farms and ranches and with many tracts where dry farming is at least being attempted. The early conditions, when there was almost unlimited room for expansion of the industry, are in strong contrast with the present situation of the sheep raiser. If he attempts to keep his sheep for a part of the year on the open range he is likely to find that it has been over-grazed, and that the watering places have been pre-empted. In driving his sheep from the winter to the summer range and back he is likely to get into trouble with settlers along the way who charge him with trespass. He will often find that the only feasible way is to send his sheep by rail. Moreover, the quota of sheep which he has been accustomed to keep in the National Forest in the summer is sometimes cut down by the Forest Service because of the demand of new settlers for privileges. It is evident that the person who does not own or lease considerable land cannot hope to carry on any substantial stock-raising enterprise.

The Homestead Acts of 1909 and 1916 have added to the difficulties of the stockmen. The Enlarged Homestead Act, passed in 1909, allowed settlers to take up 320 acres in certain areas where the previous possible allotment of 160 acres was not sufficient to afford a livelihood. The Grazing Homestead Act of 1916 fixed 640 acres as the size of the homestead where the land was not suitable for agriculture. Considerable land has been taken up under these acts.[11] Frequently it lies between the winter and summer ranges and as the sheepmen often depend on this area to supply their flocks while in transit with feed during two to four months in the year, it has seriously interfered with their systems of management. Charges have been made that much of this land was taken with the intent to force the stockmen to purchase it and with the knowledge that it was too poor to furnish a living by tillage. The policy of the Federal Government has always been to encourage the settlement of the land—a policy which has, no doubt, been socially desirable. There is grave doubt, however, whether some of the land set aside under these acts is capable of supporting a family on the number of acres designated as a homestead. As a partial relief, stock driveways have been established to enable flocks to pass to and from the summer range in the

[11] Amount of land designated and amount entered under Act of 1909 (Enlarged Homestead) and Act of 1916 (Stock Raising Homestead).

Enlarged Homestead Act (1909)

		Acres
Amount of land designated up to July 31, 1923		322,874,190
" " " entered " " June 30, 1923		72,380,256
Number of entries during fiscal year 1923		2,974
Area " " " " " "		745,721

Grazing Homestead Act (1916)

Amount of land designated up to July 31, 1923		113,115,567
" " " entered " " June 30, 1923		36,665,982
Number of entries during fiscal year 1923		10,541
Area " " " " " "		4,183,922

Figures furnished by U. S. Interior Department, Commissioner of General Land Office.

mountains; but this does not solve the problem of feeding in transit.

The resulting curtailment of the open range, together with the lack of regulation of grazing, inevitably led to the excessive use of the free land which remained. Close grazing by sheep often destroys the roots of vegetation and when this has occurred, considerable time is necessary to restore the range to its former carrying capacity. This compels the purchase of winter feed and helps to swell the cost of keeping flocks. "Tramp" sheepmen sometimes add to the burden on the pastures. These are usually aliens who have formerly been herders and have succeeded in securing small flocks of their own for which they find pasturage by trespassing on the land of other stockmen and settlers. They contribute to the overcrowding of the range and are an annoyance difficult to eliminate.

The National Forest system has done more to alleviate the land difficulties than any other factor. The original purpose of the National Forests was the preservation of timber and the protection of the water-sheds, but it was found that there was actual advantage in allowing stock to graze in the forest because of fire protection afforded. There are now nearly 200 million acres in National Forests, and 75 per cent of the total summer range of Far Western flocks is obtained on these areas.

Grazing in the National Forests is regulated under a system of permits. In order to obtain grazing preference, live-stock owners must own and reside on improved ranch property and be dependent on the National Forest for range; or they must have been users of the range before its inclusion within the forest; or they must have purchased stock which has previously been permitted in the forest in connection with improved range property. There is a charge of a few cents per head for a season's grazing, and the number of stock which the owner may run in any forest is limited. The number allowed varies from 25 to 300 head of cattle or horses and from 500 to 2,000 sheep or goats.

This system has been a boon to the small owners, although the "permittees" are frequently obliged by the Forest Service administrators to decrease the number of stock which they run in order to make room for new settlers. The business is thus tending constantly toward smaller scale operations. It is an invaluable adjunct of ranching and small farming operations, and the general agreement that the number of stock per owner should be limited shows the growing predominance of the small holder in the sheep industry.

Other remedies for the growing shortage of free range have been proposed. It has been suggested that the government should regulate grazing on the remaining free range, issuing permits to users as it does in the case of the National Forests. Control of this kind is probably essential if the grazing land is not to be permanently impaired. Other suggested measures involve the sale or lease of remaining range lands to the present users and the creation of grazing homesteads in units large enough to allow a good living to a family. It has been proposed to allow the several states to take control of the grazing lands within their borders. This, however, would in itself not help unless each state should adopt some practical remedy. It is probable that all of the measures suggested would have beneficial results if applied in certain sections, but no one of them is applicable to all parts of the range country.

If grazing homesteads are to be allotted, the size should be increased. The experience of many who have taken up 640 acres under the Act of 1916 has been disappointing. Frequently failure has clearly been due to the inadequacy of the grant. That the establishment of grazing homesteads hampers the present users of the range may not be considered good reason for the alteration of public policy, and the encouragement of small holdings at the expense of the stock raisers will probably continue. But it is obviously a mistaken policy to make the holdings too small to be self-sustaining. The settler should be given a "fighting chance."

In some instances, either sale or leasing of public land might be resorted to with advantage. Bills have been introduced in Congress to permit the leasing of public lands to stockmen in sufficiently large areas and for long enough periods to encourage

the industry.[12]   The objection raised to the plan
of sale to the present users is that it would favor the
large operators.   It is not at all certain, however,
that sale of the remaining public land would result
in any greater control by large operators than they
now exercise.   Many large stock raising companies
have already secured control of considerable land
by grazing their flocks near the holdings of smaller
operators and thus taking away their feed.   Sale of
the land is not likely, however, to commend itself
to the majority of the stockmen because of the
increase in investment which it would entail.   Probably the most promising remedy proposed is the
extension to the open range of the permit system.
Regulation of the forests has resulted in such conservation of grazing resources that it is highly probable that the same result can be obtained with the
rest of the public lands.

VII.   THE OUTLOOK FOR THE RANGE SHEEP INDUSTRY

The disadvantages in competition of the American range wool grower almost all originate from

[12] The Kent Bill, introduced in Congress in December, 1913, provided for the establishment of grazing districts on the remaining
public domain and the issuance of ten-year permits for grazing on
such areas. "It also granted the right to fence and otherwise improve the range and especially provided for the equitable disposal of necessary improvements when the permit should be
cancelled." "As this plan was not in accordance with the established policies for the utilization of the public domain, and as it
was considered to conflict with the grazing homestead acts, this
bill was never reported out of the Senate Committee on Public
Lands." U. S. Tariff Commission, *The Wool Growing Industry,*
1921, pp. 161-2.

the reduction in grazing land. Closer settlement and utilization of land for agriculture restrict the ranges, interfere with the movement of flocks, and bring about over-grazing of the land still available for sheep. Smaller bands of sheep have to be kept, the breeds must be different, and only partial relief is found in the use of government reserves of forest land for summer grazing. The greater investment in land and equipment causes a heavier financial burden for the owner, and the fact that he is frequently pressed for ready money helps to place him at a disadvantage in marketing his product.

Even if all practicable palliative measures are applied, sheep raising by the range system is far past its zenith in this country. Sheep raising primarily for wool production can be conducted profitably only where there are great tracts of un-tilled country. The settlement of the land and development of agriculture inevitably crowd out such an industry. An increase in the output of wool and mutton therefore can come only from the adoption of methods which bring sheep raising into conjunction with tillage under irrigation or with other diversified farming operations.

In certain sections of the Far West where irrigation is not feasible and where the arid climate may prevent even dry farming, "islands" of untillable country may be left where the methods of an earlier period will continue to be economically justifiable. A shortage of wool, due to the long-run decrease in the number of sheep in foreign countries, is likely to keep the price so high that there will be a profit in sheep raising in places especially adapted to it. These regions will be few, however, because in many places where land is not suitable for agriculture the discovery of mineral deposits or oil has made it far too valuable for use as pasturage. As settlers keep coming in and the value of land increases, the industry will either become subsidiary to general farming or it will be crowded out to the "fringes" of usable land. The future of the industry will, therefore, be determined by the competing uses of available land.

CHAPTER II

SHEEP RAISING ON THE FARM

Farm sheep husbandry in the United States has undergone many vicissitudes. The enthusiasm for sheep, during some periods and in various regions, has been unbounded, only to be followed by severe and long-continued prejudice. Although the number of sheep on farms has decreased in the past thirty years, there are good grounds for believing that sheep husbandry will gradually come to play a more prominent part in the country's diversified agriculture than at present.

The foreign market for most American agricultural staples has been curtailed in recent years, and the farmer has become more predominantly a producer for the home market.[1] Greater diversification in some sections and more intensive farming in others probably will both lead to an increase in the number of sheep. The stimulus to the industry which would come from an increased price of wool, we shall consider later.[2] The present

[1] See Nourse, E. G., *American Agriculture and the European Market* (Publications of the Institute of Economics, Washington), 1924.

[2] See Chapter IX.

chapter is devoted mainly to a consideration of the place which sheep husbandry occupies in various schemes of diversified agriculture.

I. THE PROBLEMS OF FARM SHEEP HUSBANDRY

The principal problem of the farmer is to combine sheep raising judiciously with other lines of production. In his choice or rejection of sheep, personal preference seems to play a larger part than with many other varieties of farm enterprise. Some men regard sheep as stupid animals and as a nuisance generally, while others are willing to lavish attention upon them. Hardly any other type of farm animal seems to arouse so much affection or animosity. But though individual preference plays a prominent part, costs and prices are the long-run determining forces. The question of profit or loss is more complicated, however, than it is when sheep-raising is conducted as an independent industry. In the latter case there is but one set of operations and one balance sheet. On the farm the multiplicity of operations makes it difficult to apportion costs, especially the items of labor and management. Therefore the farmer may not know, over a period of several years, whether he is really making anything out of his sheep or not. If he once becomes convinced that it is a losing venture, he will not try it again for a long time.

When the farmer begins to consider whether he

should adopt sheep-raising, or should enlarge his
flock, there are many factors which he must take
into account. One of the most important is the
comparative price of sheep products and of other
crops. If the prices of dairy products are high
while the prices of wool and lamb are not, he will
not divert any forage from his herd to his flock.
He may, however, have an old pasture full of brakes
or with thin and rocky soil. Such grazing he can
utilize for sheep, or he can run them with his cows,
to "clean up the corners" of the pasture. If, then,
there is no question of diversion of the feed from
the dairy herd to the sheep, the question may
become one of management: how much of his time
does he want to spend in looking after sheep?
They will require considerable attention: to keep
them free from disease, to prevent dogs from making havoc with the flock, to provide quarters and
to feed them through the winter, to look after
breeding and shearing, and to market the lambs
and wool.

But even if the farmer is willing to make the
outlay of time and effort, local conditions may prevent his undertaking to keep a flock. Sheep may
be particularly susceptible to parasites in that region, or dogs may be too troublesome. On the
other hand, local conditions may be unusually favorable. The climate may be mild and the pasturage abundant; or it may be easy to provide some
special crop for feed. In such case, he may find

raising early lambs very profitable. Again, he may find sheep useful in some variety of crop rotation which he wishes to adopt.

If the farmer finds that his scheme of diversification and the prevailing scale of costs and prices favor flock husbandry, his next problem is to ascertain the breed best adapted to the situation. Under present conditions he will almost inevitably find that some breed which furnishes a large and easily fattened lamb is the one which he wants. The breed or cross which he adopts will depend also, of course, on local conditions of soil and climate. The way in which these problems have been worked out in various sections of the country will form the principal subject matter of this chapter; but first it will be well to review briefly the course which farm sheep raising has taken in the past in the United States.

II. REVIEW OF FARM SHEEP RAISING IN THE UNITED STATES

Until the development of the ranges of the Far West after 1860 the sheep industry of this country was almost altogether incidental to diversified agriculture. It is true that in some instances sheep raising was a very important part of farming, but it was seldom conducted as an independent enterprise. Farm sheep of colonial days were often scrawny and ill-conditioned, and the clip was only two or three pounds per head. Improvement in breeding was accomplished by the importation of Spanish Merinos shortly before the outbreak of the War of 1812, and later by the importation of Saxony Merinos. Sheep of the English mutton breeds—Southdowns, the "New Leicesters," developed by the famous sheep-husbandman, Bakewell, and other varieties—were imported at the end of the eighteenth and early in the nineteenth century.

New England led in number of sheep between 1830 and 1840, while from 1840 until 1860 the Middle Atlantic and Middle Western sections were most important. Flocks increased in the East during the years 1861-65, but it was only a temporary revival. The industry continued to develop in the West after the Civil War, but in the East it receded to a more unimportant position than before.

About 1869 began the importation of mutton sheep from Canada to the tobacco-growing regions of southern New England, where they were fattened for slaughter. The sheep were bought in the fall, fed on roughage and meal, and sold in the spring. The value of sheep manure in tobacco culture made this combination of operations very profitable. The number of sheep kept in New England as a whole was not, however, greatly increased.

During the following decade the Middle West suffered a slight decline. Mutton breeds gained steadily at the expense of the Merinos. There were many more sheep in Kansas, Nebraska, and Minnesota in 1880 than there were directly after the

Civil War, due to the increase in settlement. An increase in the South was mainly the result of restoration from the havoc wrought by the war. Kentucky, Tennessee, Virginia, and West Virginia were the leading sheep-raising states in this period, and were even then exhibiting a preference for the mutton breeds. In Ohio the Merinos remained predominant.

Between 1880 and 1890 there was a slow decline in the number of sheep in the farm states. During this period and well into the nineties, prices of agricultural commodities declined greatly. Wool, together with wheat and corn, suffered a greater relative decline than dairy products. The expansion of wool production in other parts of the world had been rapid. From 1890 to 1900 the decrease in flocks was pronounced in this country, except in Iowa, Nebraska, and the Dakotas, where there was an increase due mainly to a growth in diversified agriculture at the expense of "one-crop" wheat raising.

During the first decade of the twentieth century the total number of sheep in the country remained about the same. There was a substantial growth of the industry in a few states, however. Among these were Maryland, Virginia, West Virginia, Kentucky, and Tennessee. The production of early market lambs was found profitable in these regions. The business of fattening for market lambs bought in the Far West expanded in the West Central states, and brought about an increase in the flocks of Iowa, Minnesota, Missouri, and Kansas.

In spite of the high prices for wool and mutton during the World War, the number of sheep in the United States remained nearly stationary. A slight decrease in the three years after 1914 was followed by a small increase in 1918 and 1919. Then the drop in price of 1920 caused a great reduction.[3] During the period of expansion from 1917 to 1918 flocks were enlarged the most in the "spring lamb" region of Kentucky and in the "feeding" states of Minnesota, Iowa, Missouri, South Dakota, and Kansas. Ohio, Pennsylvania, Maryland, Virginia, and West Virginia also had a substantial increase, while the growth in New England was large proportionately, though not important in absolute figures.

III. PRESENT STATE OF FARM SHEEP HUSBANDRY

Throughout the Middle West small farm flocks are maintained, and sheep and lambs brought from the western ranges are fattened for market. Sheep in the corn belt are often infested with parasites. But the principal reason for failure to expand the industry in that region has been the greater profit of using the land for other purposes, such as raising corn or grain and keeping hogs and dairy or beef cattle. The competition of the dairy business with sheep raising is very marked in southern Wis-

[3] See Chapter V.

consin. The flocks have been almost driven out of that section by the butter and cheese factories and by the business of supplying milk to Chicago. There is considerable sheep raising in those areas which are not suited to intensive cultivation, such as the hilly land along the rivers, the Ozark region, and the cut-over land of northern Michigan and Wisconsin.[4] In some of the less fertile sections, such as northern Missouri and southeastern Iowa, flocks of 50 or more are frequently kept with herds of beef cattle. The chief use for sheep in the Middle West is, however, to turn the surplus feed and otherwise waste products of the general farm into meat and wool.

Although the individual farm flocks of the Middle West are small, the total number of sheep and the quantity of wool produced are large as compared with New England and the Middle Atlantic States. The average wool clip of the Middle West is about three million pounds per state. A total of 33,-319,000 pounds was the output in 1924 of the ten states, Indiana, Illinois, Wisconsin, Minnesota, Iowa, Missouri, Kansas, Nebraska, North and South Dakota.[5] Almost all of this was medium wool. The sheep of the Middle West are predominantly of the mutton breeds. The range-grown sheep are

[4] Sheep raising on the cut-over lands has been successful when carried on as part of a farming enterprise, but has not succeeded when the sheep have been run in underbrush left from lumbering operations.

[5] Bulletin of National Association of Wool Manufacturers, *Annual Wool Review, 1924*, p. 176.

more hardy than the native sheep of these states, however; a fact which has led to the practice, in some sections, notably in Missouri, Iowa, Illinois, and Indiana, of purchasing range ewes for breeding purposes. The lambs are sold each year, and when the ewes become too aged they also are fattened and sent to market. By this means some Merino blood is introduced into the flocks, and in the various states from 5 per cent to 20 per cent of the wool is graded as "fine."

The business of fattening sheep and lambs for market is very important in some parts of the Middle West. In Iowa and northeastern Nebraska, lambs purchased in the Chicago and Omaha markets are turned out in the corn-fields in September and sold in December. Part of the corn crop is thus utilized in other sections of the corn-belt.

Many "feed yards" are operated in northeastern Colorado, in the Arkansas valley of southeastern Colorado, in western Nebraska, and in parts of Kansas. In these regions there is usually little bad weather during the early winter months. Feeding begins in October or November, and shipments begin in February.[6] In the sugar-beet areas the beet tops, and alfalfa which is sown as a rotation crop, are fed to sheep and lambs.

In Indiana, Michigan, Ohio, and western New York, lambs purchased in Chicago are fed in barns through the winter, and sold in the spring in Buf-

[6] U. S. Department of Agriculture, *Year Book,* 1923, pp. 260-2.

falo, Pittsburg, and other eastern markets. These various methods of feeding provide a profitable way for farmers to dispose of surplus crops.

The Ohio Region is the one stronghold of Merino sheep which remains east of the Mississippi River. This region lies principally in the State of Ohio but also includes, as commonly understood, parts of northern West Virginia, southwestern Pennsylvania, and southern Michigan. The high land of the upper Ohio Valley is well adapted to sheep raising, but not so well to dairy farming or to grain raising, which have crowded out the sheep in many other parts of the country. The hilly land is easily eroded, and a large proportion of it is kept in better condition by use for stock than for crops.[7] Sheep are more profitable than cattle because they do not require as much winter feeding. Also, the grazing habits of cattle and sheep are different. They supplement one another, as the cattle do not fully graze the steeper areas while the sheep feed there more than on the lower levels. Sheep and cattle are often kept together in this region because of that fact.

From the first quarter of the nineteenth century, when the Saxony Merinos were introduced into this region, to the present day, the sheep industry has been very important. The State of Ohio produces more wool than the New England and Middle At-

[7] U. S. Tariff Commission, *The Wool-Growing Industry*, 1921, p. 129.

lantic States together,—a total of 13,899,000 pounds
in 1924.[8] Sixty per cent of Ohio wool is graded as
"fine," the leading breed at present being the Delaine, a large-bodied Merino which was developed
in the region. Ohio flock owners have been turning more and more to mutton production in recent
years to sustain their profits; but the Merino sheep
has always been a favorite with them. The Tariff
Board pointed out, in 1912, that wool was raised
there at higher cost than anywhere else in the
world.

Crossbreeding is not in as great favor in the Ohio
region as it is in the West. The crossbreds are
more subject to parasitic infection than the Merinos, and require a larger quantity of feed to carry
them through the winter. Unless all the lambs are
sold and Merino ewes bought for replacement, the
second or third crossbreeding brings out great un-
evenness of fleece. The Delaine, moreover, is large
enough so that the carcass does not compare unfavorably in weight with that of the crossbred.
These factors, added to the conservatism of the
sheep owners of the section, have resulted in a
strict adherence to this breed in a large part of
the Upper Ohio Valley. In those parts of the Ohio
region where it is possible to raise more winter feed,
the Down breeds are more popular than either De-
laines or crossbreeds. Wool, however, continues to
be of practically co-ordinate importance with mut-

[8] *Annual Wool Review, 1924,* p. 176.

ton in the sheep husbandry of this section—the only part of the farm area where that is true. An illustration of the status of the industry here is found in the figures for wool production. The total clip in Ohio, West Virginia, and Michigan, in 1924, was approximately 23,647,000 pounds.[9] The percentage of fine wool was 60 in Ohio, 75 in West Virginia, and 25 in Michigan. For the three states as a whole the clip was just about evenly divided between fine wool from the Merino sheep, and medium wool, principally from the mutton sheep.

In the South sheep raising encounters difficulties that are not found elsewhere. In some sections parasites are hard to control, and proper feeding is difficult. In the northern part of the region there is a favorable environment, and in the "blue grass" regions of Kentucky and Tennessee sheep are found in large numbers. The breeds in these two states vary. The sheep of Tennessee originated from the Cotswold, Down, and Merino breeds, but the fleece no longer bears any traces of Merino character. In Kentucky the predominant strains are Hampshire, Southdown, and Shropshire. "Western" blackface ewes are also largely used, but there "western" ewes come, not from the ranges of the Far West, but from the western part of the Corn Belt. On the excellent limestone pastures in the mountains of western Virginia some large flocks are found. The Downs and Dorsets are the leading breeds in this state.

[9] Ibid.

Delaine and Rambouillet Merinos were introduced into the Carolina mountains some years ago and have considerably influenced the flocks there. They seem to thrive there better than the Down breeds. In Georgia the principal pasture lands suitable for sheep are in the pine woods. Alabama and Mississippi have coastal pine woods where flocks of semi-wild sheep are found, and in the central portion of these states, where alfalfa can be grown, good-sized flocks are kept.

The production of early market lambs has been highly developed in certain regions of the South. North central Kentucky, central Tennessee, southwestern Virginia, and the valleys of West Virginia lead in this branch of sheep husbandry. The development began soon after 1890, stimulated by the growing market for mutton and lamb. The mild climate of these states favors early lambing, and winter grain affords pasturage. The sheep are often grazed upon rye which is sown as a "cover crop" after corn and tobacco. The cost of winter and spring feeding is thus reduced. The lambs are marketed from the latter part of May until the middle of August, and obtain good prices by avoiding the glut which comes when the movement of lambs from the western ranges is at its height. The receipts from mutton and lamb are much greater than the receipts from wool—often three-fourths of the total. Early lamb production has also been increasing in western North Carolina and in parts of other southern states, notably Mississippi, Alabama, and Louisiana.[10]

The wool output of the South, including the state of Kentucky which raised about one-third of the whole amount, was 8,456,000 pounds in 1923, all of medium grade except a small amount of fine wool in Oklahoma.[11] The average fleece weighed only about four pounds, which is considerably less than the average for the country as a whole. Both the light weight of the fleece, which is partly the result of the climate and partly of poor breeding, and the low quality of the wool, tend to emphasize the need of further developing the market lamb business in this section of the country.

In the Middle Atlantic States, likewise, sheep-raising is carried on as an adjunct to general farming. The English breeds prevail, and the flock receipts are usually two-thirds from lamb and mutton and one-third from wool. But in one part of this area there is a variation from this rule. Sixty per cent of the production of Pennsylvania—2,908,000 pounds in 1924—is rated as fine wool,[12] and the proportion of receipts from wool is greater than in the other Middle Atlantic States. The great sheep-raising section of this state is the southwestern corner, particularly Washington County, which is usually considered part of the Ohio region, as

[10] U. S. Tariff Commission, *The Wool Growing Industry*, 1921, pp. 103-11.
[11] *Annual Wool Review, 1924,* p. 176.
[12] Ibid.

is also the point, or "panhandle," of West Virginia.

New York ranks second in this group in total amount of wool produced—3,181,000 pounds in 1924—and in quantity of fine wool, thirty per cent of the clip being estimated as "fine."[13] Although some sheep are kept on high-priced land in western New York to utilize the fodder from the bean crop and on some of the orchard lands along Lake Erie,[14] most of them are kept to utilize roughage and to graze the fence-corners of cow pastures, as in New England. There are some pure-bred flocks; and soon after the war a company was formed in New York to raise Karakul sheep, the pelts of which are valuable as "astrakhan." But mutton and lamb are nearly always the chief source of receipts.

In the mountains of western Maryland are pastures especially adapted to sheep-raising. In that region a few flocks of pure-bred Rambouillets are found, but wool growing is subordinate to lamb production as it is also on the farms of the eastern part of the state, where the Downs and Dorsets predominate. Very few sheep are found in Delaware or New Jersey. The total wool output of New York, New Jersey, Pennsylvania, Delaware, and Maryland in 1924 was 6,643,000 pounds.[15]

These states have at their door a great market

[13]*Annual Wool Review, 1924,* p. 176.
[14] U. S. Tariff Commission, *The Wool Growing Industry,* p. 93.
[15] *Annual Wool Review, 1924,* p. 176.

for mutton and lamb in New York City. The number of sheep slaughtered at Jersey City in 1924 was 1,230,246, or nearly half as many as were killed at Chicago, which is the leading sheep market and slaughtering center.[16]

In New England the industry is carried on as an adjunct of general farming. The wool grown is of less importance to the farmers than the lambs raised for the market. The farmers are well situated for the marketing of mutton, since they are within a very short distance of many large cities; but location also favors the dairy industry, and milch cows are found to be more profitable than flocks of sheep by the majority of farmers. Sheep are, however, kept as "scavengers" in some cases; and on many farms there are rocky and sterile areas which are unproductive of forage for cattle and which are given over to sheep. A few sheep are often pastured with the dairy herd, as they clean up many corners which remain untouched by the cows.

The total wool output of New England in 1924 was only 1,077,000 pounds, almost all of which was rated as "medium." The number of fleeces clipped was estimated at 169,000. Maine produces a greater quantity of wool than any other New England State —542,000 pounds in 1924—while Vermont stands second in total amount and first in the amount of fine wool grown.[17]

Authorities on sheep husbandry, and govern-

---

[16] Ibid., p. 186. [17] Ibid., p. 176.

mental commissions which have investigated the
subject, have emphasized the opportunity for an
expansion of the industry in New England. They
have laid stress on the similarity of conditions there
and in England. In the United Kingdom there are
about twenty-four million sheep, or practically 200
per square mile, while in New England there are
less than 200,000, or about three per square mile.[18]
Massachusetts has only about 15,000 sheep, while
1,000,000 carcasses of lamb and mutton are annually
consumed in the state.[19] There are 1,000,000 acres
of waste land in the Commonwealth, and many of
the abandoned farms could be utilized better in this
way than in almost any other. Stray dogs are a
menace to the flocks, but this danger can be overcome by more stringent legislation. Sheep clubs
for boys and girls, demonstration flocks kept by
county agents, and co-operative marketing of wool,
have been recommended as appropriate means of
stimulating the industry.[20] Such measures will
prove entirely ineffective if other enterprises give
more profitable employment to the agricultural
population. It would seem, however, that the
farmers might make a substantial profit by utiliz-
ing hitherto unused resources.[21]

[18] *Report* of the Massachusetts Special Commission on the
Sheep Industry, Agriculture and Related Matters, Massachusetts
Senate Document No. 293, 1919, p. 11.
[19] Ibid., p. 12.   [20] Ibid., pp. 20-4.
[21] "Sheep men of Connecticut, New Hampshire, and Maine ad-
vise starting with small flocks of from eight to twelve, on small
farms, where the surplus stuff would be almost enough to feed

IV. ENCOURAGING NEW DEVELOPMENTS IN THE FARM SHEEP INDUSTRY

Changes which have occurred in farm sheep husbandry in the United States within the past few years are distinctly of good omen for the future welfare of the industry. Before making an estimate of the prospective trend of sheep raising in this country, our attention should be turned briefly toward these developments.

The growth of co-operative marketing of wool is one of the most hopeful indications for the future prosperity of farm sheep raisers. It is peculiarly necessary for the farm wool growers to sell their wool co-operatively because of the small size of the individual clips. The wool growers of the Far Western states are in a much stronger bargaining position, for one clip often amounts to several thousand pounds. The ignorance of the average sheep owner—particularly the smaller grower—concerning the quality of the wool which he has to sell, is another important factor which operates in favor of co-operation. Associations and wool pools hire

them. All authorities on the subject are agreed that sheep should be combined with dairy herds. From twenty to thirty ewes could be carried on a farm with only a slight increase in crop area and no increase in paid labor. It was suggested that restoration of sheep raising here might bring about the English system of common pasturage during the summer, the sheep going back to the individual farms in the winter. It was pointed out that there are tracts in Massachusetts large enough to run from 1500 to 2000 sheep, if the owners of adjoining lands would get together. Sheep breeders should rotate the pastures, as too continuous feeding on the same ground causes disease." Ibid., pp. 13-4.

expert graders and agents, and their services tend to place the seller more nearly on terms of equality with the buyer.

Before the World War, co-operative wool selling was poorly organized and unimportant in volume. The forces tending toward disintegration were much stronger than those drawing the sheep owners together. The action of the government in 1918 in taking over the entire clip of the country and grading it, may have been somewhat educative. The great urge toward co-operation after the war was, however, the depressed state of the wool market in 1920 and 1921. The movement attained its greatest proportions in 1921, when 22,298,856 pounds were marketed co-operatively in eighteen states. Since 1921 the price of wool has risen, and sellers have been in a much stronger position. Quite naturally, therefore (because depression is an urge to co-operation), the amount of wool sold co-operatively has fallen off. The experience of 1921 proved the possibilities of co-operative sale, however, and that method of marketing will again be employed if a similar situation arises. It will undoubtedly grow even under conditions of prosperity for the wool-grower, because of its obvious advantages.

Those who do not join the pool gain materially through its operations, which stimulate the local price. The co-operative movement is also useful in other ways than through price stimulation. It establishes a reputation for a locality where wool is of good grade and well prepared for market, and helps to bring about better trade relations with those who buy that grade. It arouses a healthy rivalry between sheep owners to improve their flocks and to excel in preparation of the clip for market. Furthermore, in 1920, when wool was a "drug on the market," the associations had large quantities of wool manufactured into blankets, robes, and other articles, and distributed them to members upon an equitable basis.[22]

For the efficient working of any co-operative plan it is usually necessary that a contract should be entered into, between the grower and the association. The Iowa Fleece Wool Growers' Association is a typical successful organization. Their "producer's contract" provides that the grower shall market his wool through the association for three years. He agrees to deliver it, packed in standard wool sacks, f. o. b. at the selling point, which may be designated by the association. The latter agrees to furnish the grower with sacks and twine on a cost basis, and to instruct him in preparation of the wool for market; to store the wool, and grade it into the lines most suitable for advantageous sale; to sell it according to best judgment; and to deduct only the actual cost of handling, including the ac-

[22] "The extent of this proposition is illustrated in the case of Iowa, which last year manufactured in excess of 10,000 pairs of double bed blankets for their consignors." *Report* of the Executive Secretary to the President, Executive Committee and Board of Directors of the American Farm Bureau Federation, Third Annual Meeting, Atlanta, Georgia, Nov. 21-3, 1921.

cumulation of necessary reserves. The grower agrees to pay his pro rata share of the marketing cost, and if he fails to market through the association is subject to a fine levied by the pound upon all the wool sold. The contract may be terminated by either party at the end of any year's operations by giving notice in November.

The Iowa association for several years entered into an agreement with a wool warehouse and storage company for the storage, grading, and sale of the wool of its members. The company received as compensation 2-¾ cents per pound on all wool held not more than five months, and an additional storage and insurance charge for wool which had to be held longer. The company advanced freight, and 50 per cent of the value of the wool, not to exceed 15 cents a pound.

It has been found that concentration of the wool of a whole state, or even of a larger area, at one point is better than a local pool. The advantages of the larger scale operation are, first, greater bargaining power; and second, opportunity to grade, classify, and assort the wool into different lines, so that the buyers are afforded a wider option and are thus more inclined to do business with the pool. The disadvantage of this form of operation is that a longer time is usually required to dispose of the wool and secure returns for the grower.

More wool has been marketed co-operatively in Ohio than in any other state. The Ohio Sheep and

Wool Growers' Association which was reorganized in January, 1918, and has its headquarters in Columbus, handled about 2,000,000 pounds of wool in 1919. In 1920, the worst year of depression, it sold approximately 3,000,000 pounds at an average price of about 40 cents a pound, and at a selling cost of 2-¾ cents a pound. In 1921, the quantity sold was 5,798,390 pounds at an average net price to the grower of 27 cents a pound, which was several cents better than probably could have been obtained in the ordinary way, through private enterprise. In 1922, the Ohio association marketed about 3,000,000 pounds; in 1923, about 4,000,000 pounds; and in 1924, 3,700,000 pounds.

The success already attained in this field of co-operation gives assurance that efforts will be continued to give the farmers the maximum return for the products of the sheep industry. And the fact that the members of the associations—as many as 45,000 in one year—have received approximately five cents a pound more for their wool than they otherwise would have obtained, is only part of the gain, for the growers are now stimulated to improve the quality of their wool by accurate knowledge of its grade and by the further consciousness that they will be compensated for efforts to improve it.

A marked advance has been made toward the establishment of standard wool grades. Experts of the United States Department of Agriculture have been working on this problem for several years.

Tentative grades have been selected and used extensively in grading wool for co-operative sale. Several hundred sets of samples of these grades have been distributed throughout the country and have been of great educational value to wool growers. The accuracy of the work has been attested by manufacturers, dealers, and growers. Conferences with representatives of the English wool industry have been held, and it is hoped that eventually the same form of standardized classification and nomenclature will be used in all English speaking countries.

The methods of sheep husbandry are being constantly improved. Agents of the Federal and state governments are engaged in experiment and demonstration. Colleges of agriculture are potent factors in improving the current standards of practice, and state agricultural and fair associations help along the work. The county agricultural agents have probably done more than any other one group to disseminate progressive ideas concerning sheep husbandry.

The movement toward the use of higher grade breeding stock is one of the most hopeful signs. The United States Department of Agriculture received reports from its agents that better rams were placed in service in the following states in 1924: Tennessee, 252; Iowa, 168; Alabama, 54; Pennsylvania, 35; California, 25. Through the influence of the Federal Extension Service 152 head of pure

bred sheep were purchased in other states.[23]   Nine
"ram rings"—a method of prolonging the useful-
ness of rams by changing their location at the end
of each two-year period—were in operation in
Pennsylvania in the same year.   More than one
hundred demonstration farm flocks have been established in New York, Kentucky, Virginia, and Tennessee.   These flocks not only serve to illustrate
the best methods to all sheep owners in the com-
munity, but they also constitute a source of higher
grade stock.   Many special meetings are held by
government agents at which wool grading, "culling"
of poorer ewes from the flock, and other useful
methods are demonstrated.   The use of copper sul-
phate and tobacco extract in remedying and elimi-
nating stomach worm is one of the innovations
which recently has been given widespread publicity.

The docking and castrating of lambs has also
been given much attention.   Kentucky, as we have
seen, is one of the leading states in the production
of early lambs.   In that state, according to reports
of the Department, 150,000 or more lambs were
docked and castrated during the year 1924, largely
as the result of demonstrations held by government
specialists.   It has been shown that the treated
lambs bring from 50 cents to $1.25 per hundred-
weight more than others, and that the percentage
of "No. 1's" is much higher.   Similar demonstration

[23] Information furnished author by U. S. Department of Agriculture, Bureau of Animal Husbandry.

work was carried on in 1924 in Iowa, Missouri, Indiana, Virginia, and West Virginia.

The supplemental feeding of early lambs is also being encouraged, and as a result market shipments are being made earlier, thus avoiding the glut which comes in September. Sheep owners have been shown how to construct their feeding pens better. The "zig-zag" type is favored because it affords more feeding space than the old straight line system. Information has also been spread concerning the best use of beet-tops, alfalfa, and corn in the feeding of sheep and lambs. Altogether, the advocacy of practical, scientific methods has done much to improve the position of the farm sheep raiser.

V. THE OUTLOOK FOR FARM SHEEP HUSBANDRY

Tendencies exhibited by sheep husbandry at different times and in many parts of the world give us reason to believe that sheep will continue to be important in diversified agriculture in the United States. The profit made from sheep raising under frontier conditions is low when it is expressed as a profit per acre of the land used. With the growth of population, land passes over to agricultural use. With the application of labor and capital to the land, the returns increase greatly over those obtained from the pastoral industry. The withdrawal of land from range use and the increase of sheep on irrigated ranches and dry farms in the West is thus in harmony with developments elsewhere.

The number of sheep kept in a region given over to diversified agriculture may be as large as when the region was entirely devoted to the pastoral industry. The breed of the sheep will be different, however. They are bred to secure the greatest possible profit from both wool and mutton, but as the latter is of greater importance, the pure mutton breeds are favorites. The wool is coarser; but the higher price received for large and early maturing lambs more than compensates for that unfavorable feature. This tendency as we have seen, has constantly manifested itself in the history of sheep raising in the United States.

There are several reasons why sheep are more valuable than any other animals in certain schemes of agriculture. It is hard to replace sheep because, first, they consume pasturage and roughage which no other animals, except goats, will eat; and goats are not as profitable. Second, sheep can be kept to good advantage on certain rotation crops. In this way, as well as by the high value of sheep manure, they help to maintain the fertility of the soil. Third, grain can be used economically in sheep husbandry. A small amount of grain creates more value when transformed into lamb and mutton than in almost any other way. Fourth, the seasonal character of the industry helps to keep it in favor in some parts of the country. Lambs can be fed in barns in the winter, when other work is slack. Shearing can be postponed until after planting time is over and before haying and harvesting begin. Fifth, climate and soil conditions bring sheep into especial favor in some localities. For example, the mild climate and rich soil which are found in some parts of the South produce an ideal situation for raising early lambs. Sheep are often useful also in preventing erosion of the soil. In hilly regions plowed ground is often washed out; while if the land is kept in pasture the sheep feed in the high places, packing down the surface and fertilizing the land. For this reason it is often well to pasture sheep and cattle together. The preference of sheep for high ground and of the cattle for the lower spots, makes them supplemental to each other.

The prevalence in parts of the United States of some of the conditions described above explains why sheep raising is successful, and their absence explains the failure of sheep raising in other sections. The neglect of sheep in some regions has not been altogether due to economic reasons, however. It has been due partly to ignorance of their value as farm animals, and partly to waste of available resources. The experience of Great Britain suggests strongly that the number of sheep in the farm states of this country may be increased with a positive benefit to the other farm operations.

It is apparent that sheep are a source of profit to farmers in many parts of the East, South, and Middle West. In New England sheep are used

as scavengers on the general farm. In the bean
growing and orchard regions of New York they
supplement specialized forms of agriculture. Corn
fields are cleared up to good advantage by sheep
in many parts of the Corn Belt. The limestone
pastures of Virginia and the blue-grass fields of
Kentucky, together with the milder climate, afford
an opportunity of producing early spring lambs.
The Piney Woods area of the Gulf states supports
flocks which, though of inferior grade, yield wool
at low cost. In Ohio the high land along the rivers
is better suited to sheep raising than tillage. The
hilly sections of the Mississippi and Missouri Valleys are adapted to a system of joint cattle and
sheep production, and in the cut-over areas of
northern Wisconsin and Michigan there is much
land better suited to pasturing sheep than to any
other purpose. The by-products of the flour mill-
ing industry, and surplus fodder, are used for fattening sheep in many localities. Sugar beet production finds a useful adjunct in flocks to consume
the beet-tops and the alfalfa raised in rotation.
These facts all point toward the continuing importance of sheep husbandry in conjunction with
agriculture.

Looking at the matter from the supply side—
that is, from the point of view of good farm organization and wise utilization of land and labor—the
conditions seem favorable for an increase in sheep
raising on farms in the United States. The pro-

duction will, of course, be greater if there is a high price of wool than it will otherwise. Yet our analysis shows that wool, and even sheep husbandry itself, is of a sufficiently by-product character so that there probably will be a substantial output even if the price of wool is low. The nature and extent of the demand for the products of the industry, and their influence on the amount produced, we shall consider later.[24]

[24] See Chapter IX.

CHAPTER III

COMPETING SOURCES OF SUPPLY

The principal wool-growing regions of the world are undergoing a transition from range conditions to diversified agriculture, similar to the transition which has long been in progress in the western United States. This development brings with it a larger number of crossbreds and mutton sheep. Also, it has become apparent that even when tillage is not employed there is a greater profit in raising a combination mutton and wool sheep than in raising sheep for wool alone. As long ago as 1912, when the Tariff Board made its report,[1] there existed an almost world-wide tendency toward keeping more of the mutton breeds of sheep and crossbreds of the Longwool-Merino or Down-Merino types.

In consequence of this transition there has been both a change in the kind of wool and an arrest of the increase in the world's wool supply. The tendency for a long period has been toward a slackening of the increase in production, and for several years before the war the world output was prac-

[1] U. S. Tariff Board, *Report on Schedule K*, 1912, p. 394.

tically stationary. Since the war it has actually
declined. It is the object of this chapter to trace
these changes and to draw conclusions as to their
effect on the competitive position of the American
wool-growing industry.

I. AUSTRALIA

Australia has a soil and climate, and is in a stage
of economic progress, which favor wool-growing by
extensive methods over large areas. Sheep were
imported from the Cape of Good Hope in 1788, and
the exportation of wool to England began before the
nineteenth century. English manufacturers were
impressed with the high quality of Australian Merino wool from the beginning, and the industry
made rapid strides. By 1880 Australia was the most
important among wool-producing countries.

*There is little prospect of an expansion of wool
production in Australia.* It is true that in 1917 there
remained 875,000,000 acres of unused Crown land
out of a total area of about 2,000,000,000 acres.[2]
But these figures taken alone indicate a greater opportunity for the increase of sheep raising than
actually exists, for the nature of the unused land,
which is mainly desert, acts as a limitation. The
number of sheep kept in connection with diversified farming is increasing, and there is more prospect of growth in this direction than of a marked

[2] U. S. Tariff Commission, *The Wool Growing Industry,* 1921,
p. 301.

expansion of sheep raising in the "bush" or in the great "out-back" plains. The production of wool in Australia decreased from 720,000,000 pounds in 1909 to 650,000,000 pounds in 1924, while the acreage under cultivation and the output of agricultural crops steadily increased. The indications are, therefore, that in spite of considerable space for the expansion of the sheep industry, the low carrying capacity of the land which is left and the competition of other crops will prevent its development.

There has been a marked tendency in late years toward the production of crossbred wool. The paramount influence in bringing about this change has been the superiority of crossbred sheep for mutton purposes. The growth of the frozen meat business has greatly stimulated mutton production at the expense of the "fine" wool production. In 1890, practically all the wool grown in the Commonwealth was Merino, while in 1918-19, 30.25 per cent of it was crossbred.[3] In subsequent years the proportion has been about the same, although there is evidence of some reaction toward fine wool. The frozen meat trade was at first only a means of getting rid of surplus sheep, and in 1890 the exports from Australia numbered only 200,000 carcasses. Yet just before the late war, 4,000,000 carcasses were exported annually.[4] In 1916 the meat supply, as well as the wool, was taken over by the British

---

[3] *Dalgety's Wool Review,* 1918-1919, p. 59.
[4] Ibid., 1914-15.

Government.   Large amounts of mutton had to be
stored on account of shipping conditions during the
war, but the Government purchase relieved the situation for the producers.[5]

There is a noticeable tendency toward the breaking up of the large estates, especially in the
southern coastal region.   This is due, first, to the
increase in the value of the land, which makes grazing less profitable than other uses; and second, to
the tax policy of the Government, which is especially designed to discourage large holdings.[6]

With the subdivision of the large "stations,"
where there was formerly one large clip, usually
of Merino wool, there are now often 15 or 20 small
clips, mostly of crossbred wool.[7]   The small flocks

[5] "The Imported Meat Trade," *Royal Agricultural Journal*,
1916, p. 73-8. Total imports of frozen mutton into Great Britain
from all sources in 1918 were 2,442,804 carcasses as compared
with 3,221,483 in 1917, and 7,377,454 in 1913.

[6] NUMBER OF HOLDINGS IN THE STATE OF VICTORIA

Size of Holding	1904	1913
1 to 500 acres..................	39,105	50,848
501 to 1,000 acres..................	7,971	10,161
1,001 to 2,500 acres..................	4,055	4,544
2,501 to 5,000 acres..................	834	820
5,001 to 10,000 acres..................	309	267
10,001 to 20,000 acres..................	180	116
20,001 to 50,000 and over..............	121	34
50,001 and over.......................	23	1
Total	52,598	66,791

Dalgety's Wool Review, 1912-13.

[7] In New South Wales, for example, one of the older states, the
day of the "sheep king" has passed. In 1891, there were 73 flocks
of 100,000 sheep or more. In 1900, the number of such flocks had

are kept, as in the United States, to utilize surplus crops in connection with diversified farming or grain raising. In recent years, more attention has been paid to water conservation, and to the storage of fodder in the form of hay and ensilage.[8] This breaking up of estates and closer settlement had proceeded far before the war. Some of the wool-growers of the country were even alarmed lest the business of breeding high grade fine-wool stock be curtailed, and the supremacy of Australia in the production of the best grade of wool be endangered. Although new territory is being opened up in the interior of Australia, and the tendency in that region is toward the "extensive" system, yet the increase is not great enough to offset the stronger tendency toward small flocks of crossbreds in the older sections. (See Map of Wool Growing Regions of Australia, p. 74.)

The transition to crossbreds was promoted by the enormous demand for crossbred wool during the war to make khaki and blankets. The kind of wool in greatest demand for uniform cloth for the rank and file was 40's to 46's (that is, common to low 1-4 blood in American classification). The finer grades, used for officers' uniforms, called for 56's to 58's. The price of the crossbred wool dur-

decreased to 14, and in 1912, there were only four. It is doubtful if there is one such flock in New South Wales at present. The total number of flocks, on the other hand, increased from 13,187 in 1891, to more than twice that number in 1923.

[8] *The Pastoral Industry*, published by Commonwealth Government of Australia, October, 1914, pp. 36-9.

ing the early part of the war, so great was the demand, rose to a higher point than the price of
Merino wool. The price of Merino wool was depressed also at that time by diminished demand
from the continental European countries which

WOOL PRODUCING REGIONS OF AUSTRALIA

formerly took 60 per cent of the Australian Merino
clip, and by an embargo for several months on the
exportation of wool to the United States. Later,
the scarcity of fine wool caused some readjustment
and after the Armistice the price of fine Merino
rose to a very high point. For most of the time
from 1919 to 1924 the spread between the prices

of Merino and Crossbred wools was greater than the pre-war normal.

The fundamental condition which favors the increase of Crossbred wool at the expense of Merino was well expressed in *Dalgety's Wool Review* for 1911-12:

"The continued expansion of the frozen-meat trade has led to a further increase in the proportion of the crossbred wool produced. Experience has proved that the Merino cannot compete with the crossbred for all-around returns on country which is suited to the latter, and as the pastoralists of Australia are engaged in sheep-raising for profit and not for sentiment, a continued decrease in the production of Merino wool must be expected. Each year finds the crossbred flocks penetrating further into the back country, and districts which, five years ago, were considered utterly unsuited to them, now graze and fatten thousands annually. Even Queensland, hitherto regarded as an impregnable stronghold of the Merino, is steadily increasing her crossbred flocks and though, as yet, they are not of any great consequence, the significant fact remains that they are on the increase."

Since 1912 this increase has continued.

II. NEW ZEALAND

Crossbred sheep have long been the dominant type in New Zealand. The Merino was the first sheep kept, and it is still bred in the hill country and on the downs of the South Island. The Merino ewe furnished the foundation of the crossbred stock which has made "Canterbury" mutton famous; but only about 4 per cent of the New Zealand wool is now Merino.[9] The export of refrigerated meat began in 1887, and mutton soon became more important to the sheep raisers than wool. The climate is excellent for mutton production; there is not much snow; and the English breeds, which thrive best in a cool, moist climate, were found to be admirably adapted to the country. The Romney, a long-wool sheep, is the most popular breed.

Though there is a possibility of some slight increase in the output of wool in New Zealand, the area of the country will not allow an expansion which will much affect the world's supply. There is considerable general farming in the country, and practically all farmers are, to some extent, sheep raisers. Dairying is important in the North Island and grain and root crops are raised on a large scale in the South Island; these operations are also combined with sheep raising. There are, however, millions of acres of land in the highlands which are unsuited to tillage but are well adapted to grazing sheep. Also, there are large areas in tussock grass the carrying capacity of which might be increased by seeding to "tame" grass. The number of sheep in the country is about 25,000,000, and the wool output is about 200,000,000 pounds a year. The

Dalgety's Wool Review, 1918-19, p. 59.

tendency is toward reduction of the average size of flocks, which is a little over 1,000 head.

New Zealand has followed, in general, the same policy as Australia in attempting to keep the land from being consolidated into great estates. The average size of all holdings is about 540 acres; but the average size of holdings devoted principally to sheep raising is about 1,500 acres. In the highlands much more land than this is required, however, and most of the "stations" occupy land held under pastoral leases from the government.

III. SOUTH AFRICA

South Africa is the country which seems to afford the greatest promise of an increase in the total number of sheep. It is also the only wool-growing country of importance where the tendency does not seem to be unmistakably toward the crossbred. Sheep raising is an old industry in South Africa. Native flocks were found there by the early settlers, and were improved by crossing with sheep from some of the best flocks in Holland. English breeds were brought into the country about 1820. There were also importations of Merinos from Saxony and France. The greatest improvement in the flocks of South Africa has been brought about by the importation during recent years of pure-bred Merino rams and ewes from Australia. Wanganellas, Tasmanians, and Rambouillets are the popular breeds. Vermont Merinos were tried some years ago, but they exaggerated the tendency of South African wool to shrink heavily—a tendency due partly to breeding and partly to the sandy character of the range. The shipping situation during the war made it difficult to secure pure-bred stock from abroad and stimulated the production of such stock for breeding purposes at home.

In South Africa the freehold land is less than half of the total area, and only about three per cent of it was cultivated in 1919. Considerable room, therefore, is left for expansion of the sheep industry. But since water is scarce and the carrying capacity of the land is low, there is doubt whether the number of sheep will much increase unless there is a greatly increased production of feed on the farms. Up to 15 years ago practically all sheep were herded on the open range; but the paddock system is now coming into use, which indicates a tendency toward more efficient methods. The original cost of fencing for the paddock system is heavy; but it is economical in the long run, because more stock can be kept on the same area, because labor is reduced, and because the wool is kept cleaner. The number of wooled sheep increased from 12,000,000, in 1904, to 29,343,675 in 1922.[10] There were also about 6,000,000 "native" or haired sheep which may gradually be replaced with improved sheep.

The Parliament of the Union passed the Land

[10] *Bulletin* of National Association of Wool Manufacturers, March, 1923, p. 241.

Settlement Act in 1912, and amended it in 1917. Under the terms of this Act the government is empowered to acquire land from private individuals and to resell on easy terms to settlers. Crown lands are also allotted to settlers, and the government assists in the development by boring wells or erecting buildings, and by purchasing stock and implements which are also to be sold on easy terms to settlers. The Land and Agricultural Bank of South Africa, known as the Land Bank, also extends financial help to farmers and to co-operative societies of farmers. In these ways the Government is materially promoting the cultivation of the soil.

The mutton industry is growing in South Africa. For some time there has been a large demand for home consumption, and the Union has imported considerable mutton. New freezing works have been established, and during the war the cold storage and chilled meat facilities in Pretoria, Bloemfontein, Maritzburg, and Durban were increased. Imports of fresh mutton into South Africa in 1908 were valued at $607,554; in 1915 at $1,158; but in 1917 there was a small export.[11] Exportation has not continued regularly, although it promises to develop. South Africa is nearer the London market than South America or Australasia, and this advantage should help to encourage the trade. Although the Merino sheep probably will

[11] U. S. Department of Commerce, Special Agents' Series, No. 146, by Juan Homs, p. 108.

remain numerically more important in the districts where the rainfall is light, in the sections where dairying and tillage are becoming common there may be a gradual increase in the number of the mutton sheep.

IV. SOUTH AMERICA

The principal wool-growing countries of South America are Argentina and Uruguay. Other countries which produce some wool for export are Chile, the Falkland Islands, Peru, Paraguay, Bolivia, and Brazil. The remainder of the continent has a climate unsuitable for wool-growing.

Argentina has been for many years one of the greatest wool-producing countries of the world; but the increase of tillage has lately much curtailed wool-growing. The war encouraged wool-growing through high prices for wool. Immigration was checked, somewhat hindering the development of agriculture. Yet in spite of these factors, the sheep-raising industry has not gained in importance, and the production of wool decreased from a pre-war average of about 360,000,000 pounds to 280,000,000 pounds in 1924.

The northern provinces of Buenos Aires, Santa Fe, Entre Rios, and Corrientes, were the first to develop the sheep industry; but the industry has been growing in the southern provinces, where there is considerable room for its expansion. The sheep first introduced into the country were of the

Merino type.   About 1885 the frozen meat trade began, and, in consequence, the Lincoln and other English breeds were introduced.   Most of the frozen mutton produced has been exported to the Unifed Kingdom.   About 75 per cent of the sheep are now crossbred, and the greater part of the wool now exported from Argentina is crossbred of high yield.

While the wool-growing industry of Argentina is bound to continue of great importance, and the country will probably remain one of the great wool-exporting regions of the world, such increase in strength and importance as the industry shows will be due to greater care in breeding and to more attention to details, rather than to any great augmentation in numbers of sheep.   There are fewer sheep in Argentina now than there were in 1875; and the constant growth of agriculture is causing less attention to be paid to the industry even though the great northern agricultural provinces could probably now carry more sheep than ever.

The physical characteristics of Uruguay stamp it as predominantly pastoral, and the sheep-raising industry has always been of great importance there. The climate is favorable; there are comparatively few wild animals; and the soil is better adapted to grazing than to agriculture.   About 98 per cent of the exports of Uruguay are normally made up of livestock products and meats.   Although the smallest independent country in South America, Uruguay has supported as many as 26,000,000 sheep; but the last census, taken in 1916, showed less than half that many head.[12]   Agriculture has increased, especially near the coast and river cities. The shipments of wool from Uruguay went, before the war, principally to Dunkirk, Antwerp, Hamburg, and ports of the United Kingdom.   Most of the Uruguayan wool was used on the continent of Europe.   After the war had been in progress for about two years, the United States took most of the Uruguayan wool; but a surplus was left at the close of the conflict, and the wool output declined rapidly.   In 1921 it was 125,000,000 pounds,[13] as against a pre-war average of more than 150,000,000 pounds.

The paddock system of handling the sheep is in use in Uruguay as it is in Argentina, and the breeds of sheep kept have also been much the same.   The "Criollo" (or native) sheep were first improved by the introduction of Merinos, and later, after the frozen mutton business became important, by the introduction of the English breeds.   The meat industry, which was in the beginning only a means of disposing of surplus stock by the preparation of salt meat, has grown in importance.   The combination wool and mutton type will probably be the sheep kept in Uruguay in the future.

Chile has never been a large exporter of wool, but

[12] The accuracy of these figures is questioned by some authorities on sheep husbandry.

[13] U. S. Tariff Commission, *Recent Tendencies in the Wool Trade*, 1922.

during the last few years, with the development of the southern territories which lie about the city of Punta Arenas, the industry has increased in importance. The industry in this southern territory was started by Scotch shepherds from the Falkland Islands. The wool-growing region, which is partly in Chile and partly in Argentina, produces from 30,000,000 to 40,000,000 pounds of wool annually; and the five freezing works in the district kill each year about 1,300,000 head of sheep.

The Falkland Islands have from 800,000 to 900,000 head of sheep, with an annual output of wool of 4,000,000 to 5,000,000 pounds. Peru has an annual production of between 10,000,000 and 15,000,000 pounds, but the exports of alpaca wool have been greater than those of sheep's wool from the latter country. Llama and vicuna wool are also produced in Peru; but the llama wool is inferior, and the vicuna is almost extinct. The wool industry of Peru is conducted principally on the table lands, at a very high altitude. The alpaca is not suited to an altitude of less than 5,000 feet. Paraguay, Bolivia, and Brazil export small quantities of wool. In the production, for export, of wool suitable for making clothing, South America, as a continent, is second only to Australia, but there is little prospect of an increase in the supply from that source.

V. CANADA

The sheep industry of Canada shows a marked predominance of the mutton breeds. Most of the sheep in the Dominion are kept on farms, the average flock being 25 head. There are only about 200,000 Merinos out of 3,000,000 head in the entire country. The Merinos are on the ranges of the Northwest, while in Ontario and Quebec, which have about two-thirds of all the sheep in Canada, and which are farming provinces, mutton breeds are kept. The range sheep industry is seriously handicapped by the large amount of snow, which precludes keeping sheep out of doors during most of the winter.

Sheep raising has been a declining industry in Canada until the past few years. The number of sheep was considerably less at the beginning of the war, in 1914, than it was in 1871, and only in 1918 did the industry regain the position it held nearly fifty years ago. The pre-war output of wool was about 11,000,000 pounds a year. The wool clip amounted to about 18,000,000 pounds in 1918; 24,000,000 pounds in 1921; and 15,000,000 pounds in 1924. Most of the clip is classed as "combing." The Longwool breeds have been giving way somewhat, in the past few years, to the Down breeds, because of the excellent mutton characteristics of the latter.

The Dominion Government has done a great deal

to stimulate the industry during recent years. A central warehouse at Toronto, controlled and operated by the Government, is a center for wool purchases by manufacturers. Financial facilities, through banking channels, have been provided, so that 75 per cent of the value of the wool may be advanced after appraisal by a Government agent. The authorities also encourage the conservation of breeding sheep; and if an owner must dispose of female stock, measures are taken to enable him to hold the ewes until a suitable purchaser can be found. Pure-bred rams are loaned to breeders' associations when the farmers cannot otherwise obtain them. Uniformity in the type of sheep in a locality—which represents an advance in efficiency —is often secured by the efforts of the breeders' associations. Co-operative purchase of feeds and of dipping and shearing apparatus is a progressive step which has been made in some places.[14] These measures have resulted in an increase in the output, which has been almost altogether in the direction of farm flocks yielding market lambs and a medium grade of wool.

VI. GREAT BRITAIN

There has been a decrease in the number of sheep in Great Britain in the past few years, largely because sheep are proving unsuccessful in competi-

[14] Arkell, J. Reginald, "Present State of Sheep Breeding in Canada," *International Review of Science and Practice of Agriculture,* Vol. VIII, No. 10, October, 1917, pp. 1333-8.

tion with dairy cattle. The pre-war output of wool was about 125,000,000 pounds a year, while in 1924 it was only 106,000,000 pounds. In spite of this decrease it is probable that the sheep industry will continue to occupy about the same place in the agricultural organization of the United Kingdom that it has for many decades past.

The experience of England shows conclusively that sheep-raising for the joint production of mutton and wool, with the emphasis on the former, is profitable, under proper management, in countries which have an intensive form of agriculture. The sheep-raiser who conducts the industry with the joint product in view must, however, be satisfied with a wool clip of somewhat coarse grade. Sheep farming in Great Britain is conducted with two principal aims—the production of mutton and the upbuilding of the land. Wool growing is of less importance than either of the foregoing objects. The methods of sheep husbandry in the southern and central part of Great Britain differ considerably from those of the hill country of northern England and Scotland. In the former sections, sheep are kept as one feature of a system of intensive agriculture. The climate permits sheep to be kept out all the year; but winter feeding with chaff, straw, hay, or roots is often necessary, and in the case of fattening lambs, grain, corn, and cottonseed or linseed are used. Kale, vetches, rape, cabbages, and turnips are sown expressly for the flocks, and grazing is regulated by changing the hurdles. Many of the sheep in England are kept under this "hurdling" system, which consists of enclosing the sheep within a movable fence which is changed every day so as to provide fresh pasturage. By this means the sheep are prevented from roaming about and consuming crops which are not intended for them. It reduces the amount of labor necessary in looking after the sheep and is peculiarly adapted to a country where intensive agriculture prevails.

There are a great many sheep in the Scottish Highlands, and also in the Cheviot Hills along the border between England and Scotland. Here the sheep are usually kept on land not suitable for cultivation. In some places there is a succession of different grasses and heather, so that there is fresh feed all the year; but supplementary feeding is necessary. The most popular breed in the Highlands of Scotland is the Blackface. The Blackface-Leicester and the Cheviot-Leicester crosses are also popular, and both give excellent results in mutton. The great majority of the 39 distinct breeds of sheep in Great Britain are used for crossbreeding at home, and the popularity of the exported pure-bred English sheep for crossbreeding in North and South America and in Australasia is well known. The sheep which are designated "crossbreds" in the United States—i.e. crosses between some variety of Merino and a mutton breed—are not kept in England. The crossbreds of that country are all dis-

tinctly mutton sheep.   There is no prospect of a
change in breeds, or of any marked increase in numbers of sheep, in Great Britain.

VII.   CONTINENTAL EUROPE

Sheep constitute an important feature of diversified agriculture in many parts of Europe. The number of sheep and the wool output of Europe remained
about the same for many years prior to the late war.
During the war the number of sheep was much
reduced in some countries, notably in France, while
in others there was a marked increase, especially in
Germany and Spain.   The total output of wool in
Europe in 1924 was 548,303,000 pounds as against
an average for the years 1909 to 1913 of about
520,000,000 pounds.[15]   A large increase in Spain
was partially offset by the decrease in Austria and
France.   Other countries which suffered a considerable decrease were Bulgaria, Poland, Denmark, and
Hungary.   The output of Germany, which was about
25,000,000 pounds before the war, is now double
that amount.

*Most of the sheep kept in Europe are of the mut-
ton breeds, and the recent additions to the flocks
have been largely of that kind.*   Even in Spain,
where the Merino originated, crossbred and mutton
sheep have increased in number.   In Germany,
where the Saxony-Merino was developed, and in

[15] U. S. Department of Commerce, *Commerce Reports*, March 5,
1923, p. 616.   Russia excluded from estimate in 1924.

France, the home of the Rambouillet, the production of fine wools has been almost entirely superseded by the growing of coarser grades incident to mutton production. Some Merino wool is raised in the northern part of Italy, especially in Apulia and Piedmont. The number of sheep in Italy increased greatly during the war, but the flocks have been reduced since that time. Before the war a variety of Merino sheep known as the Racka breed was common in Hungary. The flocks in that country have now been reduced by one-half. Territorial changes, however, have left the Hungarian wool largely fine. Merino sheep used to be numerous in Sweden, but their number is now very small, while the Cheviots, Oxfords, Shropshires, and Southdowns are found in considerable numbers. European Russia produced more wool than any other country on the Continent before the war, but it was mainly low-grade crossbred or carpet wool; a few million pounds of Merino wool were produced but the quantity was decreasing.

The scarcity of agricultural labor during the war stimulated the sheep industry in Europe, and, in those countries which were cut off from communication with exporting regions, the inadequate supply of both food and wool were factors in bringing about the increase of the flocks. Conditions were favorable for a revival of sheep raising, except in the war zones. Although there was sufficient increase in some regions to more than offset the losses in the devastated areas, the wool production of the Continent is not much greater than it was over sixty years ago.[16]

VIII. SUMMARY

It is evident that there is a world-wide tendency toward the crossbred and mutton sheep. This tendency is apparent even in Australia, the greatest Merino wool-producing country in the world. Both the natural advance of agriculture and the policy of the Australian Government are tending to break up the large estates, to lessen the average number of sheep in a flock, and to hasten the trend toward diversified farming. The growth of the frozen mutton trade has had much to do with the increasing popularity of the crossbred sheep and has helped to stimulate the form of the industry in which this kind of sheep could be kept profitably. In New Zealand the mutton breeds of sheep have been predominant for a long time, and the production of mutton and lamb for export is as important as the production of wool. There is no indication that the character of the sheep industry in New Zealand will change.

In South America the trend is all the same way. Tillage is increasing in the northern part of Argentina. There are places where sheep raising by open pastoral methods may increase, but the larger num-

[16] The wool output of Europe was estimated at about 500,000,000 pounds a year in 1860. See Helmuth, Schwartze, and Company, *Wool Circulars*.

MERINO SHEEP IN SALTBUSH PASTURAGE, AUSTRALIA

Courtesy U. S. Department of Agriculture

ber of Merino sheep in those areas is not likely to counterbalance the decrease in the other provinces. In South Africa, although the majority of the sheep are Merinos, the raising of sheep for meat production is increasing.

Great Britain is a striking example of a country in which sheep raising has found a permanent place in diversified agriculture because it helps to maintain the soil fertility and because mutton production is profitable; wool-growing is merely incidental. Continental Europe has many more mutton sheep than Merinos; although in some places, as, for example, in Spain, the original home of the Merino, that breed is still found in considerable numbers. Northern Italy, also, has some Merino sheep; but throughout northern Europe sheep are raised as a part of general farming operations and mutton production is more important than wool. The sheep of Canada, also, are almost all of the mutton breeds.

The tendency exhibited by the sheep industry of the United States is, therefore, part of a world-wide movement. Different causes contribute to the general trend in the newer countries; it is largely the result of growth of population and of transportation facilities, with a consequent increase in agriculture. The movement is stimulated by the greater profit of keeping combination wool and mutton sheep, while, in some places, the trend is aided by soil and climatic conditions. The widespread tendency is therefore based on fundamental causes. It will

WORLD'S PRODUCTION OF WOOL, 1909-13 TO 1924.
(Source: U. S. Department of Commerce, *Commerce Reports,*
March 16, 1925.)

Countries	Annual Average 1909 to 1913	1924
	Pounds	*Pounds*
NORTH AMERICA		
United States	314,110,000	282,330,000
Canada	11,210,000	15,112,000
Mexico	7,000,000	795,000
Total	332,320,000	298,237,000
CENTRAL AMERICA AND WEST INDIES.	1,000,000	750,000
SOUTH AMERICA		
Argentina	358,688,000	280,000,000
Brazil	35,000,000	19,000,000
Chile	17,430,000	34,000,000
Uruguay	156,968,000	95,000,000
Other	19,264,000	24,984,000
Total	587,350,000	452,984,000
EUROPE		
France	80,688,000	42,361,000
Germany	25,600,000	53,600,000
Italy	55,000,000	57,000,000
Spain	52,000,000	94,798,000
United Kingdom	134,000,000	106,300,000
Russia	320,000,000	*
Other	172,744,000	194,244,000
Total	840,032,000	548,303,000
ASIA		
British India	60,000,000	60,000,000
China	50,000,000	75,000,000
Persia	12,146,000	19,000,000
Russia in Asia..................	60,000,000	195,000,000**
Turkey in Asia.................	90,000,000	60,000,000
Other	1,000,000	*
Total	273,146,000	409,000,000
AFRICA		
British South Africa.............	157,761,000	193,000,000
Other	53,806,000	81,265,000
Total	211,567,000	274,265,000
AUSTRALASIA		
Australia	705,146,000	650,000,000
New Zealand	198,474,000	188,000,000
Total	903,620,000	838,000,000
OTHER	13,000,000	15,000,000
GRAND TOTAL	3,162,035,000	2,836,539,000

* No estimate. ** Russia, European and Asiatic.

lower the quantity of fine Merino wool and will aid
the range wool-growers of the United States to some
extent in that way. It will not increase the competition from imported mutton and lamb unless the
prejudice in this country against the frozen product
is overcome.

The other important tendency is the slackening
in the rate of increase of wool production throughout the world. This is connected in some countries
with the trend toward diversified agriculture. In
the older countries wool production has long been
stationary. Even in the United States it is not
larger than it was thirty-five years ago; while in
Great Britain, Canada, and Continental Europe
conditions are similar. Even in many of the newer
countries the wool output has reached its maximum
or has declined. In Argentina wool production is
less than it was twenty years ago. Some increase is
possible in Australia and South Africa, although influences are at work to prevent it. In New Zealand,
the carrying capacity of the land cannot be much
increased, and dairying is competing with sheep-
raising. Practically everywhere throughout the
world we find a tendency toward a decline in output.
This aspect of the world situation will react favorably on the competitive position of the United
States wool-growing industry, and will mitigate the
severity of foreign competition.

PART II

HISTORY OF THE WOOL DUTIES IN THE UNITED STATES

CHAPTER IV

THE WOOL TARIFF, 1789-1912

While it is unnecessary, and would prove wearisome, to enter upon an exhaustive account of wool tariff history, a brief survey of the subject will serve as a valuable background for more recent events. There have been duties on wool, with few exceptions, in the tariff acts passed in the United States since 1816. It is the purpose of this chapter to chronicle the more important happenings and to delineate the more obvious effects of the tariff. For a more elaborate analysis of wool tariff history the reader is referred to other sources.[1]

Sheep were brought to the Colonies early in the seventeenth century, but the numbers did not increase rapidly. Natural conditions did not favor them. There was such a scarcity of wool that exportation of it was prohibited in Massachusetts

[1] See U. S. Bureau of Animal Industry, *Special Report on the History and Present Condition of the Sheep Industry of the U. S.,* 1892; Bishop, J. L., *A History of American Manufactures from 1608 to 1860,* 1866; Wright, C. W., *Wool-Growing and the Tariff* (Harvard Economic Studies V), 1910; Taussig, F. W., *Some Aspects of the Tariff Question* (Harvard Economic Studies XII), Chapter XIX, 1915; Page, T. W., "Our Wool Duties," *North American Review,* April, 1913; Connor, L. G., *A Brief History of the Sheep Industry in the United States* (Annual Report of the American Historical Association), 1918, pp. 89-197.

from 1675 to 1681. Although homespun goods were made by the colonists, the finer cloths were imported from England until just before the Revolutionary War, when the use of the English goods decreased. The domestic industry could not supply the needs of the colonists for woolens, however, and during that war large quantities of these goods were smuggled in from England by way of France.

I. EARLY HISTORY OF THE WOOL TARIFF

There was little advance in sheep raising during the early years of America's independence. The wool produced was of good strength and of medium quality, well adapted to use on the hand-loom with which the wives and daughters made cloth for the family. The duties on woolens in the earliest acts were for revenue rather than protection. A few woolen mills were built before 1800 but there was a narrow market for their products, restricted between importation of fine goods from Great Britain and the manufacture of coarse goods in the household. These beginnings of woolen manufacture stimulated a little interest in wool-growing, however, and there was some importation of Merino sheep. The activity in the breeding of Merino sheep was, however, until the Embargo of 1808, confined to a few persons who took an especial interest in fine live-stock.

The Embargo marked the beginning of a great development of wool manufacturing and wool growing. The outbreak of the war of 1812 gave a new impetus to the industry, as there was a demand for coarser goods for the army, in addition to the demand for broadcloths which had been supplied before the embargo by England. At the end of the war the output of domestic woolen mills was three or four times what it was at the beginning, although the proportion of cloth made in factories to that made in the household was small. At the same time that the demand for wool from domestic manufacturers and from the household industry, was increasing, the farmers' foreign market for other products was curtailed, so there was a double incentive to increase the flocks.

Between 1816 and 1820 the situation changed entirely. After the close of the war, in 1815, the American market was again opened to British manufactures, while the demand for woolen goods for the army was removed. Woolen goods were imported from England in great quantity and at low prices, as the English manufacturers had a surplus of goods. American mills began to close and the price of wool to decline. The tariff of 1816 was passed in the endeavor to check the flood of imports which came in after the war. The duty on wool was fixed at 15 per cent, while the duty on woolens was 25 per cent, with the proviso that after three years it should be reduced to 20 per cent. The duty did little to check the imports of woolens, and the reduction proposed for 1819 did not take place. The duty on wool was of slight account because the depression in domestic manufacturing reduced the demand for wool to a low point, and there were almost no imports. There were even some exports of wool from the United States to Great Britain during this period.

Wool manufacture in the United States had been artificially stimulated during the War of 1812, and in consequence the equipment of the mills was poor and the technical knowledge of the managers inferior to that of their English competitors. After the more inefficient had been eliminated and the methods and equipment of the surviving concerns had been improved, the condition of the American woolen manufacture began to take on a more hopeful aspect. The crisis of 1819, the causes of which were complex, occasioned temporary distress; but between 1821 and 1824 several new mills were started.

Between the years of 1816 and 1833 there was almost constant discussion of the tariff question. It was a period marked by several crises and depressions; the manufacturing industries of the country were in a formative state; and foreign competition was severe on account of a surplus of manufactured goods and the occurrence abroad of crises, notably that of 1825-26 in England. It was natural that the producing interests of the United States should seek increasing protection to relieve them from the harassment arising from these different causes. The tariffs of 1824, 1828, and 1832 were outgrowths of this situation, and were an expression of the desire to create what Henry Clay called "The American System."

By the Tariff Act of 1824 the duty on woolen goods was raised to 30 per cent (it was to be 33⅓ per cent after 1825), and the duty on wool to 20 per cent; to 25 per cent after 1825; and to 30 per cent after 1826.[2] The British woolen manufacture passed through another crisis at this time, and threw on the American market large quantities of goods at prices which in some cases did not cover the cost of production. At the same time the British government reduced the wool duty to one half penny a pound if the wool were valued at a shilling or less, and one penny if valued at more than a shilling, while British Colonial wool was admitted free.

In 1828 the "Tariff of Abominations" was passed. This act derived its bad name partly from the fact that the rates were not adjusted, in relation to each other, with any approach to equity, and partly from the fact that many of the rates were exceedingly high. This act is sometimes called "The Woolens Bill" because of the high rates on woolen goods. The duty on most classes of woolens was 45 per cent ad valorem, with a system of minimum valuations which did not prove satisfactory as it led to

[2] Wool costing less than 10¢ per pound was dutiable at the old rate of 15 per cent. See *Tariff Acts of the United States, 1789-1909,* p. 79.

undervaluation. The duty on wool was four cents a pound and 40 per cent ad valorem, to be raised to 45 per cent the next year and 50 per cent the year after.[3] By 1830 a general improvement in conditions had taken place, due chiefly to the fact that British woolen manufacture had recovered from its depression and was not dumping goods upon the American market. In addition, the survivors of the severe competition to which the domestic industry had been subjected between 1815 and 1830, were fully capable of holding their own.

II. THE WOOL INDUSTRY AND THE TARIFF, 1830-1860

The first decade of this period preceding the Civil War was a time of great prosperity for the wool growers of the Eastern states, and marks the high tide of popularity of the fine wool sheep. The twenty years immediately preceding the war were a period of expansion of the industry in the Middle West, with a corresponding decline in the East.[4]

The tariff of 1832 was of a decidedly protective character; but it was followed in 1833 by the Compromise Tariff, which provided for a gradual reduction in the rates of duty fixed in the Act of 1832 until July 1, 1842, after which there would be a uniform rate of 20 per cent on all articles.[5] The

[3] *Tariff Acts of the United States, 1789-1909,* pp. 85-6.

[4] Wright, Chester Whitney, *Wool-Growing and the Tariff,* Harvard Economic Studies V (1910), Chapter V.

[5] Taussig, F. W., *Tariff History of the United States,* p. 110. On January 1, 1834, one tenth of the excess of all rates over 20 per

duty on wool, under the Act of 1832, was 4 cents a pound and 40 per cent ad valorem on wool costing over 8 cents a pound, while that costing 8 cents a pound or less was admitted free.[6]

During the years 1830-37, the price of wool was rising both in the United States and in the world market. The wool manufacturing industry in Great Britain and in this country was prosperous. Exportation of wool from Australia had only just begun. Under these conditions the American sheep industry found itself in a favored position, and, as very little wool was shipped from the Middle West, the Eastern growers reaped the benefit. The imports of both wool and manufactures of wool increased under the Compromise Tariff; yet domestic woolen manufacture grew during that period, and the number of sheep increased from about 12,000,-000 in 1830 to 19,300,000 in 1840.[7] The increase in manufacture was partly at the expense of the household woolen industry which was now on the wane. The crisis of 1837 brought with it a sharp break in the price of wool, and, although there was some re-

cent was to be removed; one tenth more on January 1, 1836; an additional tenth in 1838, and another tenth in 1840. On January 1, 1842, one-half the remaining excess over 20 per cent was to be taken off and on July 1, 1842, the rest of the excess was to go.

[6] Minimum duties on manufactured goods were done away with, by the Act of 1832, and ad valorem duties substituted. On most goods the rate was fixed at 50 per cent ad valorem. Carpets and blankets were dutiable at 25 per cent; flannels at 15 cents per square yard; worsted stuff goods at 10 per cent. See Wright, C. W., *Wool Growing and the Tariff*, pp. 83-4.

[7] U. S. Tariff Commission, *Report on the Wool Growing Industry*, 1921, p. 417.

covery within the next two or three years, the price of wool was lower during almost all of the following decade than it had been from 1830 to 1840.

The period of decreasing duties, under the Act of 1833, ended in 1842. The Whigs had again assumed control of the government in 1841; and within a short time after the "horizontal" rate of 20 per cent went into effect under the Compromise Act of 1833, the tariff act of 1842 was passed. This was distinctly a protectionist measure, although the argument for higher duties was based partly on the deficiency of the Federal Revenue after the panic of 1837. Upon the accession of the Democrats to power a lower tariff, the Act of 1846, was passed. It embodied a considerable reduction in rates, although it was not a close approach to free trade. During the remarkably prosperous period from 1846 to 1860, there was little agitation of the tariff question. Even in 1857, when a new act was passed still further lowering rates, the division was not strictly along partisan lines, and the reduction was brought about because of the redundancy of the Federal revenues.

During the years when fine wool growing was at its height, New England had about one third of the sheep in the country and the Middle Atlantic states about one fourth. Kentucky, Tennessee, and Virginia had a considerable number, and Ohio was also an important wool growing state; but the regions to the South and West had comparatively few sheep,

The beginning of the decade of 1840-50 found the wool growing industry of the West upon the point of a great expansion. The enthusiasm for "internal improvements" had already created a series of waterways of which the Erie Canal was the most important; but up to this time population had not increased rapidly around the Great Lakes, and the capital necessary to provide a good sized flock of sheep had not been possessed by many of the pioneers in Indiana, Illinois, and the other prairie states.

The eighteen forties were not years of high prices for wool, but the West rapidly increased its output. The low price level for farm products in general led to the adoption by Western farmers of wool production, as the clip furnished them a money crop which could be marketed to advantage. Along with this growth of flocks in the West there was taking place a decrease in the number of sheep in the East. The urban population was growing, and dairying was becoming more profitable than sheep husbandry. The great development of the sheep industry in the countries of the Southern Hemisphere was then fully under way, and exports from those sources increased by leaps and bounds. The expense of keeping sheep in the Eastern states was increasing: the value of land was rising; and, in comparison with the sheep husbandry of the Western states and of the countries below the equator, much greater expense had to be incurred for fodder. The economic development of the East had reached the point where resources could be more profitably used for other purposes. The flock owners turned to the mutton breeds of sheep to augment their profits, and sheep husbandry was reduced to a minor place in the diversified agriculture of the region.

During the latter part of this period, especially from 1853 to 1860, the price of wool was much higher than in the years following 1840, but the wool growing industry of the West expanded much less rapidly than it had during the era of low prices. The prices of other farm products were so attractive that the farmers neglected sheep in the rush to produce grain and meat for export. The development of railroads reduced enormously the cost of transportation to eastern markets and the seaboard.[8] The Irish famine, the abolition of the Corn Laws in England, and the Crimean War all aided in raising the price of farm products in the years 1847 to 1855. The panic of 1857 caused a temporary decline; but prices were high, on the whole, until the end of the period.

The number of sheep in the western states increased very fast in the years 1840-50, but only slightly from 1850 to 1860. The decline in the East, which began in the forties, continued until 1860. The same factors which had been operating there in the period of low prices continued in the years of

---

[8] The fall in the cost of transporting grain and meat bore a greater proportion to the total value of the product than in the case of wool.

higher prices, and were effective in preventing any general return to sheep raising. Some sheep were kept for breeding purposes and some for mutton production, but the industry was relegated to a subordinate position.

III. THE CIVIL WAR PERIOD

The natural trend of events in the sheep industry was interrupted by the Civil War. The industry was revived in the Eastern states, and the dominance of the West in wool growing, which had been imminent, was postponed. However, the course of development apparently was not changed, in the long run, and the chief significance of the events of this period lies in the adoption of the new scale of duties which became a permanent part of the tariff system.[9]

The Tariff Acts of 1861, 1862, and 1864 were passed mainly for revenue purposes. The Act of 1861 took effect on April 1, and, as the wool duties remained the same in the Act of 1862, the rates were uniform practically throughout the war period.[10] The adjustment of rates in these acts was rather more favorable to the manufacturers than to the growers, yet the result of war-time demands was un-

---

[9] Wright, Chapter VI.

[10] The duties were: 5 per cent ad valorem on wool valued at less than 18 cents a pound; 3 cents on that valued at 18 to 24 cents; 9 cents on that valued at more than 24 cents. Sheepskins, with the wool on, paid 15 per cent ad valorem. See *Tariff Acts of the United States, 1789-1909*, p. 166.

paralleled prosperity for both. The compensatory duty on woolen goods, which has had a prominent part in tariff history, was introduced in 1861.[11]

The high duties of the Act of 1864 [12] somewhat checked importation of both wool and woolens, but in 1866 it became apparent that Congress would pass a tariff law carrying even higher rates, whereupon importations began to come in great volume. Partly as a result of these imports and partly on account of the natural reaction from war-time activity and high prices, the domestic market for both wool and woolens collapsed in the latter part of 1867.

The end of the war in 1865 had not brought with it any cessation of expansion in the sheep industry, or, apparently, any abatement of the high hopes of sheep owners for a continuation of their remarkable prosperity. Not until the price broke did signs of curtailment appear, but then the sheep were sent to slaughter in great numbers, or were driven westward to contribute to the increase in flocks which soon took place in that region. The decrease in the total number of sheep in the country from 1867 to 1871 was over one-third—from 35,800,000 to 22,-400,000—the greatest reduction being in New Eng-

[11] See Chapter VI.

[12] The rates on wool in the Tariff Act of 1864 were: on wool valued at 12 cents a pound or less, a duty of 3 cents a pound; on wool valued at more than 12 but not over 24 cents a pound, a duty of 6 cents a pound; on wool valued at more than 24 but not over 32 cents, a duty of 10 cents per pound, plus 10 per cent ad valorem; on wool valued at more than 32 cents a pound, a duty of 12 cents a pound, plus 10 per cent ad valorem. See *Tariff Acts of the United States, 1789-1909*, p. 235.

land and the Middle Atlantic states. These regions had, at the end of the period, fewer sheep than in 1860. The whole number of sheep in the country, however, was greater than at the beginning of the war, the principal increase being in the Middle West.

The wool growers and the wool manufacturers met in convention at Syracuse, New York, in 1865, and agreed to stand together in support of higher rates on wool, together with the compensatory system. The schedule passed by Congress as a separate act in 1867 contained a much more minute classification of wool than any preceding tariff law, and raised the rates very materially.[13] The perpetuation of the compensatory system was of advantage to the manufacturers because it gave them a substantial amount of concealed protection.[14] The protective duty on woolen goods levied in 1867 was 35 per cent ad valorem, 10 per cent of which

[13] See Chapter VI of this book for discussion of the "blood classification" which was adopted at that time. The rates imposed were: on Class I, Clothing, and Class II, Combing Wool, valued at 32 cents per pound or less, a duty of 10 cents per pound and 11 per cent ad valorem; valued at more than 32 cents per pound, a duty of 12 cents per pound and 10 per cent ad valorem. By the change in classification making all wool valued at less than 32 cents per pound dutiable at 10 cents per pound and 11 per cent ad valorem, a considerable increase in the effective rate of duty was brought about.

[14] An allowance of four pounds of raw wool to one pound of cloth is excessive. The compensatory duty of the Act of 1867 was 50 cents per pound of cloth. This allowed compensation not only for four pounds of wool to each pound of cloth, but also for the duties paid on dye-stuffs and oils, and for interest on the amount of duties paid, for the time between the payment of duty and the sale of the finished goods.

was to offset the internal revenue tax.[15]   The extra
10 per cent duty was continued in force, however,
after the tax was removed.

IV. FROM THE END OF THE CIVIL WAR TO THE TARIFF ACT OF 1894

The most important development in wool growing in the United States during the years following
the Civil War was the expansion of the industry in
the Far West. Wool growing followed the frontier
to its final outpost, and found in the region last
utilized a territory better adapted to it than any
theretofore occupied. The arid nature of the country precluded a rapid development of agriculture,
but livestock could be kept profitably.

The era following the Civil War was one of great
industrial expansion. Immigration increased, and
the population doubled between 1870 and 1900.
Two transcontinental railroads were completed
within a few years after the close of the war, and
these aided considerably in the development of the
western territory. Expansion in agriculture accompanied the industrial development. There was a
great increase in grain growing in the Central West,
and the export trade in cereals, beef, pork, and dairy
products grew by leaps and bounds. The growing
industries of the country furnished new markets
for the agricultural produce of the West, and the
improved transportation system and reduced freight

[15] *Tariff Acts of the United States, 1789-1909*, p. 260.

rates furnished the means of delivering the increased volume of production to the eastern markets and to the seaboard for exportation.

At the same time that wool growing was increasing in the Far West the countries of the Southern Hemisphere—particularly Australia and Argentina —were also expanding their production of wool. The price of wool in the United States was low relative to the price of other agricultural commodities during most of this period. There were two rises in price, one in 1871-72 due partly to the Franco-Prussian war and partly to the great reduction in the number of sheep after the Civil War. The other increase in wool prices came in 1879-80 as a result of the revival of business on the resumption of specie payment. The surplus from the Southern Hemisphere, however, operated to depress the price.

The wool manufacturing industry as a whole underwent a great expansion, but the most noteworthy development was the rise of the worsted manufacture. The extent of the benefit to wool growers can be appreciated when it is considered that the amount of wool used by the worsted industry increased from 3,000,000 pounds in 1860, to 100,000,000 pounds in 1890. This increase in demand would have been more potent in increasing the price of wool, despite the augmentation of supply from the Southern Hemisphere, had it not been for the increased use of cotton and shoddy in wool manufacturing.

While sheep raising was developing in the Far West from 1870 to 1885, it was declining in other parts of the United States. The reduction in the years 1867 to 1870 had been greater in the eastern states than in the Middle West. During the decade 1870-80 there was little change in the number of sheep in New England and in the Middle Atlantic states. The Middle West, with relatively larger flocks at the beginning of the period, suffered an almost continuous decline. Kentucky, Tennessee, Virginia, and West Virginia were the leading sheep raising states of the South, and there the mutton breeds made a rapid advance. Ohio had the largest number of sheep of any state in the Union from 1850 until about 1880, when California came to hold first place. Since that time one of the far western states has always held the leading position, and by 1900 several of the Rocky Mountain states had surpassed Ohio.

There was little growth in the industry in any part of the country except the Far West. The tariff may have caused a slower decrease in the numbers of sheep in the East and Middle West than would otherwise have taken place, because a comparison of domestic and foreign prices shows a difference of 8 to 11 cents per pound on comparable grades of wool. The wool duty of 1867 was aimed at the Mestiza wool of South America, and this was practically excluded. Imports of carpet wool from South America continued, but were almost wholly non-

competitive with the domestic clip. The chief
competition came from Australian wools, the clean
content of which was high. The imports both of
manufactures of wool and of raw wool increased
under the Tariff Act of 1867, but the domestic production of both also increased very fast. The proportion of foreign wool consumed was less than before the Civil War. More foreign wool came in as
manufactured goods than in the raw state, dress
goods being the largest item. A horizontal reduction of 10 per cent of all rates was made in 1872;
but the effect of this change was imperceptible, as
rates were again raised to their former level three
years later.

Surplus revenue led to tariff reduction in 1883. A
tariff commission took testimony in many different
parts of the country in 1882, and a reduction of
rates was expected. The rates enacted were, however, only slightly less than those of the Act of 1867.
On Classes I and II the ad valorem part of the duty
—11 per cent ad valorem on wools costing less than
32 cents a pound and 10 per cent on wools costing
more than 32 cents a pound—was removed.[16] The
point of separation between the value-classes was
reduced from 32 cents to 30 cents, however, which
partially nullified the reduction. The duty on the
lower grades competitive with Texas and Territory
wools was still high enough to keep out all exports,
while the reduction on the higher grades amounted

[16] *Tariff Acts of the United States, 1789-1909*, p. 337.

to little.[17] Although there was a re-arrangement of
the duties on manufactures of wool, the rates on
some classes being less and some classes more, making it difficult to estimate the total effect, still it may
fairly be said that the reduction of rates on manufactures was merely nominal.[18] Under the Act of
1883 the imports of raw wool increased, but since
the world price fell, the average value of the imports was less than under the former act. Imports
of manufactures also increased, although the average
duty amounted to 67 per cent of the value, which
was even higher than the rates paid by imports
under the previous act. Under this, as under the
previous act, the competing wool coming into this
country in the form of woolen manufactures was
much greater than the imports in the form of raw
wool.

The changes in the tariff of 1890 were very
slight,[19] so that substantially the same rates were

[17] Taussig, F. W., *Tariff History of the United States,* page 239.
The carpet wool duty was reduced from 6 cents a pound to 5
cents a pound on wool costing over 12 cents a pound, and from 3
cents to 2½ cents a pound on wool costing 12 cents or less per
pound. This was "a small but nevertheless a real reduction."
Ibid., p. 205.

[18] The compensating duty on woolen goods was reduced from
50 cents to 35 cents per pound on the assumption that only 3½
pounds of wool, instead of 4 pounds, was used in the manufacture
of a pound of cloth. The protective duty was raised from 35
per cent to 40 per cent on the better grades of woolens (those
valued at more than 80 cents per pound), while on the poorer
grades (those valued at less than 80 cents) the duty of 35 per cent
was unchanged. *Tariff Acts of the United States, 1789-1909,*
pp. 337-8.

[19] Duty on Class I wool increased from 10 cents per pound to
11 cents per pound; on Class II wool from 10 cents to 12 cents

in effect from 1867 to 1894. During this time the price of wool was low, with the exception of two brief periods. Prices of other agricultural products were sufficiently attractive to divert the attention of farmers away from sheep, but the natural advantages for wool growing in the Far West were so great that the increase in that section outweighed the decrease in other parts of the country. The supplies of wool from the Southern Hemisphere, together with the more extensive use of cotton and shoddy, might have further depressed the price of wool to the American producers had it not been for the tariff. The duties on wool and woolens were so much higher than those before the war that the tariff exercised greater influence than it had ever done previously. The American wool growers benefited by substantially the amount of the duty; yet other factors than the tariff were more influential in determining the course of events in the industry.

per pound; on Class III wool, valued at more than 13 cents per pound, it was made 50 per cent ad valorem, and valued at 13 cents or less per pound, 32 per cent ad valorem. The administrative provisions were made stricter. Carpet wool which had Merino or English wool mixed with it was to be classified as one of the latter varieties. Wool improved by rejection of any part of the fleece was subject to double duty, although this did not apply to "skirted" wool. The compensatory rates were readjusted so that on the cheap grades of woolen goods the ratio was three to one, that is, three pounds of wool were assumed to be necessary to make one pound of cloth; on the medium grades 3½ to 1, and on the better grades 4 to 1. The protective element also, in the rates on manufactures, was increased. *Tariff Acts of the United States, 1789-1909*, pp. 487-8, 504.

V. FROM FREE WOOL IN 1894 TO FREE WOOL IN 1913.

The tariff issue came to the forefront in the campaign of 1892, and, with the election of President Cleveland, revision downward was regarded as a foregone conclusion. The new tariff act was passed in 1894, and wool was placed upon the free list for the first time since 1861.[20] The compensatory duties on woolen goods were swept away, and in place of the old system of compound specific and ad valorem duties a schedule of purely ad valorem rates was instituted. The duty upon the classes of goods which were most largely imported was placed at 50 per cent, which was the same as that of the McKinley act of 1890. The woolen manufacturing industry, therefore, was not subjected to a drastic cut in its protection.

The domestic wool growing industry suffered by reason of the tariff change, but the crisis in the industry was not caused entirely by the removal of the wool duty. There had been a decline in wool prices ever since the middle eighties, and the market had taken another downward turn not long before the era of free wool began. The enactment of the new law followed the panic of 1893, and was accompanied by industrial depression to which several causes contributed.

The number of sheep was reduced rapidly in all sections of the country except the northern Rocky

[20] *Tariff Acts of the United States, 1789-1909,* pp. 504-5.

Mountain area (Idaho, Wyoming, and Montana). The decrease in numbers between 1893 and 1896 amounted to about 10,000,000, and the fall in value was so great that many flocks were butchered for the pelts and tallow. The low prices led to such neglect of the sheep that many were carried off by disease. The situation should not be regarded as having been principally caused by the tariff; it was rather the culmination of a series of events which had been lessening the profit of sheep raising. The new situation led to a readjustment in agricultural methods and in animal husbandry to correspond with changed conditions.

The former high scale of duties on both wool and woolens was restored in 1897.[21] It is very significant, however, that even after these rates were restored and after the world price of wool had risen considerably, because of a protracted drought in Australia, the number of sheep in all parts of the country except the Rocky Mountain states increased very little. In the eastern states the dairy industry had become firmly entrenched, while in certain regions of the West, such as southern Wisconsin, it had become of paramount importance. In the western states the acreage in corn and wheat continued to increase. On the Pacific Coast agriculture and fruit raising continued to crowd out the sheep. The number in the northern Rocky Mountain states continued to grow until about 1902, when

[21] *Tariff Acts of the United States, 1789-1909*, pp. 578-81.

the maximum carrying capacity of the ranges in that part of the country was reached.

The rates actually collected on imports of wool manufactures under the Tariff Act of 1897 averaged 91 per cent ad valorem; and the imports of manufactured goods fell to a very low point. The imports of raw wool increased, on the other hand; and the American wool grower for the first time in many years met with greater competition from this source than from foreign wool made up into goods. Australia continued to be the chief competitor, but the improvement in the grade of wool from Argentina and the greater demand for coarse wool, made it possible for the first time since the Act of 1867 to import large quantities from South America.

The tendencies in wool manufacture which had been made manifest in the preceding period continued during these years. The worsted manufacture gained in importance, until in 1905 it consumed a greater amount of wool than any other branch of the industry. Probably the greatest contributing factor was the increasing preference for lighter fabrics. The use of cotton also continued to grow, especially in hosiery and knit goods manufacture. The price of cotton was even lower, relatively, than the price of wool during the decade of 1890 to 1900, and this encouraged substitution. The per capita consumption of wool was less in 1900 than it was in 1860.

In 1909 came another revision of the tariff, which

was expected to lower the rates but which ended by leaving them at practically the same level as before.[22] The position of the sheep industry was about the same at that time as it had been in 1890. At the passage of this new act there were 42,000,000 sheep in the country, which was 1,000,000 less than in 1891, while the wool clip amounted to 311,000,000 pounds, or 4,000,000 pounds greater. The Rocky Mountain states had remained in the position of leadership which they had attained at the passage of the Act of 1897, but the tendency toward the reduction of available range land had become clearly apparent. The wool growing and wool manufacturing industries came up to the second free wool period since the Civil War, inaugurated in 1913, without having undergone any notable development since the passage of the Act of 1897.

VI. CONCLUSIONS

The consensus of opinion among economic historians is that the tariff was not the predominant influence in shaping the course of events in the wool growing industry during the years covered by this chapter. After the Civil War the wool duty was of more assistance to the growers than before, yet even then it seems to have been overshadowed by other forces operating in the industry. The ruling factors were: the competition of other kinds of farm enterprise, which limited the increase of farm sheep

[22] *Tariff Acts of the United States, 1789-1909,* pp. 741-44.

husbandry over most of the country; the opening of the western ranges, which caused the industry to expand in the Far West; the great growth in imports of wool from Australia and Argentina, which made it necessary for even the western sheep owners to turn to mutton and lamb to sustain their profits; and finally, the increased use of cotton and shoddy by manufacturers, which tended to keep down the price of wool and limit production.

During the time when these developments were taking place a duty was almost continuously maintained in the United States. It is impossible to say just how much the tariff contributed to the prosperity of the industry. It is probable, however, that the decline in output, which took place in the later years of the period under consideration, would have been somewhat accelerated in the absence of a duty.

CHAPTER V

WOOL UNDER THE TARIFF ACTS OF 1913 AND 1921

On October 3, 1913, the duty on wool was abolished, the removal to become effective on December 1. The change was not unexpected, as the tariff question had been agitated for several years, and in 1911 a bill had been introduced into the House of Representatives which placed wool on the free list. When the election was won by the Democrats in 1912, active discussion of the subject was renewed. The Tariff Board, in 1910-11, secured figures for cost of production of wool in both the Ohio Region and the Territory Region.[1] The cost data, taken in conjunction with other valuable information regarding wool growing during the ensuing period throw some light upon the effect of the tariff change.

I. THE TRANSITION TO FREE WOOL, 1913-1914

The period under free wool in 1913-14 was too short to afford any opportunity to draw conclusions

[1] The Ohio Region includes southwestern Pennsylvania, northern West Virginia, and southern Michigan as well as the State of Ohio. The Territory Region includes the Rocky Mountain and the Inter-Mountain States.

about the probable results of a permanent free wool
policy. The wool-growing industry of the United
States was not, however, greatly damaged by free

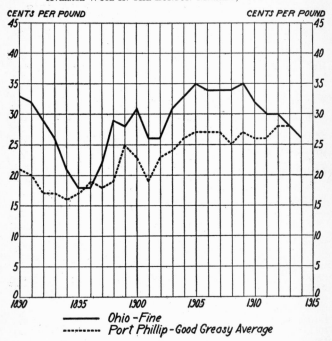

PRICES OF FINE WASHED OHIO FLEECE WOOL IN THE EASTERN
MARKETS AND OF COLONIAL PORT PHILLIP GOOD GREASY
AVERAGE WOOL IN THE LONDON MARKET, 1890-1914

—————— Ohio – Fine
- - - - - - - - Port Phillip – Good Greasy Average

wool at that time.   The only other trial of free trade
in the commodity was in 1894-97, and at that time
the general economic situation was very much dis-
turbed and the real effect of the policy was much in

doubt. Though economic conditions were more stable in 1913, the war, which followed so soon, obscured the long-run influence of a free wool policy. This much can be said, however, that free wool did not accelerate the tendency toward a smaller wool output which had existed for several years prior to 1913, nor did it lower the price of wool substantially, except, perhaps, on one or two grades.[2]

Wool production in this country had been increasing for several years prior to 1909, while from that time until 1917 it decreased. In 1917 production was about the same as it had been in 1903—281,-892,000 pounds in the later as against 287,450,000 pounds in the earlier year. The following table gives the wool output of the United States for a number of years preceding and following 1913.

WOOL PRODUCTION IN THE UNITED STATES, 1903 TO 1922 INCLUSIVE.

Year	Pounds	Year	Pounds
1903	287,450,000	1913	296,175,300
1904	291,783,000	1914	290,192,000
1905	295,488,000	1915	285,726,000
1906	298,915,000	1916	288,490,000
1907	298,295,000	1917	281,892,000
1908	311,138,000	1918	298,870,000
1909	328,110,749	1919	298,258,000
1910	321,362,750	1920	277,905,000
1911	318,547,900	1921	271,562,000
1912	304,043,400	1922	264,560,000

[2] During the time when the coming of free wool was being discounted and immediately thereafter, the price of Ohio fine wool declined by an amount approximately equal to the duty removed. See Chart on p. 122 for a comparison of prices of Ohio fine and Port Phillip average, 1890-1914.

Even if the entire decrease between 1909 and 1917 be considered due to tariff agitation, fear of free wool and its actual consummation, the effect was only 14.08 per cent decrease in the output of the United States. The entire decrease of this period can not, however, be ascribed to such a cause, for the wool duty which had been in effect ever since 1867 was re-enacted in 1909. There was no possibility of change for at least two years after 1909, even though the Tariff Board conducted its investigation in 1910. The principal reasons for the decline were the downward tendency of wool prices during 1909-13, and the increasing cost of production after the price had begun to rise again in 1913-17. The multiplication of the problems and difficulties of the growers in the range states no doubt also had much to do with the decrease in output.[3] Aside from these factors there were few disturbing elements. In fact, the years 1909 to 1914 were comparatively devoid of unsettling occurrences. Imports remained at about their usual level, except immediately preceding the removal of the duty, when they decreased, to rise again after free wool became a fact.

A study of the costs gathered by the Tariff Board in 1910 shows the marked disparity between costs of different producers, and brings out the fact that some individuals or companies were producing at a cost greater than the market price. The chart on

[3] See Chapter I.

p. 127 gives a graphic representation of the costs of production of Territory wool, as secured by the Tariff Board. The costs of 21,000,000 pounds of wool were obtained in the Far West. It will be observed that about 2,100,000 pounds of this were produced at a net credit; that is, according to the Tariff Board method of figuring cost, the receipts from "sources other than wool" (mostly mutton and lamb) more than offset the total expenses, so that there was no charge against the wool. The cost curve ascends steeply at first, then moves up gradually throughout most of its course, and rises sharply at the upper end, showing that about 1,500,000 pounds, or 7 per cent of the total, were produced at a cost greater than the average price for Territory wool at that time, 20 cents a pound. If the "bulk line" [4] were drawn at a point covering 93 per cent of the output the bulk line producer would be found producing at a cost equal to the average market price.

Between 1910, the year of the cost investigation, and 1917, the wool output of the Territory Region declined 8 per cent,—from 182,723,750 to 168,008,000 pounds. This did not occur, however, through the elimination of all growers who were producing at a cost greater than the price, a fact

[4] In a discussion of cost of production the term "bulk line" is used to indicate a line drawn at such a point that it will cover the major part of production and will presumably include all efficient producers. It may be assumed in this case that the costs obtained were representative of the western wool-growing industry as a whole.

which is borne out by the graphs of costs in 1918
and 1919, based upon the investigation of the U. S.
Tariff Commission.[5]   The explanation of this
phenomenon lies in the following facts: the "supra-
marginal" producers are partly those who have an
occasional bad year which swells their costs, and
partly the ones whose costs are nominally very high
but who are nevertheless making interest on their
investment and a fair wage of management.   Under
such circumstances they will not withdraw from the
business.   Moreover, the increasing amount of sheep
raising on irrigated farms in the Far West has
tended to give the industry a permanent place because of utilization of by-products and contribution
to soil fertility.   At any rate, most of the wool-
growers were securing returns from the joint production of wool and mutton great enough to induce
them to stay in the business.

When we turn to the chart on p. 129, which shows
the costs in the Ohio region, we find the shape of
the curve to be similar.   The average cost is much
greater, however, and the curve of costs rises more
steeply at the upper end.   The report of the Tariff
Board stated that wool was grown at a higher cost
in this region than anywhere else in the world, the
chief reason being that comparatively little dependence was placed upon lamb production.   The
Delaine sheep, the most popular breed in that section, grows a fine fleece, but the lambs are inferior

[5] See Chapter VIII.

COST OF PRODUCTION OF TERRITORY WOOL IN 1910

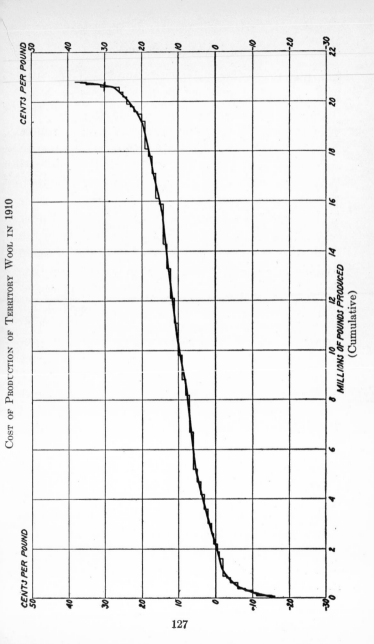

CENTS PER POUND

MILLIONS OF POUNDS PRODUCED
(Cumulative)

to those of the mutton breeds. Moreover, under the
system of sheep raising popular in Ohio, wethers
were often kept for wool production instead of being sold as lambs.[6] A larger proportion of the wool
of the Ohio region than of the Territory region was
grown by producers whose costs were greater than
the market price. During the period under consideration, we find, as might have been expected,
that the output fell off more in the Ohio than in the
Territory region. The clip of Ohio was 16,900,000
pounds in 1910 and 13,923,000 pounds in 1917, a
decrease of 17.6 per cent. Examination of the
graph (p. 129) shows that 17.6 per cent of the wool
of this section was produced in 1910 at a cost greater
than the average price of 30 cents a pound. The
reduction in output, as in the case of Territory wool,
was not brought about entirely by the elimination
of supra-marginal producers but by some re-adjust-
ment of production on the part of many producers.

The reduction in the output of wool in the whole
country between 1910, when the agitation for a
tariff change began to be evident, and 1917, when
the lowest production figure of this period was
reached, was 12 per cent—from 321,362,750 pounds
to 281,892,000 pounds. Because of the political
situation between 1909 and 1912, however, it is
doubtful if free wool began to be discounted before

[6] The method of conducting the industry in Ohio has changed
considerably since that time, especially through the reduction in
the number of wethers kept, so that the wool duty now means
less to the Ohio growers than in 1913.

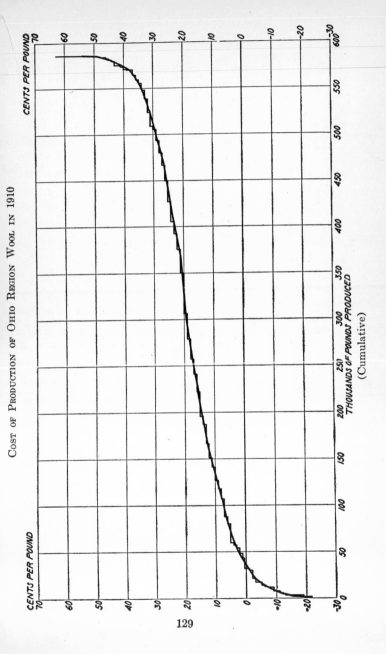

Cost of Production of Ohio Region Wool in 1910

CENTS PER POUND

THOUSANDS OF POUNDS PRODUCED
(Cumulative)

CENTS PER POUND

129

1912. The decrease in the clip between 1912 and 1917 was 7 per cent—from 304,043,400 pounds to 281,892,000 pounds. The coming of free wool did not, therefore, have a strikingly adverse effect on the production of wool in this country in these years of tariff discussion and revision. Yet we cannot tell how much more the margin of production in the industry would have changed in the years following, had not the war intervened.

II. THE WAR PERIOD AND ENSUING YEARS, 1914-1921

The experience with free wool under normal conditions was not to be long continued. The tariff history was interrupted and the record of wool growing in all countries became inextricably interwoven with military exigencies. The following account of the war period is given in considerable detail because the tariff legislation of 1921 and 1922 was the outgrowth of war conditions.

The events in wool tariff history which followed the war were likewise intimately connected with the surplus of wool which had accumulated under government control. To help us get the proper perspective as to the situation at the time of the signing of the Armistice it will be well to survey briefly the measures of control which were adopted by England and America. Control of wool by these two countries means practically world control of wool suitable for making clothing. Argentina and Uruguay are the only important sources of crossbred or

Merino wool outside the British Empire and the United States. A large measure of control of the South American market was exercised by England and the United States because of the importance of the markets they afforded to the South American growers.

The removal of the Central Empires as a market for Australasian wool, the occupation of the French and Belgian textile districts by the German army, and the readjustment to war conditions in the British and American wool manufacturing industries, kept the price down sufficiently during the first year. Strenuous measures on the part of the Government did not at first seem necessary. Complete control of the wool situation by the British Government did not come until the autumn of 1916.

Government control of wool in England as well as later in the United States was made imperative by the essential nature of the commodity which led to a great increase in the price. During 1916 the stimulation of English and American wool manufacture, due to the war demands and the opening of new export markets, had a marked effect; and as the supplies of Australasia and Argentina were short, due to drought and other causes, the price began to soar. The price of Port Phillip Average wool ("in the grease," or raw state) in London increased only from 27 cents to about 30 cents between January, 1914, and January, 1916, but by the end of 1916 it had reached 48 cents. In May, 1916, the British

Government arranged to take over the whole clip of the United Kingdom at prices 35 per cent above those of June and July, 1914. The 1917 clip was taken at an advance of 50 per cent and the 1918 clip at 60 per cent over the 1914 price. On November 23, 1916, the government purchased all available supplies of Australasian wool except what was needed for colonial manufacture. The price paid was 55 per cent higher than the 1913-14 average and 10 per cent below that then ruling in the market, or about 31 cents per pound in the grease. The entire 1917 and 1918 clips were also taken over by the British Government. The British Government also purchased some wool in South Africa, though not the whole clip. That market was left open to the United States and Japan during the war and the latter country was an especially heavy purchaser. Small amounts of wool were imported into England from other sources, but it all came under the control of the Government.

Wool prices reached a much higher level in the United States than in England. For some months after the beginning of the war in Europe the wool manufacturing industry of the United States was in a stagnant condition, but when the orders for military fabrics began to come from the foreign governments a boom period began. During the years which followed, there was an unprecedented consumption of wool by American mills, and all records for high wool prices were broken. Imports increased rapidly, and reached a record of over 500,000,000 pounds in the fiscal year 1915-16. Domestic consumption for that year was over 800,000,000 pounds, but the domestic production remained at the usual level of somewhat less than 300,000,000 pounds. American buyers purchased about 6 per cent of the Australasian clip in normal years before 1914, while in 1914-15 they purchased 15 per cent, and in 1915-16, 31 per cent. The British wool control, therefore, removed an important source of American wool imports. Some wool was released by the British Government for use in this country, under strict regulations as to the disposal of the finished product, to prevent aid to the enemy; but the supply was so limited that prices in this country were steadily climbing throughout 1917 and the spring of 1918. Territory Fine Medium Scoured reached $1.85 a pound in April, 1918, and the price of other grades was proportionately high.

The wool dealers of Boston offered their stocks to the Government at current prices soon after the entry of this country into the war, but the Government did not avail itself of the offer. The War Trade Board was empowered to permit the importation of wool upon license only, and the Government was given the option of purchasing the imported wool at the price prevailing on July 30, 1917. It did not exercise its option until the Spring of 1918. Argentina and Uruguay were at that time the only important free markets where American purchasers could secure wool suitable for manufacturing clothing, and our purchases were steadily forcing up the prices. The exercise of the Government option checked this trend. In May, 1918, the Government commandeered the domestic clip, fixing as the purchase price of the several grades the market quotations for July 30, 1917, which were nearly, though not quite, the highest prices reached during the war period. The purchased wool was issued by the War Department to manufacturers engaged on Government contracts at a price slightly in advance of the purchase price, to pay the cost of handling.

Action by the United States government after the war postponed, although it did not finally avert, a crisis for the wool-growers. The level of wool prices was higher in the United States than in England, as we have seen, because the United States Government had assumed control at a much later date. An immediate break in the American price would have involved great losses for the owners of stocks of wool or woolen goods. On the other hand, it was the desire of the officials to relinquish control as soon as possible. The United States Government instituted a series of auctions to dispose of its holdings. A minimum price was fixed which corresponded closely with the price at which the British Government was issuing similar grades. The better wools sold rapidly, the medium slowly, while the lower grades were a drug on the market for a long time.

The British Government was at the same time disposing of its stocks through the British-Australian Wool Realization Association, which did not entirely liquidate its business until 1924. Every effort was made to co-ordinate the actions of the British and American governments and to "stabilize" the market. Buyers from the United States were not admitted to the London sales for some time, and the United States suspended its auctions during the summer months when the domestic clip was being marketed.

It is somewhat remarkable, in the face of all the uncertainty and with a great surplus of wool, that the price level remained high as long as it did. Wool-growers of the United States feared that the domestic market would be flooded with foreign wool. The amount of wool in the world at the end of the war was a matter of much dispute. Subsequent events have confirmed the belief that there was about a whole year's supply on hand in November, 1918. A large part of this was, however, in Australia, and its availability was lessened by a shortage of shipping. It was not known to what extent the former enemy countries could buy wool if they were allowed to do so. As the event turned out, their purchases were very small.

The woolen and worsted manufacturing machinery of the United States was kept fully occupied during 1919, the demand for fine goods being especially strong. The wool clip of the country amounted to approximately 300,000,000 pounds, which was larger than it had been since 1913. The imports were greater than in any year except the unprecedented year of 1915-16, and the total consumption of the mills was nearly as much as in any of the war years.

The crash did not come until the spring of 1920. The reduction of demand for wool manufactures, known as the "Consumers' Strike," which became pronounced in the latter part of 1919, brought about cancellations of orders; and both the British and American mills were affected. The representatives of eastern wool firms suddenly stopped buying in May, 1920, and for several months wool was almost unsaleable. A large part of the 1920 clip was consigned to dealers. The price of sheep declined 50 per cent, and the flock owners had great difficulty in procuring renewals of loans secured on flocks. Failures were many, and the flocks were sent to slaughter in large numbers. The sheep industry entered 1921 in a more depressed state than for many years.

It is evident that war conditions, with the accompanying government control, led to the accumulation of a surplus which endangered the position of producers and owners of stocks of wool and wool goods. The continued exercise of influence over the market by the American and British governments after the war delayed the evil day for the wool producers and dealers but could not postpone it indefinitely. The inevitable fall in prices created an emergency situation which led to tariff legislation.

III. THE EMERGENCY TARIFF OF 1921

Few experiences with the tariff have been more inconclusive than that under the "Emergency Act" which was in force from May 27, 1921, until September 21, 1922, when the Fordney-McCumber Act was passed. The law restored or raised the duty on a number of agricultural commodities. An insistent demand for relief came from the farmers and stock raisers, who were suffering from the precipitous decline in the price of their products which began in May, 1920. This fall was almost simultaneous in the United States, England, France, and Canada.[7] The index number of prices of all commodities fell at the same time, and industry suffered severely from depression. Before the break came, the index number of prices of farm products was higher than that of all commodities,[8] but fell to a lower level than the latter by July, 1921.[9] The price of wool sustained a greater drop than that of any other important commodity except cotton and corn.[10]

[7] Letter from the U. S. Tariff Commission, *Operation of Rates in the Emergency Tariff Act,* United States Senate Document, No. 224, 67th Congress, 2nd Session, 1922.

[8] Ibid., p. 3. Index number of prices for "All Commodities" in May, 1920, was 247; for "Farm Products," 314 (Base, 1913).

[9] Ibid. Index number for All Commodities in July, 1921, was 141; for Farm Products, 122 (Base, 1913).

[10] Ibid. Index number for Wool (Ohio ¼—⅜ Blood, Scoured) in March, 1920, was 263. In August, September, and October, 1921, it was 100 (Base, 1913).

The demand of the wool-growers for assistance was, therefore, especially urgent. In response to it, a duty was enacted which, because of an administrative provision, became practically prohibitive. The rate was 15 cents per pound unwashed, 30 cents washed, and 45 cents scoured, with a compensatory duty of 45 cents per pound on manufactures of wool. The feature of the law which almost excluded imports was the stipulation that wool improved by the rejection of any part of the original fleece was to pay double duty. Since nearly all imported wool is "skirted," [11] a duty of 30 cents per grease pound was, in effect, levied. This resulted in keeping most of the shipments to this country in bonded storage in the expectation of a lower permanent rate. Only such lots were withdrawn as were especially in demand on account of quality.

A large surplus existed in the home market during most of 1921, for over 200,000,000 pounds of wool had been imported between January 1, and May 28, 1921, in anticipation of the passage of the Emergency tariff, and a considerable proportion of the 1920 domestic clip was still unsold when the 1921 clip was shorn. Moreover, the United States Government had not entirely disposed of its after-war surplus.[12] The American wool textile mills consumed much less than their normal pre-war amounts

---

[11] Skirting is the process of removing the poorer quality wool around the edges of the fleece.

[12] The last of it was not sold until March 2, 1922.

of wool from the middle of 1920 until the spring of 1921, and stocks in the hands of dealers and manufacturers were large. Altogether, the situation was very bad for the domestic wool-growers.

The Boston price of Territory Fine Staple was only about one cent in excess of the price of comparable Australian wool in London, on January 15, 1921.[13] Before the Emergency Tariff Act was passed on May 27, the excess of the American over the foreign price increased, but this diminished toward the end of 1921. Upon the revival of manufacturing early in 1922, wool prices became stronger, and soon after the passage of the Tariff Act of 1922 the difference between London and Boston prices amounted to about the duty plus freight charges. The table on page 140 gives representative quotations on comparable grades in Boston and London during 1921 and 1922.

The wool markets both at home and abroad were so disorganized during the Emergency Tariff period that it is difficult to trace direct effects of the law. It is reasonable to suppose, however, that the practical embargo on imports which resulted from the double-duty provision enabled the American wool-growers to dispose of their surplus more quickly than they otherwise could have done,[14] and that

[13] Territory Fine Staple was $.8250 per scoured pound (*Commercial Bulletin*): 64/67's Medium Fleeces (Australian) were quoted at $.8169 per scoured pound (*Wool Record & Textile World*) converted at current rate of exchange. The difference between Boston and London prices was about ⅘ of a cent per pound.
[14] National Association of Wool Manufacturers, *Annual Wool*

PRICES OF AMERICAN AND ENGLISH WOOLS *

Date	Boston (½ Blood Territory Combing)	London (58/60's and 60/64's Good Medium Fleeces)	Spread (Difference Between Prices of American and English Wool)
1914			
July	$0.5900	$0.5980	$0.0080
1921			
Jan. 15............	.7000	.6065	.0935
Jan. 27............	.7700	.6060	.1640
March 5..........	.7700	.4884	.2816
April 15..........	.7250	.4493	.2757
May 12............	.7750	.4990	.2760
June 18..........	.7100	.4907	.2193
July 28............	.7000	.4169	.2831
Sept. 15..........	.7000	.5163	.1837
Oct. 15............	.7000	.5924	.1076
Oct. 29............	.7000	.6392	.0608
Nov. 25..........	.7250	.5575	.1675
Dec. 8.............	.7650	.5720	.1930
1922			
Jan. 12............	.8250	.6878	.1372
Feb. 2.............	1.0000	.6980	.3020
March 10..........	1.0000	.7082	.2918
March 30..........	.9750	.7148	.2602
May 8............	1.0250	.7880	.2370
May 19............	1.0750	.7972	.2778
June 9.............	1.1500	.7773	.3727
June 28............	1.1250	.7790	.3460
July 21............	1.1250	.7892	.3358
Aug. 3.............	1.1250	.7875	.3375
Sept. 8.............	1.1250	.8261	.2989
Sept. 15............	1.1250	.8568	.2682
Oct. 13............	1.1750	.8956	.2794
Oct. 25............	1.2150	.9535	.2615
Nov. 24............	1.2750	.9173	.3577
Dec. 15............	1.2750	.9375	.3375

* American wool prices from *Commercial Bulletin*—Boston market—at dates as near as possible to those given for the English prices. English prices from the *Wool Record and Textile World* —values at Colonial wool sales in London—converted at current rates of exchange.

the duty helped to create the excess of domestic over foreign wool prices which existed during part of the time. Also, without doubt, the Emergency Tariff had a favorable psychological effect upon the sheep industry. The slaughter of sheep and lambs under Federal inspection fell to 9,345,000 in 1917, rose to 10,320,000 in 1918, and to 12,691,000 in 1919. In the latter year the severe drought in the West prevented carrying the usual number through the winter. In 1920, partly because of the abnormal slaughter of 1919, the number fell to 10,982,000, but after the depression of 1920 it increased again to 13,005,000, in 1921. The Emergency Tariff, or the expectation of passage of the new law—perhaps both—helped to check slaughter in 1922, which was 10,929,000 head.[15]

IV. SUMMARY

The immediate decrease in the wool clip of the United States, after removal of the duty in 1913, was not large. War conditions intervened to prevent a full trial of free wool, however, and the history of the industry for the next few years is one of government control in the interest of the military establishments of the various countries. A surplus

Review, 1922, p. 150, shows domestic wool stocks and consumption for 1918-22. Consumption of domestic wool was greater than consumption of foreign wools from the middle of 1921 to the middle of 1922. The reverse was true for almost all of the rest of the period.

[15] U. S. Department of Agriculture, Statistical Bulletin No. 3, *Sheep, Lamb, Mutton and Wool Statistics*, Washington, D. C., May 9, 1924, p. 14.

of wool was gradually accumulating, which amounted at the end of the war to practically a year's supply. The British and American governments co-operated in the effort to dispose of their stocks without a precipitate decline in price, and were successful, because of favorable business conditions, for more than a year. The bottom fell out of the market in 1920, however, and for many months there was severe depression in the wool-growing industry. Upon the revival of activity in wool manufacturing in 1921 the price of the raw material rose; and the flocks, which had been much reduced in 1920 and 1921, were slightly enlarged. The Emergency Tariff amounted practically to an embargo on wool imports and probably helped the domestic growers to dispose of their surplus, although the economic situation was so confused during that period that it is difficult to draw definite conclusions.

CHAPTER VI

WOOL AND THE TARIFF ACT OF 1922

The wool schedule of the Tariff Act of 1922 is the result of compromise between conflicting forces, rather than the product of scientific investigation. In the form which "Schedule K" [1] assumed under a number of previous acts it was praised by some as the most admirable of all American official documents, with the one exception of the Constitution, and condemned by others as iniquitous favoritism to special interests. The burden and incidence of the wool duty are not easy to determine, and the real nature of the compensatory system of duties on goods manufactured out of wool is obscure and difficult of comprehension.

In the last chapter we have considered the occurrences in wool tariff history between the enactment of free wool in 1913 and the passage of the Tariff Act of 1922. The present chapter will continue the narrative with an account of happenings under this latest tariff law; but first it will be necessary to describe the method of levying the duty which vitally affects its amount, and also to explain the nature

[1] Under the Tariff Act of 1922 the wool schedule is known as "Schedule 11."

143

and effect of other changes in the structure of the schedule. The desirability of a carpet wool duty will be considered; but a decision as to the advisability of maintaining a duty on the principal classes of competing wool will be postponed for later chapters.

I. AMOUNT AND FORM OF THE DUTY OF 1922

A tariff bill was introduced into the House of Representatives on June 29, 1921. Congress struggled with the bill for 18 months. The confused economic situation, both at home and abroad, enhanced the difficulty of making decisions upon the rates. Another great obstacle in the way of the legislators was the clash of interests between the agricultural and manufacturing "blocs."

The rate on wool as passed by the House was 25 cents per scoured pound, with the provision that the maximum ad valorem rate collected should be 35 per cent. After the bill had been reported to the Senate an amendment was presented which provided for the assessment of the duty by a "step-rate" plan, under which the rate would have depended in each case upon the shrinkage of the wool. This would have been very cumbrous in operation and was discarded after debate. A flat rate of 33 cents per scoured pound was substituted before the bill was sent to conference. The rate adopted in conference and enacted into law on September 21, 1922, was 31 cents per scoured pound—that is, per pound of clean fiber contained in the wool. There was no "maximum ad valorem" as in the House bill.

Most of the wool imported is in the raw state, or "in the grease," as it is called; but the amount of clean wool in each lot can be closely estimated. The duty under the Act of 1909, as under most of the tariff acts since the Civil War, was 11 cents per pound in the grease, 22 cents on washed wool, and 33 cents on wool imported in the scoured state.[2] Though this might appear upon superficial consideration to be higher than the present duty, further examination shows that such a conclusion is erroneous.

The duty on wool under the tariff law of 1922 is higher than in any previous act except the "Emergency Act" of 1921. The effective protection to the growers of the old rate of 11 cents per grease pound, was only about 7 cents per pound. The way this came about was as follows: the imported wools were "skirted"—that is, the poorer parts around the edges of the fleece were taken off—and were especially selected for their light shrinkage. The clean yield of such wools was 60 per cent, on the average—that

[2] These were the rates on Class I wool, the kind which comprised most of the imports. It should be noted that there is a difference between the duty on scoured wool and the duty on the scoured content of "grease" wool. Some imported wool shrinks in scouring as much as 66⅔ per cent. On such wool, imported in the grease, the equivalent duty on a scoured pound (at 15 cents on the "grease" pound) would be 45 cents, equal to the duty imposed by the Emergency Act on wool imported in the scoured state. Much of the imported wool, however, does not shrink over 40 per cent and on such wool a duty of 15 cents per grease pound would be 25 cents a pound on the scoured content.

is, it took one and two thirds pounds of the imported grease wool to make one pound of clean wool.
The average clean yield of domestic wool on the
other hand, was only about 40 per cent—that is, it
took two and one half pounds of grease wool to make
one pound of clean wool.   Therefore, the domestic
wool would make only two-thirds as much clean, or
scoured, wool as the competing imported product.
It followed, necessarily, that the duty could raise the
price of domestic wool over the price of foreign wool
(comparable in all other respects except the yield)
by only two thirds of the nominal rate.

The former rate was equal to about 18 cents per
scoured pound on the wools actually imported as
against 31 cents, the present rate.   Wools imported
under the Tariff Act of 1922 yield, on the average,
about 55 per cent of clean content.   The rate of 31
cents per scoured pound is, therefore, equal to 17
cents nominal protection on the grease pound as
against 11 cents nominal (and seven cents actual)
protection under the Act of 1909.   The fact that the
duty is now levied upon the scoured basis tends to
make this nominal protection coincide with the real
protection enjoyed.   The fact that the difference in
price between domestic and foreign wools has not
been equal to the duty part of the time since 1922 is
not due to the form in which the duty is levied.

The price of wool is higher than before the war,
and this raises the question whether the present
ad valorem equivalent is any greater than that of

the former tariff act. The statement can be made at this point in the discussion that it is higher, on the whole. In order to understand the present situation it will be necessary to describe the operation of the act somewhat more fully. Consequently this phase of the question is here passed over. (See table on page 153.)

The carpet wool rate is increased over that in the Act of 1909.[3] It is 12 cents per pound "in the grease," 18 cents per pound if washed, and 24 cents per pound if scoured. The grease pound and washed rates are the ones chiefly effective, as most of such wools are imported in the original or washed state. They are of very unequal shrinkage and value, and a scoured content duty would be more difficult to administer than it is in the case of crossbred and Merino wools. Carpet wools are much further from standardization than Australian or domestic wools. If any duty is to be levied, therefore, the present form of duty is the best for administrative purposes.

All carpet wool should be admitted free because it is almost altogether non-competitive with domestic wool. The problem of the carpet wool tariff is of comparatively little importance in this study, and therefore it may be disposed of at this point. So far as wool of this class is actually used for making carpets, it is now free from duty. The tariff act

[3] The Payne-Aldrich rates on Class III wools were: four cents per pound on wool the value of which was 12 cents per pound or less; seven cents per pound on wool the value of which was over 12 cents per pound.

provides: "That such wools may be imported under bond in an amount to be fixed by the Secretary of the Treasury and under such regulations as he shall prescribe; and if within three years from the date of importation or withdrawal from bonded warehouse satisfactory proof is furnished that the wools have been used in the manufacture of rugs, carpets, or any other floor coverings, the duties shall be remitted or refunded." To the extent that it is competitive, the wool manufacturing industry should be allowed to substitute it for domestic (or other foreign) wool. This would have the effect of offsetting slightly the discrimination which exists against dutiable low-grade wool. Free admission would also simplify administrative procedure,— a consideration of some importance.

II. CHANGES IN THE STRUCTURE OF THE SCHEDULE

The present method of levying the duty does away with certain inequities which resulted from the old method of levying the duty on the "grease pound." The duty on wool is accompanied by compensatory duties, in addition to those intended as protective, on "tops" (the intermediate product in the process of making clean wool into yarn), and on yarn, woolen and worsted goods, and clothing.

The compensatory rates of former acts gave some "concealed" protection to manufacturers. This concealed protection arose from the fact that the compensatory rates were fixed on a false assumption.

They presupposed that it took four pounds of raw wool to make one pound of cloth, while as a matter of fact, it took much less than four pounds of the kind of wool commonly imported. As the duty on raw wool was 11 cents per pound, the compensatory duty on cloth was 44 cents per pound.[4] Since the present law levies the duty according to the scoured content, the compensatory duties are framed on the assumption that about one and one-half pounds of scoured wool goes into a pound of cloth of the better quality. The results of an investigation made by the Tariff Board were used in determining the amount of clean wool used in making a pound of cloth of each of the different grades, so that there is probably little if any concealed protection in the duties of the present act.

The old form of duty—that on the "grease pound"—discriminated against the carded wool manufacture. That branch of the industry uses proportionately more of the "heavy-shrinking" wool—that is, wool which has a comparatively small content of clean fiber; and a specific duty levied on the "grease pound" obviously bears more heavily on such wools. It may be said, however, that the worsted industry has grown to much larger proportions in this country than the carded woolen in-

[4] The Act of 1909 levied on woolen cloth, of a value of not more than 40 cents a pound, a compensatory duty of three times the duty on Class I wool, or 33 cents a pound; on cloth valued at more than 40 cents a pound the compensatory duty was four times the duty on Class I wool, or 44 cents a pound. The more expensive cloth, however, was the kind most largely imported.

dustry, and the total quantity of heavy shrinking
fine wool which it now uses is absolutely though
not relatively greater than that used by the carded
woolen branch.   Therefore, the discrimination between the two branches would now be less pronounced than formerly.   Nevertheless, the chief opposition to this form of duty has come from some
of the carded wool manufacturers.   There would be
discrimination against the users of heavy-shrinking
wools, whether they were woolen or worsted
manufacturers.[5]

[5] The two great groups of wool manufactures are the worsteds
and the woolens.   The primary distinction between the two
branches of the industry is that in making worsteds, yarns of
combed wools are used, while for woolens, the wool is carded
instead of being combed.   The combing process causes the fibers
to lie parallel; and when spun, a harder twist is given to the
yarn.   The woolen yarns are softer, and the fibers are tangled
and intertwined by the carding process.   Until about 1850 more
of the English long wools than of any other variety were used for
making worsteds.   About that time a series of inventions began
which made it possible to comb shorter wools.   Progress in this
direction has continued until, at present, very short and fine
Merino wool can be used in making combed yarn.   The development of the process of combing made it possible to turn out a
standardized product, "tops," which is the name given to the
strands of wool when ready for spinning.   This was one of the
most important steps in the advance of the worsteds to an ultimate position of greater importance than the woolens.   "The very
possession of a homogeneous material facilitates the use of highly-
perfected and quasi-automatic machinery in the later manufacturing stages.   In all countries the worsted branch of the industry
is conducted on a larger scale than the woolen branch; it is more
capitalistic, more in line with the general trend of modern industry."   (Taussig, F. W., *Some Aspects of the Tariff Question*,
1915, p. 339.)   Fashion was also an important influence acting in
the same direction.   The form in which customs duties were levied
in this country may have been partly responsible for the stimulation of the worsted manufacture, but that it was not the dominat-
ing cause is shown by the fact that the same tendency appeared
in England, France, and Germany.   (*Ibid.*, p. 337.)   The worsted

The former method of levying the duty on the grease pound deprived the wool growers of some of the protection contemplated by the law. Thus, under the law of 1909, the grease wool rate of 11 cents per pound was the one actually operative, as practically all wool was entered in the raw state. Due to the fact that the wools imported were selected for light shrinkage, while competing domestic wools shrunk heavily, the amount of effective protection was, as has been shown, several cents a pound less than the nominal protection. With the rate levied as at present on the clean content of the wool, the actual protection is substantially increased; and the duty will tend more strongly to

industry in this country had its inception about 1850, and grew slowly for some years. After 1869, it increased in importance rapidly; but the woolen branch of the industry continued to have a larger production than the worsted branch in the United States until about the end of the nineteenth century. In 1899, the value of the output of the worsted mills was $120,314,344, while that of the woolen mills was $118,430,158. In recent years the importance of the woolen relative to the worsted branch has increased, principally on account of the demands occasioned by the war. In 1919, about one-half of the total output of cloth and dress-goods was woolen. (*Summary of Tariff Information,* 1921, p. 974.) The total value of the domestic production of woven fabrics of wool in that year was $692,179,000. (Ibid.) In this country not only is the average business unit in the worsted branch of the industry much larger than in the woolen branch, but there is also much greater specialization in it. In the typical woolen mill all the processes, from raw wool to finished cloth, are performed. Some worsted mills, on the contrary, buy yarn and do weaving only; some carry the process only as far as spinning. Only a few mills combine all processes from raw wool to finished cloth. (U. S. Tariff Board, *Report on Schedule K,* p. 220.) An even more pronounced degree of specialization is found in English mills. In the former, only one stage in the process of turning the raw material into the finished goods is usually found in any one establishment.

make the price of wool in this country higher than the price of foreign wool by the full amount of the duty.

A new form of discrimination is permitted under the present act. Wools of exactly the same shrinkage often vary widely in value. The ad valorem equivalent of the present duty on wool worth $1.24 per scoured pound is only 25 per cent, while on wool worth $.62 per scoured pound it is 50 per cent. The present law, it will be seen, discriminates against the cheap wools. Now, these are in many instances the same grades which were discriminated against by the former grease-pound rate. This is not true in all cases, however, because some of the fine and high-priced wools were kept out by the earlier law, whereas the discrimination is now chiefly against the coarse wools. It is a serious defect of the law, however, because these wools are much used in low-priced fabrics.

The situation is illustrated by the table on page 153.

This effect of the duty led to the presentation in November, 1923, of a petition by the carded wool manufacturers to the President asking for the establishment of an ad valorem duty on wool. The petition was made under the section of the Tariff Act of 1922 known as the "flexibility" provision by which the President was granted the authority to raise or lower the rate by 50 per cent of the duty levied in the Act. He was not empowered, however,

SPECIFIC AND AD VALOREM DUTIES ON WOOL.

Kind of Wool	Shrinkage	Yield	Foreign Price Nov.-Dec., 1923		Scoured Pound Equivalent of 11 Cent Grease Duty	Ad Valorem Equivalent of Specific Duty	
			Grease	Scoured		11 Cents per Grease Pound	31 Cents per Scoured Pound
	Per Cent	Per Cent	Cents	Cents	Cents	Per Cent	Per Cent
South American—Buenos Aires [a]							
54-60's—fine crossbred from South...	40	60	36	60	18.3	30.6	51.7
46-50's—medium crossbred from South	35	65	26	40	16.9	42.3	77.5
36-40's—coarse crossbred from South.	30	70	19	27	15.6	57.9	114.8
Australian—London [b]							
64-70's—good medium fleeces	50	50	62	124	22.0	17.7	25.0
50-56's—fine crossbred fleeces	40	60	40	66	18.2	27.5	47.0
46-50's—crossbred fleeces	35	65	30	46	16.9	36.7	67.4
36-40's—crossbred fleeces	25	75	23	30	14.3	47.8	103.3
New Zealand—Christchurch [b]							
58's—ordinary	40	60	50	84	18.5	22.0	36.9
50's—super	35	65	40	62	17.1	27.5	50.0
44-46's	35	65	23	36	17.2	47.8	86.1
36-40's	28	72	22	30	15.0	50.0	103.3
South Africa—Port Elizabeth [b]							
64-66's	55	45	48	107	24.5	22.9	29.0
Second fleeces	60	40	43	108	27.6	25.6	28.7
Best shorts [c]	67	33	33	99	33.0	33.3	31.3

[a] Review of the River Plate, Nov. 23, 1923; Quotations reduced to U. S. money at current rate of exchange.
[b] Wool Record and Textile World, Nov. 29, 1923. [c] New York Journal of Commerce, Dec. 22, 1923.

to change the duty from specific to ad valorem, or *vice versa,* so that the request of the carded wool manufacturers could not be considered. The operation of the Act is obviously not satisfactory, however, and something should be done to remedy it. Its working is all the more unequal when the price of low grade wools is abnormally low, as it has been for much of the time since the Armistice. Even when normal price relations exist, however, the ad valorem equivalent of the specific duty on the low grade wools is so high as to be a serious bar to importation.

A "maximum ad valorem" rate is proposed to remedy this situation. A simple ad valorem duty would do away with discrimination between wools of different values and also between wools of high and low shrinkage, since the amount of shrinkage affects the grease price of the wool. However, there are objections to the ad valorem rate.

First, it is difficult to fix a compensatory rate on cloth when an ad valorem rate is levied on wool. To levy a 20 per cent compensatory duty on cloth, for example, when there is a 20 per cent ad valorem duty on wool, is not equitable. The value of the cloth is not always proportionate to the value of the raw material used, because varying amounts of labor and skill may be expended on it. It is not feasible to use a definite ratio, for example, 1 to 3, as the proportion of raw material cost to the cost of the cloth. The use of any average would be unjust, because in practice the departures from it would be numerous.

Second, the ad valorem rate would give the wool growers greater protection during a period of rising prices when they need less, and diminished protection in a time of falling prices when they need more. The specific duty, on the other hand, works in the opposite way and gives the wool growers more protection when prices are falling. It is one of their strongest reasons for favoring a specific duty.

For these reasons it seems best to turn to some other remedy. A step-rate graduated according to the fineness of the wool has been suggested. For example, if the grades could be standardized as coarse, medium, and fine, different specific scoured content rates might be levied on each grade. In this connection, the work of the Department of Agriculture in establishing standardized wool grades is important. However, the plans of the wool experts have not developed sufficiently so that this is possible.

Since neither of these methods will remedy the situation, a maximum ad valorem rate is proposed. The specific duty on the scoured content should be retained (as long as a duty is kept in force), as it does away with the inequality between light-shrinking and heavy-shrinking wools. If a maximum ad valorem rate were fixed (at, say, 50 per cent), the pronounced discrimination against the low grades would be abolished. Until greater standardization of wool is brought about, which may take some years, this offers the best means of securing justice in the operation of the law.

The present act abolished the antiquated basis of classification of previous acts. The "blood classification" which was in force during all the periods when wool was dutiable, from 1867 until the passage of the Act of 1922, divided wool into three groups—class one, clothing wool; class two, combing wool; and class three, carpet wool. The first class was further defined as "wool from sheep having any admixture of Merino blood," wool of this variety being easily identified by its crimp and by its oily character. It also included the Down wools, which were put in class one because they were not suitable for combing under the methods then in use. Class two included only the English long-wools. Class three included all wool from unimproved or "native" breeds of sheep.[6]

[6] The classification of the Act of 1867 was more than a "blood-classification." It was a three-fold classification, for in addition to the arrangement in classes according to the breed of sheep from which the wool was shorn there was a suggestion of the purpose for which the wool was to be used, in the names "clothing," "combing," and "carpet," and an enumeration of the countries from which the different classes of wool were ordinarily imported. For example, the wools of class one were defined as, "Such as have been heretofore usually imported into the United States from Buenos Ayres, New Zealand, Australia, the Cape of Good Hope, Russia, Great Britain, Canada, etc.," and class three wools were defined as, "Such as Donskoi, native South American, Cordova, Valparaiso, native Smyrna and * * * such as have been heretofore usually imported into the United States from Turkey, Greece, Egypt, Syria, and elsewhere." It should be noted that

FARM FLOCK OF SOUTHDOWNS IN MARYLAND

At the time when the Act of 1867 was passed, the classification conformed to the situation which actually existed in the wool trade and manufacturing industry. It soon became obsolete, however, because of changes in combing machinery, which was improved so that shorter wool could be utilized by the worsted branch of the industry. In 1867, Merino wool, which is rarely more than two and one-half inches long, was used altogether for carded woolen goods, but at the present time it is much used for worsteds. The worsted industry has, moreover, grown to such size that it uses a greater quantity of Merino than the woolen industry. The English long wools, which at that time were used in making worsteds, are frequently blended with other wools to give a lustrous finish, and are also

the use of the term "clothing" as the designation of class one wool did not signify that this was the only kind of wool used for cloth to be made into wearing apparel. It was used because "cloths" were distinguished in the trade parlance from "stuffs," such as worsted goods.

The principal cause of the blood classification was the varying degree of competition with American wool offered by the different classes of imported wool. The foreign wools competitive with American-grown wools fell mainly within the first group. The native or carpet wools have been largely non-competitive, while at the time the Act of 1867 was passed the combing wool which was placed in the second group was partially competitive. It was used principally by the worsted industry, then in the "infant" stage; and as a concession to that industry it was accorded somewhat more favorable treatment than class one wool. If the class one wool was imported without having been subjected to any cleansing process, the rate was 11 cents per pound. If, however, it had been washed, it was subjected to double duty, and if scoured to triple duty. The combing wool, however, was not subjected to double duty if imported in the washed state, since most of it came from Canada where wool was almost always marketed in that condition.

employed in the manufacture of dress goods and braids.

The primary reason for the creation of a separate class for combing wool disappeared, therefore, many years ago. The persistence of the old classification can perhaps be explained by fear of disturbing the peace established between opposing interests. A partial recognition of changed conditions is found in the fact that in 1890 the terms "clothing," "combing," and "carpet" were dropped from the text of the Act, and the titles of the three divisions became merely class one, class two, and class three. Although the classification remained substantially the same down to the Act of 1922, certain minor changes were made. For example, in 1897 some of the native wools—namely, Bagdad, China lambs' wool, Castel Branco, and Adrianople wool—were transferred to class one because it was found that they were sometimes used interchangeably with certain domestic wools in the manufacture of clothing fabrics.[7] By

[7] Under a Treasury decision of July 1, 1923, such wools are placed in Paragraph 1102 of the Act of 1922, with Merino wool. "The Tariff Acts of 1890, 1897, and 1909 in the classification of wools, provided that the standard samples of all wools which were then or might thereafter be deposited in the custom houses under the authority of the Secretary of the Treasury should be the standards for the classification of wools under the respective acts mentioned. While a corresponding provision does not appear in the present tariff act, because of the fact that the wools mentioned in Paragraph 1101 are similar to those enumerated in the acts mentioned, as of class 3, and because of the further fact that under Paragraph 1104 the Secretary of the Treasury is authorized and directed to prescribe methods and regulations for carrying out the provisions of the wool schedule relating to the duties on wool and hair, the Department is of the opinion

the Act of 1890, also, any carpet wool which was improved by mixing with it clothing or combing wool was made subject to the same duty as those classes respectively. If two kinds of wool were mixed the entire lot was made subject to the higher duty, and if it was improved by the rejection of any part of the original fleece the duty was doubled. A distinction was made, however, between such wool and "skirted" wool. That is, the inferior wool around the edge of the fleece might be removed without making it liable to double duty.

Under the Act of 1922, wool is divided into two classes.[8] The first consists of all wools not improved by the admixture of Merino or English blood; the second of wools not especially provided for.[9] Paragraph 1101 covers substantially the same ground as the old classification "carpet" wools. Paragraph 1102 covers wools suitable for making fabrics for wearing apparel. This change is commendable, as it simplifies the classification and abolishes the distinction, no longer useful, between the former Class II, English wools, and other combing wools.[10]

that the classification of wool does not depend upon commercial designation but rather is controlled by the character of the wool itself, and that under the provisions of Paragraph 1104 the standard samples now in the custom houses should control the classification of wools imported into this country."

[8] Paragraphs 1101 and 1102.

[9] In the statistics of imports (U. S. Department of Commerce, *Commerce and Navigation Reports*) the three classifications, clothing, combing, and carpet, are still used, but under combing is now placed all wool actually suitable for combing, not merely the English long-wools, as formerly.

[10] Experts of the United States Department of Agriculture have

It is apparent that, although the Tariff Act of 1922 abolishes the discrimination between light-shrinking and heavy-shrinking wools, does away with the "concealed protection" to the manufacturers, and introduces a better classification, yet the rate is higher than any hitherto imposed, with one minor exception; and a new discrimination is created between wools of high and low value. If it is found desirable to continue a duty on wool, the method of levying the duty should be changed. A maximum ad valorem limitation should be imposed upon the specific scoured content duty. The carpet wool duty should be abolished, regardless of the action taken toward other wool. The principal question remains, whether we ought to change the rate on the principal classes of competing wool, maintain the present duty, or abolish it altogether.

III. IMMEDIATE CONSEQUENCES OF THE DUTY OF 1922

The general business situation tended to promote a rise in the price of wool and to restore prosperity to the wool-growing industry in 1922 and the early part of 1923. Manufacturing activity was increas-

made a marked advance toward the establishment of standard wool grades. They have selected samples of fine, medium, and coarse wools, the grading being made on the basis of diameter of wool fibre. Samples of combing and clothing wool have also been selected. Conferences with representatives of the English wool industry have been held; and it is hoped that eventually wool grades will be standardized and terms adopted which have the same significance in all English-speaking countries. At some future time it may be possible to use such international terms in the classification of wool for tariff purposes.

ing, and the index number of wholesale prices of all commodities was rising.[11]

Conditions were not as favorable during the latter part of 1923 and early months of 1924. Unseasonable weather helped to reduce retail sales, and the general hesitancy of business which exhibited itself shortly after the French occupation of the Ruhr extended also to the wool trade and industry. Depression in the wool manufacturing industry became severe in the middle of 1924, followed by some recovery in the later months. Early in 1925 another downward trend set in. Consumption of wool, employment, and the activity of cards, combs, and spindles through February, March, and April, 1925, was even less than in the corresponding months of the preceding year. Looms, however, were somewhat more active. The season was marked by great hesitancy in trade and by "hand-to-mouth" buying.[12] The depression in wool manufacturing during 1924 and 1925 was considered by many the worst since the post-Civil War crisis.

The imports, both of wool and manufactures of wool, continued to come in large volume after the passage of the Act of 1922. The average value per pound of the imported cloths and dress goods remained about the same, as might be expected, because the trade is largely in specialties.

[11] Harvard Economic Service, *The Review of Economic Statistics,* January, 1924, Vol. VI, No. 1, p. 9.
[12] *Bulletin,* National Association Wool Manufacturers, July, 1925, Vol. LV, No. 3, p. 404.

CONSUMPTION OF WOOL *

(Grease pound equivalent in thousands of pounds)

Month	1920	1921	1922	1923	1924	1925
January	72,344	24,049	52,280	63,348	53,845	51,435
February	63,404	30,600	53,774	57,916	50,633	46,415
March	67,387	39,510	60,368	62,859	47,630	45,853
April	66,725	43,466	42,574	56,411	44,361	43,287
May	57,419	48,183	52,533	59,682	36,507	38,246
June	46,439	47,103	52,621	52,649	30,972	38,176
July	37,438	42,126	46,902	46,347	33,778	40,781
August	37,558	48,141	57,340	48,233	40,064	42,149
September ...	35,484	49,824	54,771	46,616	45,638	44,383
October	38,337	53,589	59,282	51,815	54,854	47,327
November	27,926	53,463	63,313	50,279	48,380	43,471
December	24,316	49,441	58,367	45,452	51,097	44,762

* Source: U. S. Department of Commerce, *Survey of Current Business,* May, 1922, and subsequent issues. The figures do not include consumption by the American Woolen Company and a few small firms.

IMPORTS OF UNMANUFACTURED WOOL *

Class	1921 (Calendar Year)		1922 (Calendar Year)	
	Pounds	Value	Pounds	Value
Clothing ...	207,866,615	$45,772,325	38,401,590	$9,471,786
Combing ...	10,837,821	2,202,081	155,101,038	44,357,492
Carpet	97,900,496	11,499,175	173,035,833	29,267,134
Mohair, etc..	4,060,819	1,008,106	10,257,024	3,457,717
Total	320,665,751	$60,481,687	376,795,485	$86,554,129

* Sources: *Bulletins* of National Association of Wool Manufacturers for May 9, 1923, Feb. 29, 1924, Aug. 6, 1924, and Feb. 28, 1925.

Class	1923 (Calendar Year)		1924 (Fiscal Year Ended June 30)	
	Pounds	Value	Pounds	Value
Clothing ..	30,850,916	$11,406,349	17,785,144	$8,128,556
Combing ..	235,094,858	89,180,994	103,909,514	48,393,260
Carpet	122,398,919	26,303,545	140,960,360	34,174,758
Mohair, etc.	5,905,702	2,819,823	5,557,722	2,454,694
Total ...	394,250,395	$129,710,711	268,212,740	$93,151,268

Class	1925 (Fiscal Year Ended June 30)	
	Pounds	Value
Clothing	24,446,000	$12,256,000
Combing	117,991,000	70,070,000
Carpet	138,461,000	39,980,000
Mohair, etc.	3,809,000	1,858,000
	284,707,000	$124,164,000

IMPORTS OF PRINCIPAL MANUFACTURES OF WOOL INTO THE U. S.*

Class	1921 Value	1922 Value	1923 Value
1. Wool Cloths and Dress Goods	$13,668,571	$14,702,931	$20,851,522
2. Yarns	6,952,638	4,393,661	8,293,506
3. Tops, etc.	9,878,400	3,292,197	2,553,424
4. Wearing Apparel	6,304,614	9,975,140	9,126,632
5. Carpets	7,739,374	10,568,895	13,952,227
6. Rags, Wastes, Noils, etc.	3,542,049	13,188,748	11,270,016
Total	$48,085,646	$56,121,572	$66,047,327

* *Bulletins* of National Association of Wool Manufacturers for May 9, 1923. Feb. 29, 1924, Aug. 6, 1924, and Feb. 28, 1925.

Class	1924 (Fiscal Year) Value	1925 (Fiscal Year) Value
1. Woven fabrics of wool (term used to supplant "wool cloths and dress goods")..........	$19,830,000	$22,669,000
2. Yarns	5,586,000	3,078,000
3. Tops [a]	....	....
4. Wearing Apparel	9,086,000	11,076,000
5. Carpets	14,726,000	16,554,000
6. Rags, Wastes, Noils, etc......	8,085,662	20,162,000
7. All other manufactures of wool and hair	2,333,000	1,772,000
Total	$59,646,662	$75,311,000

[a] Figures not comparable with 1921, 1922, and 1923.

For nearly a year after the passage of the Act of 1922 the difference between Boston and London prices was not far from the amount of the duty plus freight and insurance. In the latter part of 1923 there occurred a slump in the American price, consequent upon a slackening pace in the manufacturing industry and in general business. Imports of wool had been heavy during the early part of 1923, when the swing of the business cycle was upward; and some of the surplus stocks were exported in the later months of that year. Ordinarily not more than four million or five million pounds of wool are re-exported in a year from the United States, but in 1923 the amount was 24,-187,994 pounds.[13]

The British wool manufacture was active and prosperous during the latter part of 1921 and in

[13] *Annual Wool Review,* 1923, p. 91.

1922; but like the industry in the United States, it became less active in 1923. The disturbance of England's pre-war European markets for yarns and goods has kept the British industry from entirely re-adjusting itself, although exports of some classes of goods are larger than before the war. The outstanding feature of the British wool market in 1924 was the fact that wool prices were for much of the time higher than had been the price of the raw material in the finished goods then being sold. This, of course, slowed up manufacturing.

The price received by American growers in 1924 and 1925 was 5 to 6 cents per grease pound, or 10 to 12 cents per scoured pound, less than in 1923; and for most of the time the difference between Boston and London prices was substantially less than the duty. In June and early July, 1924, the domestic and foreign prices became almost equal, but a differential was soon restored. The difference between domestic and foreign prices has been great enough under the Act of 1922 so that the president of the National Wool Growers' Association said at the annual meeting in January, 1925: [14] "For the first time in our history domestic wools have reached a parity on the Boston market with the price of foreign wools plus the entire tariff levied by law. During the past year many growers have made their own low markets by selling too cheap. If

[14] Address of President Hagenbarth at the association convention in San Francisco.

growers will co-operate and pool their wools and properly warehouse them, they can be financed for a reasonable per cent of their value and then sold when the market is ready to take them on a fair basis of value."

Large quantities of wool were re-exported from the United States in 1924 because of the slack demand in this country and the comparative activity in the British wool trade. The price of wool in London held its own or advanced slightly during almost all of 1924; but in the spring and summer of 1925 came a sharp decline, following the marketing of a larger wool clip for 1924-25 in Australasia. The low state of the American wool manufacturing industry, with decreased consumption of wool and declining prices for the raw material, may be partially attributed to general business conditions and partly to curtailed use of woolen goods on account of the high prices.[15]

Throughout the years 1922 to 1925 the American sheep industry was gradually recovering from the slump of 1920-21. The total number of sheep increased, but the expansion in flocks was not common to all the states. For example, New York, Maryland, Virginia, Illinois, Indiana, and Missouri all had substantially larger clips in 1924 than in 1923. Ten states showed a small increase—that is, the clip was from 100,000 to 300,000 pounds larger than two years before. These states were Kentucky,

[15] See Chapter X.

COMPARATIVE WOOL PRICES, BOSTON AND LONDON MARKETS *

Date	Boston ½ Blood Terri- tory Combing	London 60/64's Good Medium Fleeces	Excess of Bos- ton over Lon- don Price
1914			
July	$0.5900	$0.6084	$0.0184 [a]
1923			
Jan. 26........	1.2750	1.0078	.2672
Feb. 9........	1.2750	.9745	.3005
Mar. 9........	1.3100	.9614	.3486
Mar. 23........	1.3100	1.0171	.2929
Apr. 27........	1.3250	1.0620	.2630
May 11........	1.3250	1.0576	.2674
June 29........	1.3250	1.0118	.3132
July 19........	1.2750	.9953	.2797
Sept. 7........	1.1750	1.0001	.1749
Oct. 26........	1.1750	1.0126	.1624
Nov. 4........	1.1750	1.0224	.1526
Dec. 7........	1.2400	1.0192	.2208
Dec. 20........	1.2500	1.0368	.2132
1924			
Jan. 25........	1.2750	1.0560	.2190
Feb. 12........	1.3000	1.0758	.2242
Mar. 21........	1.3000	1.1117	.1883
Apr. 1........	1.2750	1.1472	.1278
May 9........	1.2400	1.1455	.0945
May 20........	1.2400	1.1445	.0955
July 4........	1.1250	1.1185	.0065
July 11........	1.1750	1.1428	.0322
Sept. 19........	1.3250	1.3002	.0248
Oct. 9........	1.3250	1.3054	.0196
Nov. 28........	1.5000	1.3905	.1095
Dec. 12........	1.5250	1.3860	.1390
1925			
Jan. 23........	1.5250	1.3010	.2240
Feb. 3........	1.5250	1.2975	.2275
Mar. 20........	1.4100	1.1154	.2946
May 8........	1.1100	.9698	.1402
May 14........	1.1100	.9706	.1394
July 10........	1.1750	.9720	.2030
July 23........	1.1750	.9315	.2435

* American wool prices from *Commercial Bulletin,* Boston, at dates as near as possible to those given for the English prices. English prices are averages compiled by Krelinger and Fernau for London auctions of Colonial (Australasian) wool, and published in the *Wool Record and Textile World.*

[a] Excess of London over Boston.

Tennessee, West Virginia, Ohio, Illinois, Iowa, Minnesota, North and South Dakota, and Nebraska. But there was a decrease in the size of the clip in Pennsylvania, Michigan, Wisconsin, Kansas, and North Carolina. In the unenumerated farm states the clip was too small for an increase or decrease to be significant. Most of the far western states increased their output, although Wyoming and Colorado showed a smaller production. The total clip of the 12 far western states—Montana, Wyoming, Colorado, New Mexico, Texas, Arizona, Utah, Nevada, Idaho, Washington, Oregon, and California—was 147,915,000 pounds in 1922 and 165,388,000 pounds in 1924, an increase of 11-⅘ per cent. The largest number of sheep in the United States for any year since the war was reached in 1919, with a total of 48,866,000.[16] On January 1, 1922, the number had been reduced to 36,327,000, but by January 1, 1924, it had risen again to 38,361,000, and on January 1, 1925, to 39,134,000.[17] The wool output was over 275,000,000 pounds in 1919 and in 1920, but it fell to 264,560,000 pounds in 1922, and was only two million pounds larger in 1923. In 1924 it was 282,330,000 pounds, and in 1925, 11,000,000 pounds greater, increases of 6.72 per cent and 10.87 per cent, respectively, over the

[16] It should be noted that this estimate is based on the 1910 census which was taken so late as to include lambs. The number is therefore not comparable with later figures based on the 1920 census, which did not include lambs. The decrease in sheep numbers is consequently exaggerated.

[17] Estimates of U. S. Department of Agriculture.

1922 output.[18]   Although the price of wool was high relative to other farm products during these years, prices of lamb and mutton were not correspondingly high.   This may explain the failure to expand flocks more rapidly in the farm states.   The debacle of 1920 was also doubtless in the minds of farmers as a deterrent to rapid increase of flocks. Nevertheless, the sheep industry enjoyed a fair degree of prosperity in the years 1922 to 1925 inclusive.   The most important facts to note at this point are that a price difference between domestic and foreign wool was created by the duty, and that the output of wool was thereby somewhat stimulated.

[18] Ibid.

PART III

THE PRESENT PROBLEM

CHAPTER VII

ELEMENTS OF THE WOOL TARIFF PROBLEM

In preceding chapters the various steps in the development of the wool tariff problem have been set forth, and present conditions in the sheep industry in the United States and foreign countries have been described. There is necessarily some difference of opinion over the actual conditions which exist as well as over the effect which the duties have exercised in the past. But there is more likelihood of common agreement in regard to these matters than about the proper course of action for the future. We come, therefore, at this point to highly debatable ground.

The wool tariff problem still exists in full vitality. At every tariff revision in recent years wool has been one of the commodities upon which a large amount of interest has centered and over which violent difference of opinion has been disclosed. Talk about the "crime of Schedule K" has been bandied about freely, while extremely laudatory comments on the wool duties have been no less frequent. In this chapter we shall consider some of the differences of opinion, their causes, and the plan of analysis for the present problem.

Confusion of thought on tariff questions often has arisen from failure of the disputants to recognize the fundamental assumptions of their opponents. The two sides have thus chased one another around the proverbial "Robin Hood's barn," never getting any nearer a solution of their difficulties. To avoid joining this procession we must define carefully our position on the elemental issues which form the background of the present problem.

I. DIVERGENT OPINIONS ON THE WOOL TARIFF

The nature of the controversy and the wide divergence of views may be illustrated by the positions taken on various aspects of the question by certain individuals and associations. The groups most actively concerned are the wool-growers, the wool manufacturers, a minority of manufacturers who make carded woolen goods, farm organizations, and public men.

The majority of the wool-growers have long maintained that the duty is of vital interest to them. In fact, they have regarded it as essential to the successful operation of the industry. Even if the domestic production has not increased in the last forty years they believe that without a duty it would have markedly decreased. They regard the experience with free wool in 1894-97 as an indication of what might be expected if the duty were now abolished. They hold that only the intervention of the war prevented this result in 1913 and in the following years. Their position on the present tariff law is expressed as follows:

"Fair rates of duty upon imported wools have been established by the Sixty-seventh Congress. The President, through the Tariff Commission, may raise or lower such rates by 50 per cent, according to the occurrence of changes in the relation of home-production costs to those found to obtain in exporting countries. . . .

"These fair and impartial provisions of the wool duty form a part of the enlightened new policy expressed by the Congress just adjourned toward the agricultural industry, giving the rural citizenship the same consideration in commercial policies as was previously accorded only to the manufacturing industries." [1]

The wool manufacturers have generally stood with the wool-growers for duties on wool since the Syracuse Convention of 1865.[2] At various times, however, they have differed from the wool-growers in regard to the proper amount of the duties or the form in which they should be levied.

Some of the carded wool manufacturers have actively favored the use of an ad valorem instead of a specific rate. These manufacturers make large use of the heavier shrinking wools, which were discriminated against by the specific duty on the grease

---

[1] Advertisement by the National Wool Growers' Association, entitled "Giving the Public the Facts About Wool," in *The Outlook* for Nov. 15, 1924.

[2] See Chapter IV.

pound. Ad valorem duties, however, have been consistently opposed by the wool-growers, as we have seen.[3]

In 1882, although the joint committee of the National Wool Growers' Association and the National Association of Wool Manufacturers agreed upon the basic soundness of the duties on wool and woolens adopted in 1867, a representative of the wool manufacturers' association appeared before the Tariff Commission and advocated a plan which favored reduction of the duty on wool of the first class.[4] A minority of the manufacturers have at various times, when the tariff was under consideration, presented petitions favoring free wool.[5] Again, the manufacturers have sometimes advocated lower rates of duty than those favored by the growers. For example, when the revision of 1897 was under way the wool manufacturers opposed the wishes of the growers. The latter advocated the enactment of a duty, on unwashed wools of Classes I and II, which should increase by one-half cent a year until it reached 15 cents a pound. The manufacturers believed that these rates would fatally hamper the industry and would excite such opposition as soon to bring about another tariff revision. At this time the representatives of the manufacturers stated, before the Ways and Means Committee, that previous

[3] See Chapter VI.
[4] The U. S. Tariff Commission, *Report on the Wool-Growing Industry*, p. 424.
[5] Ibid., p. 427.

to the experience under free wool they had not realized the full extent of the disadvantage they suffered by reason of the wool duty.[6] In answer to this Senator Lee Mantle of Montana said,[7] "Never, until he had experienced the disadvantage which he suffered under free wool, did the wool-grower realize the impossibility of offsetting this disadvantage by the compensatory benefit derived from being able to buy his clothing a few cents cheaper."

The opinion of the majority of the wool manufacturers as to the present duties is shown by the following statement of the National Association of Wool Manufacturers:

"Unquestionably the present tariff act, so far as the duties on raw materials are concerned, is the work of the agricultural interests. This is particularly true of Schedule Eleven, in the framing of which nearly every suggestion made by representatives of wool manufacturers was rejected. Having secured what they wished, the burden now rests upon the wool-growers of the country to fulfill their promises to improve their flocks, produce greater clips, and furnish a larger proportion of the wools consumed by our expanding wool manufacture."[8]

Various public men have been ardent in advocacy of a duty on wool or in opposition to it. President Cleveland referred to the wool duty as a "tax, which,

[6] Ibid., p. 431.
[7] Speech of June 4, 1897, in the United States Senate.
[8] *Annual Wool Review,* 1922, p. 140.

with relentless grasp, is fastened upon the clothing
of every man, woman and child in the land." [9]
President McKinley was equally positive in his
declaration for a duty. Different organizations have
issued statements in regard to the benefit or detriment of the wool duty. For example, the American Farm Bureau Federation issued a statement in
1922 [10] regarding the cost of the duty to the American public, while protective organs have denied that
the cost of clothing was substantially increased by
it.

II. CAUSES OF THE DISAGREEMENT

When different groups of estimable citizens are
found with such widely divergent opinions about
an important matter, it is natural to inquire into
the cause of the conflict. As Henry Clay said: "In
the discussion and consideration of these opposite
opinions for the purpose of ascertaining which has
the support of truth and reason, we should, therefore, exercise every indulgence and the greatest spirit
of mutual moderation and forbearance." [11]   In this
case it is quite clear that there are four principal
reasons for the lack of agreement. First, the fact

[9] Message to Congress, 1887. See Taussig, F. W., *Selected
Readings in International Trade and Tariff Problems*, 1921, p. 533.
[10] The Federation estimated the total cost to the public at
$91,000,000; the share of this borne by farmers at 30 per cent of
the whole, or $27,300,000; and the increased price received by all
wool growers at $37,500,000. *American Farm Bureau Federation
Weekly News Letter*, Jan. 11, 1923, Vol. III, No. 2, p. 1.
[11] Speech of Henry Clay on American Industry, in the House of
Representatives, March 30 and 31, 1824.

that some of those involved in the controversy have a special interest at stake. Second, the existence of wide differences in opinion as to the desirability of a tariff in general and disagreement over what it will actually accomplish. Third, a like divergence of view over the status of wool-growing and its needs. Fourth, the preoccupation of some persons with the more absolute and permanent aspects of the case and of others with the temporary features—the policy of the moment.

1. Special Interest

It is evident that one of the principal causes of disagreement is the special interest of various groups. It is to be expected that those who are engaged in any one branch of industry will see its needs in sharp relief. They are entirely honest in believing that the welfare of the country is jeopardized when their interests are threatened: and they are right in holding that belief to the extent that they occupy an important niche in the national economy. To plead the cause of a private interest may be laudable, so long as other rights are not encroached upon. Nevertheless, it is well to remember that the eagerness of the parties in such a controversy is apt to lead to exaggeration.

2. Assumption as to General Tariff Policy

The second pitfall is that of the fixed opinion on tariff matters. It is almost as difficult to lay aside

preconceptions about the tariff as about race or
religion.   The average man walks "by faith and
not by sight" in regard to the tariff.   He is satisfied with such phrases as "maintenance of the
American standard of living" and "difference in cost
of production at home and abroad"; or, on the other
hand, "the tariff is a tax" and "the tariff is the
mother of the trusts."   A great number of tariff
discussions offer no food for thought more nourish-
ing than this, and it may well be said that the public mind suffers from chronic malnutrition on the
subject.

*Prevalent opinions on the tariff are stereotyped
to a surprising degree.*   The leading tariff creeds
or platforms are protection, free trade, downward
revision, and tariff for revenue.   The main positions
are so widely at variance that the basic proposals
of one group are often entirely rejected by the
others.

The protectionist believes that the national
wealth is increased by applying a stimulus to many
branches of production.   He affirms that the tariff
is a large factor in enabling the American work-
men to enjoy a higher standard of living and holds
that the tariff does not constitute a real tax upon
consumption because of the higher degree of
prosperity which is enjoyed under it.   He believes
that domestic industry should be protected by
a duty at least equal to the difference in cost of
production at home and abroad, although he may

concede that some industries operate under such a great disadvantage that it is not worth while to protect them.

The free trader maintains as the paramount article of his faith that protection diverts productive energy into less profitable channels and thus decreases the national wealth. He believes that this country has become rich and great because of its wonderful natural resources and its virile population, and in spite of the tariff; that duties tend to create misunderstandings between nations; that they foster monopolies behind the tariff wall and impose a heavy burden upon consumers; and that this burden is the more grievous because it is "regressive"—i. e., falls more heavily upon persons of small or moderate income.

Those who believe in "downward revision" usually hold that the free trade doctrine is theoretically sound and that this country would be better off if, from the beginning, it had held consistently to freedom of trade. While industrial development would have taken place more slowly, it would, they say, have been upon a sounder basis. On the other hand, they recognize that many industries depend to some extent upon the tariff and they fear harmful effects from sudden changes. For this reason they advocate a gradual lessening of the rates. Among this group are found some who do not admit the soundness of free trade theory, but nevertheless believe that the United States has passed the point where it needs to apply a strong protective stimulus to many industries.

The adherents of tariff for revenue usually subscribe to the free trade theory concerning the diminution of national wealth by the system of protection but uphold the imposition of duties for the purpose of raising revenue; and since a comprehensive scheme of revenue duties often gives some aid to domestic industry, the members of this school commonly uphold "incidental" protection.

The majority of economists, since the time of Adam Smith, have upheld the free trade theory. There have been exceptions, as in the case of Friedrich List and other German writers who defended the system of "National Economy," and of two American economists, Henry C. Carey and Simon Patten, who favored protection. The basic argument of economists has always been that protection diverts the productive forces of a country into comparatively unprofitable channels. Some have conceded that there were variations from the general rule, as in the case of young industries which can not gain a foothold without the aid of a tariff. Also, industries vital to national defence have sometimes been held to constitute an exception, for, as Adam Smith said, "Defence is better than opulence." The consensus of opinion has, however, been in favor of free trade or lower tariffs.

Business men, on the other hand, have, in the United States and several of the leading European countries, strongly favored protection. There has been much suspicion of economists for their views on the tariff. Business men have tended to look upon them as impractical theorists, while the economists have returned the suspicion, regarding the business enthusiasts for protection as selfish seekers of government bounties who have no true conception of, or interest in, the long run economic welfare of the country. Because of this sharp conflict of opinion it has been nearly, or quite, impossible for anyone to reach a conclusion for or against any duty without being branded as either visionary or opportunistic.

3. Disagreement as to the Facts About the Wool-Growing Industry

The third cause of conflict is a real difference of opinion over the state of the industry and the needs of the wool-growers. One person may regard sheep raising as a declining, and another as a progressing, industry, because each is familiar with conditions in a particular area only. Constant disagreement is likely to arise over the probable success of new methods proposed; and a sharp division of opinion sometimes appears when two persons sum up the results of past experiments. There has been much dispute over the question whether the continuance of sheep raising on a considerable scale in the Ohio Region was economically justifiable. Some have asserted that the high costs of the industry, disclosed by the Tariff Board in 1910-11, showed that the persistence of wool-growing in that region was due largely to custom. Others have just as strongly maintained that the conditions of soil and climate, and the local handicaps to dairying, were adequate reason for the presence of large numbers of sheep. There is a difference of opinion over the extent to which the carrying capacity of the western ranges can be increased, over the policy which should be followed in handling the grazing on public lands, over the most desirable methods to be followed in breeding and managing the flocks, and even in regard to the policy to be followed in regulating the number of sheep at the present time.[12] When there is such a lack of agreement over basic facts, it is not strange that there is no unanimity of opinion as to the wool tariff.

4. Varying Emphasis upon Long-Time or Short-Time Policy

The fourth cause of disagreement is found in the preoccupation of one group with the permanent and of another with the temporary features of the problem. One group fixes its attention upon the long-run development of industry, advocating changes which will be eventually beneficial. The other group sees principally, in any proposal for change, the threat of immediate disturbance. The latter are prone to argue that nothing should be

---

[12] See in Chapter IX account of difference of opinion between President Hagenbarth of the National Wool-Growers' Association, and Dr. S. W. McClure, former Secretary of the Association.

done to alter present conditions because of the temporary discomfort which will follow, while the former condemn the cautious ones as cowardly temporizers.[13]

III. PLAN OF ANALYSIS FOR THE PRESENT STUDY

We must now define the position taken in this study with respect to the fundamental causes of

[13] The element of time which is necessary to work out any considerable change in commercial policy has been recognized by both sides in the tariff controversy. President Cleveland said, in his message of December 6, 1887: "It is not proposed to entirely relieve the country of taxation. It must be extensively continued as the source of the Government's income; and in a readjustment of our tariff the interests of American labor engaged in manufacture should be carefully considered, as well as the preservation of our manufacturers. It may be called protection or by any other name, but relief from the hardships and dangers of our present tariff laws should be devised with especial precaution against imperiling the existence of our manufacturing interests. But this existence should not mean a condition which, without regard to the public welfare or a national exigency, must always insure the realization of immense profits instead of moderately profitable returns." Taussig, F. W., *Selected Readings in International Trade and Tariff Problems*, pp. 529-30.

Thomas B. Reed said, in his speech on the Mills Bill, in the House of Representatives, May 19, 1888: "You tell us, they say, that protection is for the purpose of enhancing prices to enable high wages to be paid, and yet you say that protection lowers prices. This is flat contradiction. So it is as you state it. But your statement, like all revenue-reform statements, flourishes only by assumption.

"In order to make yourself clear, you have utterly omitted the element of time. You assume that we say that both our statements of higher prices for higher wages, and lower prices for consumers are for the same instant of time. Not so. When you begin there are higher prices for higher wages, but when you establish your manufactories, at once the universal law of competition begins to work. . . .

"That lower prices will come at once, we have never said. That they will come and grow lower and lower so that in the series of years which make up a man's life all he needs will cost him less than under revenue-reform we asseverate and maintain, and all history is behind our asseverations." (Ibid., p. 558.)

disagreement which have been outlined. First, in regard to the special interests of various groups: while it is perfectly legitimate for different organizations and groups to seek their own interest, it is apparent that statements coming from such sources must be interpreted in the light of their origin. In this study we desire to avoid, so far as possible, considerations affecting the balance of political forces, and to determine, upon the basis of ascertained facts, what is good for the whole country. Consequently, the point of view taken must be as far removed as possible from that of the special advocate.

Second, in regard to general assumptions about the tariff: It is not the intention of this study to pass judgment on the protective system as a whole. There is no assumption as to the wisdom or unwisdom of any of the policies described. We are not concerned with the question whether the protective system has justified itself or whether, as the free trader says, the diversion of capital and labor into less profitable channels nullifies all the arguments of protectionists and leaves the balance in favor of free trade. If anything is herein set forth which seems to stamp with approval certain of the broad assumptions of any tariff group it is because they are peculiarly applicable to the case in hand, not because they are universally or even generally valid.

The third cause of disagreement mentioned was

difference of opinion over the status and needs of the industry. A large part of this study has been directed toward ascertaining the existing conditions in the industry at home and abroad and determining the effects which different rates of duty have had in the past, and probably would have in the future, upon the extent of, and profit in, sheep raising in the United States. In spite of the hopelessness of securing unanimity of opinion on these matters, it is upon the basis of the facts, as herein set forth, that we must draw our conclusions.

One of the greatest difficulties in charting a wise course over the sea of tariff policy is the lack of indisputable proof of the effects of most rates. A determination of the wisest course of action in regard to the tariff does not depend upon such proof as that obtained by experimenters in the exact sciences. We are concerned with establishing facts beyond a "reasonable doubt." These facts can be ascertained as satisfactorily with respect to wool as to almost any other commodity. Upon a foundation of such information it should be possible to formulate a policy which will achieve the greatest public benefit.

The fourth cause of divided opinion is the varying emphasis placed upon long-time and short-time policy. In considering immediate policy in regard to the wool tariff, it must be recognized that the sheep raising industry is a part of the economic fabric of the country. An interdependence exists between wool-growing and banking, transportation, merchandising, and other economic activities.[14] The industry is financed by large extensions of credit from banks, wool dealers, and commission men. It furnishes part of the revenue of railroads, serving a wide expanse of territory and is, in turn, dependent on their services. The wages, interest, and profits which constitute the share of the national income accruing to the sheep industry flow into the channels of trade in the wool-growing regions and make up the receipts of many merchants and manufacturers.

The production, marketing, manufacture, and consumption of wool forms a continuous process, and failure of any part of the process to operate smoothly results in a disorganization of other parts of the machinery. A change in the method of doing business at any step, or a change in the amount of business done, will affect many individuals. For example, a sudden decrease in the amount of wool grown will throw some herders and shearers out of work, impair the business of merchants in the wool-growing region and of manufacturers who sell the sheepmen supplies, cause a readjustment of the business of bankers who extend credit to the growers, decrease the freight receipts of wool-carrying roads, affect conditions somewhat in the wool-marketing centers, and cause labor and capital to seek new employment all along the line. Cog-

[14] See Chapters I and II.

nizance must be taken of these realignments in considering a change in the duty.

On the other hand, the permanent is more important than the temporary situation. When a corporation gives evidence of being in an unsound condition the stockholders do not think of immediate dividends. The policy which would afford the largest dividends this year might mean the continuance of the company on the road to ultimate disaster. The company can hardly begin at once to do business on an entirely new plan. It can not produce its goods in a totally different way or sell them in altogether new markets. It is more difficult to deal with a "going concern" than with one which is newly started or merely projected. However, an entirely different method of conducting the business may be followed if the change is brought about with circumspection.

Transfers of labor and capital between industries are constantly taking place, irrespective of tariff revision. The price of a commodity having an international market rises and falls through influences entirely apart from the tariff, and domestic production is consequently stimulated or discouraged.[15] A growth of population and a shift in the use of land affect agricultural enterprises. There is, therefore, no permanence in industry, even in the absence of tariff revision. An alteration in the tariff is overshadowed before many years by really fundamental

[15] See Appendix A.

economic developments. That which is important in a short-run view of an industry may become relatively insignificant when considered in the light of inevitably changing conditions.

Keeping in mind the essential facts which have been stated, we must formulate a plan of attack upon the present problem. In this case, as in most tariff discussion, there are three group interests which should be considered—first, the producers', second, the consumers', and third, the public's, using the latter term to cover the national welfare in a sense which is more inclusive than either of the other categories.[16]

We propose to balance the possible gain to producers against the possible loss to consumers and then to inquire whether there is any other aspect of public policy which materially affects the conclusion. The ground-work for a study of the present wool tariff has been laid in Parts I and II, which dealt, respectively, with conditions in the wool-growing industry at home and abroad and with the history of the wool tariff, including the Act of 1922. Even when all the facts have been ascertained, however, it is not always easy to interpret them.

Judgment must be exercised as to the important issues to be treated, and the relative weight of the

[16] For example, if it is necessary to increase the production of wool to make the United States less dependent on foreign sources of supply in war-time, a duty benefits, to the extent that it secures the desired end, producers and consumers alike.

facts established. Thus it comes about that even a scientific inquiry, when it deals with a subject so contentious as the one under consideration, must partake of the nature of a forum where both sides are given an opportunity to be heard. However, the principal issues can be made so clear, and the essential facts so firmly established, that any dissent from the conclusion must arise from a differing emphasis on the various elements of the problem.

Before striking the balance of gain and loss from a wool duty we must consider some of the proposed "scientific" bases for a duty. If there were any mathematical or statistical rule by which the proper amount of duty on a commodity could be ascertained, it would greatly simplify the work of tariff makers. Tariff revision would become the application of an all-embracing formula, and tariff controversies would be merely arguments over detail. The hope for such a settlement of major issues has been so often expressed, and the announcement of the discovery of such a rule has been so confidently made, that we ought not to ignore that phase of the problem.

After considering different proposed bases for a duty, we shall ask what influence a wool duty exerts upon the sheep industry. If it raises the price of wool we must inquire how much it stimulates the domestic output. The nature of the demand for and supply of the products of the industry must be examined, and specific effects of different rates of duty must be estimated. Then we must follow the wool through the various stages of manufacture and sale to ascertain the effect of the duty on these departments of industry, and to find out whether the prices of wool products, especially clothing, are raised to the ultimate consumers.

Even an accurate balance of gain and loss to producers and consumers will not, however, solve the problem finally. We must weigh all other pertinent facts and decide whether they tell in favor of, or against, the duty. The wool duty has been called "the keystone of the arch of protection." An attempt will be made to consider it, so far as possible, apart from its political connotation, and to recommend a policy which shall be both beneficial in its long-run effect and practical in its immediate application.

CHAPTER VIII

PROPOSED BASES FOR A WOOL DUTY

It has been shown in preceding chapters that the attempt to maintain the present volume of wool production in the United States means that the last increments of the output are produced under conditions less advantageous than those under which the bulk of the wool is grown in the chief competing countries. Now two questions naturally arise: first, whether it is possible to measure this disadvantage accurately; and second, whether if a quantitative expression of the disadvantage can be secured it is a suitable basis for a duty. More extensive investigations for tariff purposes have been made of the cost of producing wool than of any other commodity, and earnest attempts have been made to apply the "cost rule" in fixing duties. In this chapter the difficulties encountered in this procedure will be shown, and other bases for a duty will be considered.

It will appear that the duties levied upon wool have been empirical and experimental in character, and that there is no scientific method of determining the proper rate of duty. The way will then be cleared for the consideration of the actual effects of a duty.

I. "DIFFERENCE IN COST OF PRODUCTION" AS A BASIS FOR THE DUTY

The most widely advocated basis of a protective tariff is "the difference in cost of production at home and abroad." This phrase is used very loosely, but those who advance the theory usually profess to desire to establish "equality of competitive conditions." They do not seek to enact prohibitory duties, so they say, but to allow competition in the home market "on even terms" between the domestic and foreign goods. The first difficulty in applying this theory is to secure accurate costs. To carry out the program rigorously would require investigations on a scale never attempted. The estimates submitted as "costs" by interested parties are seldom worthy of scientific consideration. Foreigners can hardly be expected to co-operate in furnishing cost figures which are to be the excuse for raising duties against their products; and the expense of conducting all such investigations is very great. Costs are constantly fluctuating, moreover, so that the work must frequently be repeated. It is sufficiently difficult to secure accurate costs for the home production.

Assuming, however, that the costs can be secured and that the labor and expense are not prohibitory, what costs are to be taken as the basis of the tariff rate? The difference between costs of foreign producers is so great, the variation in the costs of the domestic producers is also so large, and the question of the separation of costs between joint products, as in the case of wool and mutton, is so difficult, that the duty which will actually represent the "difference in the cost of production at home and abroad" is extremely difficult to ascertain. Thus there is enough trouble in applying such a theory even if another problem did not arise—namely, what degree of ineffectiveness should be supported by the tariff. It is apparent that the less efficient a domestic producer is, the higher his costs will be, and the greater his claim, under this theory, to tariff support.

Assuming, for the moment, however, that it is possible and feasible to secure foreign and domestic costs of wool production, and that it is desired to encourage the production of wool in this country under the prevailing disadvantageous conditions, how shall we go about the task of determining the cost of production? It is obvious that it is not easy to determine just what constitutes the cost of producing one of two joint products like wool and mutton. Some of the most interesting and difficult questions connected with the wool duty center about this issue. The manner of determining the cost is of paramount importance if difference in cost is to be used as the basis of the duty. A divergence is shown between the practice of the

Tariff Board of 1911 and of the present Tariff Commission.

II. THE TARIFF BOARD AND TARIFF COMMISSION. METHODS OF COST ALLOCATION COMPARED

The method of ascertaining the cost of production of wool which was adopted by the Tariff Board in 1911 is open to serious objection. The method was as follows: The receipts from other sources than wool were set off against the total expenses of sheep husbandry, and the difference was called the "cost" of producing the wool. There are thus three factors in the problem, the returns from wool, the returns from other sources (principally mutton and lambs), and the expenses per head. A change in any one of the three will cause a change in the net cost per pound of wool.[1] The weakness of the method was freely admitted by the members of the Board, but it was maintained that there was no method which was essentially more accurate. As the report on Schedule K says: [2]

The conclusion is inevitable that when the woolgrowers' receipts are derived partly from wool and partly from mutton, it is impossible to apportion the cost between the two products and that therefore we can not obtain a result which can accurately be termed the cost of producing a pound of wool. However, this need occasion no concern, since the bearing of the receipts from wool on the returns from flock husbandry, as carried on in the region

[1] See Appendix D.   [2] Vol. 1, p. 312.

under consideration, can be ascertained and the object of this investigation can thus be accomplished.

The Tariff Board method of ascertaining cost ascribes all the profit of the industry to one of the products. If the converse of the method were used to ascertain the cost of mutton, all the profit would be ascribed to that product. If we should wish to obtain the cost of both of the products at the same time in order to determine the "proper" (based on difference in cost of production) duties on wool and mutton respectively, we should be confronted with a duplication in our figures which would entirely nullify the results.[3]

The Tariff Commission method was superior to that of the Tariff Board of 1910-11. The method which was adopted by the Tariff Commission, in its investigation of 1919-21, had the advantage of being in consonance with the facts of flock management and also of obviating the difficulty mentioned above, that of ascribing all the profit to one branch of the business. This method was to charge expenses directly to mutton or wool if it were possible to ascertain that they were properly so chargeable; the remaining expenses were apportioned to mutton or wool in the same proportion that receipts from each bear to the total receipts. Some expenses—shearing, woolsacks, twine—are evidently "wool" expenses, and were charged as such. It was

[3] See Appendix D.

not possible to allocate any expense directly to mutton as there are no such expenses which do not also contribute to a better or larger clip of wool. Consequently, all expenses except those charged directly to wool, were apportioned. This method corresponds roughly with actual practice in flock management. The owner incurs them, so far as he knows how to do it, in the proportion in which they will contribute to the increase in the output of each product. If more careful grading of the wool will enhance the price, the good manager will increase the outlay for grading. If better lambing sheds or feeding of lambs en route to market will improve his crop of lambs, he will incur the necessary expenses.

III. RESULT OF USING THE TARIFF COMMISSION'S METHOD

Applying the method of apportionment of non-separable expenses on the same basis as receipts, the Tariff Commission found the cost of wool in 1919 to be as shown in the table on page 199.[4]

The difference in cost of production between the United States and Argentina was 17-⅔ cents per pound, in the grease, including interest. Cost figures were found in this country for flocks numbering 699,627 sheep. The average cost per pound of wool was $0.4503 including interest, and $0.3723 exclud-

---

[4] Tariff Commission's Report, *The Wool Growing Industry,* 1921, p. 200.

State	Ratio of Receipts (Per Cent)		Wool Expenses (Per Pound)	
	Wool	Mutton and Lambs	Including Interest in Cost	Excluding Interest from Cost
Arizona [a]	56	44	$0.5450	$0.4370
California	32	68	.4064	.3189
Colorado	43	57	.4320	.3120
Idaho	39	61	.4880	.4061
Montana	61	39	.7620	.5823
New Mexico [a]	52	48	.3211	.2665
Texas	43	57	.3209	.2141
Utah	45	55	.3627	.3019
Washington	32	68	.3336	.2708
Wyoming	54	46	.4834	.3906

[a] For the year 1918. Representative costs for 1919 not obtained.

ing interest.[5]   The average cost of wool in Argentina was estimated, by an agent of the Tariff Commission who visited that country, at 27-⅓ cents a pound.   If interest had been eliminated from both costs, the difference between them would probably have been somewhat less.[6]

[5] The average cost of production of 45 cents per pound for the Range States, obtained by the U. S. Tariff Commission in 1919, was higher than the average domestic price at several periods between 1919 and 1924. In 1920 the price dropped to about 20 cents per pound, by 1923 it had risen to about 45 cents per pound and in July, 1924, it fell again to about 35 cents per pound. Cost of production may not have fluctuated as widely as prices but presumably it decreased during these years. This illustrates one difficulty in using difference in cost as the basis of the duty. The figures are obsolete almost as soon as the investigation is finished.

[6] The inclusion or exclusion of interest makes a vital difference. The allowance of interest on land owned or of rentals paid is objectionable from the tariff point of view. There are two possible situations.

1. *When the land can be used for nothing else but sheep raising.* In this case the value of the land is fixed by the profit of sheep raising; it is merely the capitalization at the current rate of in-

The diagrams on pages 202-3 illustrate the range of costs in the Territory Region in 1918 and 1919. These were constructed from the returns of 19 representative companies, since the material is not available for a schedule of all the costs obtained by the Tariff Commission. That most of these companies were efficiently managed appears probable from the fact that their average cost was $.3968 per pound of wool in 1918 as against a cost of $.4503 per pound for all the wool included in the Commission's investigation, and $.3915 in 1919 as against $.4509 for all. The companies are further representative in that they are both large and small outfits and are distributed among eight states—

terest of the annual net return from the use of the land. If interest (or rent) is allowed as a cost and a high tariff is imposed, it increases the profit, raises the valuation of the land and consequently the interest charge. The higher cost may be made the basis of a demand for a still .higher duty.

2. *When the land can be used for something besides sheep raising.* In the case of possible alternative uses for the land, its value is not fixed by sheep-raising alone. But if we concede interest as a cost in such a situation, we are encouraging the production of wool under disadvantageous circumstances. Where genuine pastoral conditions exist, the return per acre is usually smaller than under the most primitive form of cultivation. The farm sheep industry is usually such a subsidiary undertaking that the interest (or rent) to be charged to the flock is quite negligible.

It is probably not feasible to eliminate interest in cost comparisons between countries, because we cannot determine the exact extent to which the profit of the sheep industry helps in each case to establish the current return on land. Nor can we tell the degree to which the profit in the sheep-raising industry helps to establish the rate of return which is considered adequate for industry in general. It is evident, however, that in allowing interest on the investment in land and to some extent also in allowing it on the investment in the sheep, we are "begging the question." The very thing which we accept as a criterion of disadvantage may be due to the profit of the industry.

Colorado, Wyoming, Utah, Idaho, Montana, New Mexico, Washington and California. The average price received for the wool shown in these charts was $.5389 per pound in 1918 as against $.5427 received for all wool included in the investigation, and $.5148 per pound in 1919 as against $.5260 for all wool the cost of which was ascertained. The figure on page 202 represents 1,252,229 pounds or 22 per cent of all the wool included in the Commission's study of costs in the Territory Region in 1918, and the figure on page 203 represents 1,247,-631 pounds or 44 per cent of the total amount covered by the 1919 investigation.

The supply schedules given in these charts portray the typical dispersion of costs among companies. They are similar in shape to the charts constructed upon the basis of the costs collected by the Tariff Board in 1910-11. They emphasize the fact that in any year a portion of the output is produced at a cost greater than the market price. In 1918, 16 per cent of the wool shown in the chart was produced at a cost greater than the average price received, and in 1919, 37 per cent was so produced. It is not strange, therefore, that when the price of wool fell precipitously in 1920-21, the output of wool declined rapidly.[7]

The bulk of the wool here represented was produced at a higher cost in 1919 than in 1918. The average was kept at the same level in 1919 as in

[7] See Chapter V.

1918, however, by the fact that costs were lowered at both extremes—among both the lowest cost and highest cost producers. Also, it should be noted the

COST OF PRODUCTION OF TERRITORY WOOL, 1918
(Cumulative)

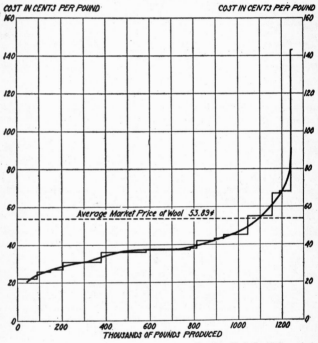

COST IN CENTS PER POUND

COST IN CENTS PER POUND

Average Market Price of Wool 53.89¢

THOUSANDS OF POUNDS PRODUCED

Courtesy U. S. Tariff Commission

average cost (including interest) of all wool included in the Commission's investigation was approximately the same in both years—45 cents. But the figure for 1919 indicates clearly a tendency toward higher costs, which was reversed suddenly by the deflation of 1920.

The ratio of cost to price in 1918 (for all wool

COST OF PRODUCTION OF TERRITORY WOOL, 1919
(Cumulative)

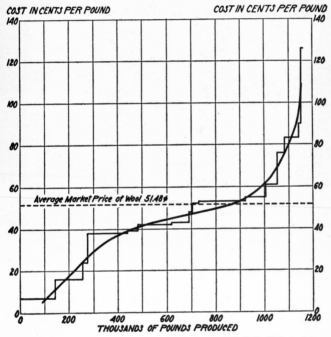

Courtesy U. S. Tariff Commission

included in the Commission's investigation) was 5 to 6—cost 45 cents and price 54 cents. If this same ratio still prevailed in 1924, the average cost per pound must have been about 30-35 cents, as the market price of Territory wool was 36-42 cents per pound in the grease. It is certain that costs were much below the 1918-19 level; otherwise one-half of the output would have been produced at a cost greater than the average price.

The charts illustrate the difficulty, mentioned above, of determining what cost is to be taken as typical of domestic costs when it is desired to equalize foreign and domestic costs by a duty. If the arithmetical average were selected (approximately 39 cents in both 1918 and 1919), a large number of domestic producers and a large proportion of the output would be left unprotected. The selection of 45 cents (average cost for all wool investigated) would still leave some presumably efficient producers exposed to foreign competition. And the selection of a bulk line,[8] as for example 55 cents or 60 cents, would be purely arbitrary; and even then a portion of the industry would be above the margin.

IV. INCONCLUSIVE NATURE OF THE RESULT

Even if all other objections are ignored, the result of the Tariff Commission's investigations is inconclusive for two reasons. First, no costs were secured from Australia, although that country is the leading competitor. Second, the Tariff Commission method does not eliminate entirely the first objection made to the Tariff Board method, namely,

[8] See Chapter V.

that a change in the proportion of receipts from wool and mutton respectively, changes the "cost of production" of wool. The cost in the state of Washington, where 68 per cent of the total receipts came from mutton and lambs, was only $.3336 per pound. A slight increase in the receipts from mutton in Washington would have reduced the "cost" of wool in that state to as low a point as the Argentine cost. The price per pound which the growers of Montana received for their wool in 1919 was $.5884 (higher than the average for any other state) according to the Tariff Commission's figures, but the ratio of receipts from wool was so high— 61 per cent as against 39 per cent for mutton receipts—that the "cost" of wool was $.762 per pound.[9] It would require an enormous duty to offset such a production cost. The "cost" of wool is almost uniformly lower where the proportion of receipts from mutton and lambs is high.

The duty of 31 cents per scoured pound, fixed by the Act of 1922 does not, therefore, represent any scientifically ascertained difference in costs. So far as it is something other than the result of political influences it is a guess, based upon information fairly complete upon the domestic side but utterly inadequate upon the foreign side.

The Tariff Commission method is merely the most convenient working formula. There is no better

---

[9] A net loss was shown for Montana growers unless interest were excluded, in which case a profit of $.13 per head was secured.

way of fixing tentative "costs" than apportionment of joint expenses on the basis of receipts for the respective products; yet because of the constantly changing relations between the products the effects of duties based on such assumed "differences in cost" must be extremely variable.[10] But even if the true differences in costs had been found, that does not prove the desirability of maintaining the part of the domestic industry which operates at such a great disadvantage. That depends upon questions of public policy which we must later consider.[11]

V. OTHER PROPOSED FORMS OF DUTY

The proposal has been made that the difference in cost per head of raising sheep in this country and foreign countries should be found—this difference to be offset by an ad valorem rate on both mutton and wool. Irrespective of any merit which this method may have, it can only be carried out through an ad valorem duty, which has never been acceptable. The wool growers fear undervaluation of the imported wool, and the manufacturers regard an ad valorem duty on wool as an unsatisfactory basis for compensatory rates on woolen goods.

Exclusion of foreign wool is not proposed by even the most enthusiastic advocates of a high duty on wool. It might be possible to enact a duty which would be absolutely prohibitive of imports, but

[10] See Appendix D.   [11] See Chapter XI.

domestic manufacturers are to a large extent dependent upon foreign grown wool. About half of the wool consumed by the American woolen and worsted mills comes from outside our borders. Special varieties of wool are demanded, also, which cannot be supplied by the domestic wool growing industry. In the course of economic development this country has come to have trade relations with certain wool growing countries, and it would disturb this trade and tend to curtail our exports if we should stop all such foreign purchases.

The determination of the rate of duty which will produce the most revenue for the Government is possible, within limits. In attempting to fix such a duty, however, we should be forsaking the point of view of those desiring protection for the wool industry. It is evident that as the imports of wool are reduced the protection to the domestic industry increases, while the Government cannot secure a large revenue from the tariff unless the imports continue in considerable volume. The purposes of protection and revenue-production are, to a large extent, contradictory. A tariff-for-revenue cannot be considered a scientific way of protecting the domestic wool growing industry.

The enactment of a rate which will fix a definite ratio between the imports and the domestic production is not possible. Conditions are constantly changing both at home and abroad. A rate which would allow 40 per cent of the domestic consumption to be imported next year might admit 60 per cent the following year.

All the important elements in competition—the difference in cost of production at home and abroad, conditions governing the demand and supply of the product, relative prices, marketing advantages, and other factors [12] must be considered in fixing a rate which will permit equality in competition between home and foreign producers. Even then the rate cannot be fixed with exactness. Moreover, even if it is determined in such a manner as to convince producers of its essential fairness, the case in favor of such a rate is not proved. We have still to settle the question whether it is advisable to encourage competition on those terms.

In spite of the impossibility of securing any general agreement upon a "scientific method" of levying the tariff, any rate which raises the price of wool will help domestic producers. The duties on wool, which have been imposed for such a long period, usually have had the effect of raising the domestic price distinctly above the level of the foreign price.[13] Often the margin has not been equal to the duty. However, variations in quality, and in the care with which the wool was prepared for market, frequently have been sufficient explanation of failure to secure a price higher by the full

[12] See Page, Thomas Walker, *Making the Tariff in the United States* (Publications of the Institute of Economics, Washington), 1924, pp. 218-9.

[13] See Chapters V and VI.

amount of the tariff. At other times the market conjuncture has robbed the duty of its full effect. In the case of the present duty it is a fair question whether the rate has not been placed so high as to fail of its full effect through some elasticity in the demand for woolen products.

The fact that the wool duty has raised the domestic price of the product is, however, the most important fact to wool growers. Therefore, attempts to construct a tenable theory with which to reconcile opposing views on tariff rates may be laid aside. We should attempt to discover how much real assistance is given to wool growing by an experimental and "unscientific" rate.

CHAPTER IX

EFFECTS ON SHEEP HUSBANDRY OF A DUTY ON WOOL

It is proposed to discuss in this chapter the effects upon the sheep raising industry of a duty on wool. It was shown in the preceding chapter that there is no scientific method for the establishment of a correct rate of duty, but it was stated that any rate which raises the price helps the domestic industry. It will now be shown that even though the price may be raised by a duty, no great increase in output is to be expected at the higher price. The effects of the retention, increase, or reduction of the present rate of duty will be estimated as closely as possible, and the probable developments in the absence of a duty will also be outlined.

I. THE DEMAND FOR AND SUPPLY OF WOOL

The influence which a wool duty exerts upon sheep husbandry is consummated, first, through a change which it brings about in the supply of wool by the stimulus of a higher price; second, through a probable decrease in the demand for wool as a higher price range is attained; third, through an increase in the supply of mutton and lamb as the number of sheep is increased to take advantage of the higher price of wool; and fourth, a possible drop in the price of the meat consequent upon an augmentation of the supply.   Consequently, the subject matter of this chapter is constituted largely of an analysis of demand and supply.   Mutton and lamb are just as important as wool, but since the latter is traditionally the main product, we shall turn attention to it first.

The demand for wool usually continues at first but little diminished in the face of an increase in the price.[1]   The experience with the tariff on wool has demonstrated that the domestic price is usually raised to the full extent of the duty,—when differences in grade and condition between the domestic and the foreign article are taken into account.   This indicates that the price can be raised by a duty without materially decreasing the domestic consumption.[2]   If the domestic wool-growing

[1] There is a strong presumption that the demand for wool is inelastic.   That is, changes in the price cause a less than proportionate change in the amounts purchased.   If the price rises, the natural tendency is toward a decrease in the amount taken and vice versa; but when the demand is inelastic, an increase of 1 per cent in the price may cause, for example, a decrease of only ¾ of 1 per cent in the demand, while a fall in the price of 1 per cent would only cause ¾ of 1 per cent more of the commodity to be taken.   With an elastic demand, on the other hand, a change in the price causes a more than proportionate change in the amounts purchased.   If substitutes are readily available for a particular commodity, the demand for it is likely to be elastic.   There is a greater possibility of substituting other food products for lamb and mutton than of substituting other textile fibers for wool.

[2] That this rule is subject to some limitation is indicated by experience under the Tariff Act of 1922.   (See Chapter VI.)   It

industry increases its output it can, therefore (provided domestic grades are largely comparable with those now imported) supplant much of the foreign wool and enjoy the benefit of the protection granted.

The domestic wool-growing industry produces grades of wool which can be thus utilized when a duty is effective in enlarging the output and reducing the amount of foreign wool used. The wools of Australia, New Zealand, and, to some extent, those of South Africa and Great Britain, are competitive with wools grown in the United States. The fine wools of Montana, Wyoming, Idaho, and Oregon meet with direct competition from the 64's-70's wool imported from Australia. The Merino combing wools of Australia compete with the Delaine wools of the Ohio region, Merino wools of Montevideo with Ohio fine clothing, and the Sydney and Adelaide 64's with "Michigan fine combing." The amount of domestic wool which competes thus directly with the foreign fine wool is variously estimated at 30,000,000 to 90,000,000 pounds annually. The possibility of using an increased output of domestic wool in the case of a reduction of imports, is undeniable.

The world conditions of supply of and demand for wool also point to the future effectiveness of a

is quite possible that the demand for certain grades of wool is elastic, or that when the price of wool rises beyond a certain point the demand becomes elastic.

wool duty. The supply of wool is less than formerly, both absolutely and relatively to the demand. The per capita consumption of wool decreased considerably in the years before the beginning of the European War, but the price was well maintained. The substitution of other materials for wool may have worked toward the decrease in per capita consumption; but it is probable that such substitution has proceeded about as far as it will. Large quantities of cotton and reworked wool are now used by the woolen and worsted industries (particularly the former), and great skill has been exercised in the creation from such materials of fabrics having a good appearance and durability. The standard of living is rising in many countries, however; and as the better goods are usually those having a higher percentage of wool (either new or the better grades of reworked) it is probable that the demand for them will considerably increase. Japan, for instance, uses 100,000,000 pounds more of wool annually than before the war. All the conditions point to a strong demand for wool in the future.

The supply is, of course, responsive to price. A stronger demand manifesting itself in a higher price might increase the production, especially in Australia or South Africa. This could, however, only be at greater cost, under the conditions existing in those countries.[3] The increase of agriculture is a sign of diminishing returns from wool

[3] See Chapter III.

production, for it represents the choice, by a growing number of persons, of the former as a more profitable occupation than the latter. Both the change in the nature of the wool produced throughout the world—the tendency toward crossbred—and diminishing production, will tend to lessen the severity of the foreign competition to which domestic producers of fine wools are subjected during the period of transition from range to farm sheep raising.[4]

Up to this point our analysis has indicated that conditions are favorable to a large increase in the domestic output of wool through the application of a protective tariff. However, one important point has not been touched upon. Nothing has been said to indicate that the costs of additional supplies of wool and mutton might not be the same as costs of previous units of the output. This is obviously contrary to fact so far as the range industry is concerned.

Conditions governing the domestic supply are unfavorable to an increased output. All the conditions in the Far West indicate that the sheep industry has been pushed into the stage of diminishing returns. More profitable uses for the land are constantly appearing; the investment in fixed capital has multiplied; more herders are necessary in proportion to the number of sheep; and a greater amount of raised feed must be used. If the in-

[4] See Chapter I.

dustry is expanded these costs will rise even higher. The farm sheep industry stands in a different position. In so far as it can be expanded by the use of roughage and surplus fodder, costs will be constant rather than increasing. It cannot be greatly extended, however, without competing with other lines of production for the use of land, capital, and managerial ability. Some increase seems possible, however, without such encroachment. But wool is the by-product of a by-industry in this case, and a rise in its price will have less influence in expanding the farm flocks than a rise in the price of lamb and mutton or a drop in the price of other farm commodities, particularly dairy products. A quantitative estimate concerning the effect of a duty must be postponed until later in this chapter. It may be noted at this point that the tendency toward increasing costs will go far toward keeping down the desired growth in domestic supply.

II. DEMAND FOR AND SUPPLY OF MUTTON AND LAMB

In forming a judgment as to the probable effect of a wool duty, the demand for and supply of mutton and lamb are fully as important as the same conditions with respect to wool. While the industry is depending more and more upon receipts from the meat, the market for it is narrowly restricted both by its price and the prejudice of a large group of consumers. The per capita consumption of mutton and lamb in the United States is small. For the 10 years from 1912 to 1921 it averaged only 6.2 pounds, while in the United Kingdom during the period 1895-1908 it averaged 26.7 pounds.[5] In Canada in 1910 the per capita consumption was 9 pounds; and in France the latest figures, for 1904, place it at 9 pounds. The greater part of the lamb and mutton eaten in the United States is consumed in the cities east of the Allegheny mountains. California also takes a fair proportion of it, but the great central and western areas of the country consume little. Moreover, consumption of all meat has declined in the United States from 167.4 pounds per capita in 1907 to 162.3 pounds in 1924. So far has the tendency toward the substitution of other foods proceeded, with the rising cost of meat, that the producers have inaugurated extensive advertising campaigns to stem the tide.

If the flock owners appreciably increase the number of sheep, in an effort to reap greater returns from the higher price of wool, they face the necessity of disposing of a larger number of lambs in a market which will not readily absorb them. By withholding ewe lambs from market for two or three years in order to increase the flocks, the supply of lambs for slaughter would be temporarily reduced; and if demand remained the same, the price would rise. In the long run, however, the supply of lambs would be increased, and a drop in the price would follow.

[5] U. S. Department of Agriculture, Department Circular 241, *Food Animals and Meat Consumption in the United States*, by John Roberts, 1922, p. 18.

The chart on pages 218-219 shows the close inverse correlation which exists between the number of sheep slaughtered and the price.

This does not prove that the demand for mutton is either elastic or inelastic. It does, however, indicate that a considerable degree of elasticity would be necessary to prevent serious losses by the sheepmen from a fall in the price of mutton if the flocks are greatly expanded.[6]

So many factors enter to disturb the calculations that it can not be proven statistically that at any period in the history of the sheep industry of this country an increase in the price of wool, when followed by a growth in the number of sheep, has at first caused a higher price of lamb and mutton through ewes and lambs being withheld from slaughter, and later, when more lambs were sent to market in consequence of the enlarged flocks, a lower price for the meat. Fluctuations in the general price level, droughts and other climatic conditions, the price situation in other livestock industries (since beef and pork compete to some extent with mutton, although only slightly with lamb), wars and other events which have changed the direction and amount of international trade in these

[6] "So far as mature mutton is concerneed consumers demand even less than they require of mature beef. Even in the case of lamb there is a well-defined limit to urgent demand and when that demand has been satisfied, the value of the entire production depreciates at a ratio out of proportion to the excess." Poole, J. E., "Twenty-five Years of Progress in Sheep Husbandry," *The National Wool Grower*, November, 1924, p. 19.

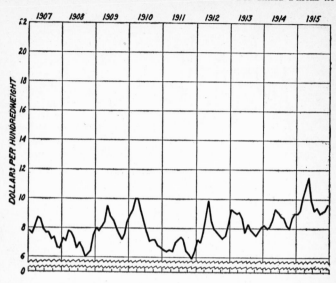

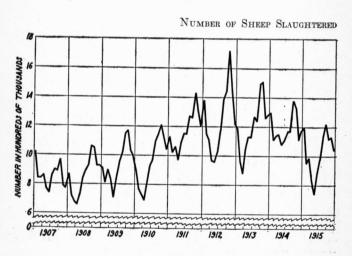

218

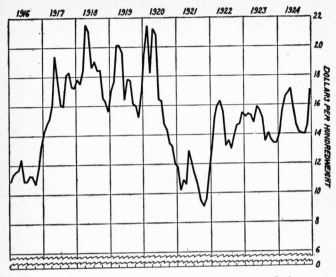

Source, Drovers' Journal Year Book

Under Federal Inspection,—1907-24.

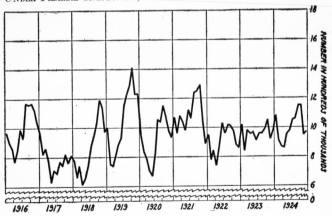

Source, Department of Agriculture Year Book

commodities—all these factors prevent the accumulation of the data necessary to test the rule. However, for almost all of the time during the last 35
years the index number [7] of wool prices in this country has been substantially above the index for "all
commodities," while the index number of mutton
prices has been well below "all commodities." There
has been practically no foreign competition in mutton or lamb, to curtail the domestic production,
while there has been foreign competition in wool in
spite of the tariff. If, in the face of these conditions,
the price of wool was so much better than the price
of lamb and mutton relative to "all commodities," it
is good evidence that the raising of sheep for the
purpose of meat production could not have been
much expanded. An enlargement of the flocks
would have depressed the price of mutton even if it
did not affect the price of wool.[8]

---

[7] Bureau of Labor Statistics Index Number; Base, 1890-99.

[8] At the convention of the National Wool Growers' Association
in San Francisco in January, 1925, F. J. Hagenbarth, President,
expressed the opinion that the demand for wool would justify an
increase of our sheep flocks by about 15,000,000 head. With this
view S. W. McClure, former secretary of the Association, dis-
agreed. Writing in the *National Wool Grower* for March, 1925,
Mr. McClure said:

"I note that at the national convention in San Francisco it was
stated that there was room in the United States for about 15,-
000,000 more sheep. I feel that this is bad advice, for it would
result in decreasing the price of lambs by around 50 per cent.
If our sheep stocks were to be increased by 15,000,000, it would
mean an increase of ewes by 12,000,000 head, that ought to yield
annually 7,000,000 marketable lambs, after making deduction
for loss and carry-over to maintain the stock. We are now
slaughtering in this country around 14,000,000 sheep a year. An
increase of 7,000,000 would be just 50 per cent. In my judgment,

The sheep business is known as one of sharp fluctuations and vicissitudes. The cycle of prosperity and depression in the industry usually lasts about nine years [9]—that is, it is nine years from

a 50 per cent increase in lambs would mean a decrease of fully 50 per cent in the present price of fat lambs. *In my opinion, if our lamb supplies were increased by even 2,000,000 head, a remarkable decrease in the price would follow. Aside from the decrease in price, there would be increased cost of handling all the sheep in the West.*" (The italics are ours.) "Labor would be scarcer, pasture rentals higher, hay and grain dearer. In every way the cost of handling sheep would be increased; yet the income, by reason of overproduction, would be decreased.

"Anyhow, I am of the opinion that the ranges of the West are fully stocked, or nearly so. If there is any spare range, someone will find it, and, if they do not, no harm will be done, as some of our range needs a short rest.

"Let us not lose sight of the fact that the lamb market is extremely fickle. The appetite for lamb is not general. Only a small portion of our people eat lamb, and before the general public will eat lamb it must sell at about the same price as beef or pork, which would be far below cost of production.

"As to the wool side of the question, there is no shortage of wool, when the situation is analyzed. We import about one third of our wool used for clothing; but remember that much of this consists of grades of wool that we do not produce in this country —70's and above, 40's and below, and wools having peculiar qualities. When these grades are subtracted from our imports, it is seen that we are fairly well taking care of domestic needs with domestic wool.

"The law of supply and demand regulates prices, and any increase means lower prices."

[9] *Cyclical Trends in the Sheep Industry*, Monthly Letter to Animal Husbandmen, Vol. 5, No. 12, March, 1925, Published by Armour's Livestock Bureau, Chicago. This bulletin states that: "The best measure of prosperity in the sheep industry is not the simple price quotation at any given time. Prosperity for the wool grower depends on the volume of necessary commodities which a given unit of his sheep will purchase." Accordingly the cycles of purchasing power of sheep in terms of other commodities were studied. It was found that since 1867 there have been six cycles, "although the first two are not definitely separated." "The first peak was reached in 1874, and the others respectively in 1883, 1892, 1899, 1908, and 1917. The period from peak to peak is nine years, as is the period from trough to trough, although the latter is less regular."

the peak of prosperity through the trough of depression to another peak of prosperity. These cycles appear to have no definite relation to the tariff. Rather, they seem to occur because the sheep business is one which is easily "overdone." Flocks can be expanded or contracted quickly. Discouraging conditions soon cause reduction of the numbers; shortage of the products then causes their prices to rise, and, in the rush to get into the business again, the sheepmen soon reach an undesirable point of expansion. In this adjustment of production to demand, mutton and lamb must be watched as carefully as wool. Wool production can be expanded only when, and insofar as, the lamb and mutton market (as well as the demand for wool) will permit.[10]

The history of the meat industry in the United States in recent years indicates that the most the sheep husbandmen can expect is to keep the per capita consumption at its present point. This will mean a gradual increase in the number of sheep and lambs slaughtered annually to keep pace with the increase in population. This is based on a further assumption—namely, that the domestic market will continue to be supplied by domestic producers. Hitherto, the prejudice against frozen mutton and lamb has been so great that imports have been

[10] This requires some qualification because wool production can be somewhat extended by the keeping of wethers if wool prices are very high.

negligible. Only in the years immediately following
the late war have the imports been of consequence,
and even then the demand for the frozen product
was so slight and stocks accumulated so rapidly that
large quantities were re-exported.

Great Britain imports frozen mutton and lamb in
huge amounts, however, and the United States may,
in time, follow her example. If, as seems probable,
the demand for lamb and mutton is somewhat
elastic, a duty upon those products [11] would raise
the price by less than the duty.[12] Therefore, unless
the whole tendency in food consumption of the past
two decades is reversed, the sheep owners of this
country can not rely upon much expansion in the
demand for one of the co-ordinate products of their
industry. And if they increase the flocks to any
great extent, the drop in the price of lamb will
neutralize part of the gain in the returns from
wool.[13]

[11] Tariff Act of 1922, Paragraph 702. Fresh mutton 2½ cents
per pound; fresh lamb 4 cents per pound.

[12] If the demand is elastic a small increase in price will cause
extensive substitution of other food products for lamb and
mutton.

[13] The conclusion seems inevitable that whether the demand for
lamb and mutton is elastic or inelastic, the sheep raisers can not,
even under present conditions when they are in undisputed possession of the home market, hope for a large increase in profits
from the meat department of their industry. In the case of an
inelastic demand, any attempt to market larger numbers of lambs
will cause the price to decline rapidly. If the demand is elastic
the price will fall more slowly in the face of a greater number
of lambs slaughtered; yet the tendency, even then, will be for
the price to decline.

III. EFFECTS UPON SHEEP HUSBANDRY OF DIFFERENT RATES OF DUTY AND OF FREE WOOL

It has been shown that a duty increases the production of wool in the United States, but that the effect, even of a high duty, is not very marked.[14] It is now pertinent to ask just what results would follow the retention of the present rate, a higher or lower duty, or the abolition of all duties. Answers to these questions can not be made dogmatically. It has long since become apparent, from this study, that many factors may enter to nullify the effect of the tariff. There are strong reasons, however, for expecting certain definite results from different courses of action.

If the present duty of 31 cents per scoured pound is maintained the domestic production probably will increase slowly for several years. Under the Emergency Tariff and the Act of 1922 there has been a slow growth in the number of sheep and output of wool. The former increased 5.6 per cent and the latter 6.7 per cent between 1922 and 1924. It seems reasonable to expect this tendency to continue until the margin of production has become thoroughly readjusted to the duty. Because the number of sheep

[14] "Two of our major crops, and one of our major livestock products, have reached the stage at which increased prices no longer bring about material increases in production. These are cotton, corn, and wool." Spillman, W. J., Agricultural Economist, U. S. Department of Agriculture, "A Balanced Agricultural Output in the United States," *The Annals of the American Academy of Political and Social Science,* January, 1925, Vol. CXVII, No. 206.

and output of wool are both less than the average maintained for the last forty years, we are led to believe that the readjustment is not complete. During that time the average number of sheep has been 47,268,600, and the average annual output of wool has been 292,182,000 pounds. The smallest wool clip between 1883 and the end of the World War was in 1897, when it was only 259,000,000 pounds. After the price decline of 1920 the number of sheep fell to 36,327,000 in 1922, and the wool clip to 264,-560,000 pounds. By 1924 the number of sheep had recovered to 38,361,000, and the production of wool to 282,330,000 pounds. There is still some room for expansion, however, judging by the figures for the past forty years, as well as by the following comparison with production prior to and during the World War.

WOOL PRODUCTION IN THE UNITED STATES BY FIVE YEAR AVERAGES
1900-1919 *

Years	Production	Years	Production
1900-1904	297,343,000 pounds	1910-1914	306,064,000 pounds
1905-1909	306,349,000 pounds	1915-1919	295,400,000 pounds

*U. S. Tariff Commission, *Report on the Wool Growing Industry,* 1921, p. 49.

The price of wool is high, relative to the price of other agricultural and pastoral products, which should cause a trend in the direction of more sheep and wool. Furthermore, the world situation, with a low production of wool relative to the demand, will create a temporarily favorable state of affairs for the domestic producer, even though eventually he encounters a greater disadvantage in competition with the foreign wool growers. It would be a reversal of the whole trend in wool growing in this country for the last forty years, however, if the domestic output should rise much above an average of 300,000,000 pounds a year.

A much higher duty, say 50 cents per scoured pound, probably would not increase the domestic output greatly over the present amount. We must not forget that the demand for wool might prove to be very elastic as a higher price range is reached. The fact that the present duty has not been fully effective, and that the demand for wool clothing has been slack in 1924 with a consequent depression in wool manufacturing, point in this direction. Such an elastic demand, coupled with rapidly increasing costs, would tend to prevent any notable expansion of the wool output if the duty were much increased over the present rate.

The margin of production has been extended in the Range territory nearly to the limit.[15] Little unused grazing land remains. On the other hand, the resources have been injured by unwise and too intensive use. The principal way in which sheep raising can be extended in the Far Western country is by the use of more hay, grain, and root crops raised on irrigated ranches and dry farms. An increase of demand for this feed would mean such a

[15] See Chapter I.

rise in its price that the costs would nearly keep pace with the mounting price of wool. More wool might be produced on farms without a great increase in its cost, but "constant cost" would soon give way to "increasing cost." [16] Resources could not be diverted from other crops and farm animals to sheep without presently raising the cost of the latter. While we may expect some growth in the farm output, therefore, the outlook for a substantial increase is not roseate.

If the present duty were abolished, the immediate effect probably would be a decrease of 10 or 15 per cent in the domestic output. Upon removal of the duty we might expect an immediate decrease in price. It is unlikely that this drop would equal the amount of the duty, for the domestic price has not been continuously higher than the foreign by the full duty under the act of 1922. The decrease would be substantial, however, and enough to subject the industry to some temporary embarrassment, at least.

After the duty on wool was removed in 1894 the domestic output fell about 25 per cent: from 348,538,000 pounds to 259,153,000 pounds between 1893 and 1897.[17] It must be remembered, however, that this came at the end of a long price decline and was accompanied by general business depression. No such result need be expected in the event of free

[16] See Chapter II.
[17] U. S. Department of Agriculture, *Year Book*, 1923, p. 1001.

wool under present conditions. When the duty was removed in 1913, the wool output of the country fell about 5 per cent: from 304,043,400 pounds in 1912 to 290,192,000 pounds in 1914.[18] Production in the high-cost Ohio Region was reduced by about 18 per cent, however. The flaw in the comparison with present conditions is that the European war began in 1914, and the price of wool rose in response to war demand.

A third case of sudden drop in price was the recent "disaster of 1920." The clip of the whole country fell from 298,258,000 pounds in 1919[19] to 264,560,000 pounds in 1922, or 11.2 per cent.[20] An objection may be raised in regard to the value of these figures, also, in that the Emergency Tariff of 1921 and the Act of 1922 followed to prevent a further decrease. All these instances, however, establish a strong presumption that a sudden fall in price would be quickly followed by a decrease in output. It is more than likely, therefore, that there would be at least a temporary decrease if the present duty were removed.

The Tariff Commission investigation of costs in 1918 showed that 5 per cent of the wool in the Range States was produced at a loss.[21] This propor-

[18] See Chapter V.

[19] 1919 figure is taken because the crisis occurred before the shearing was completed in 1920 and the clip may have been somewhat less on that account.

[20] U. S. Department of Agriculture, *Year Book,* 1923, p. 1002.

[21] U. S. Tariff Commission, *The Wool Growing Industry,* 1921, Table XXX, opposite page 201.

tion probably was minimized by the fact that the costs were averaged by states. Now, 1918 was a prosperous year for the wool growers. Though costs were high, prices were even higher by comparison. If 5 per cent of the Range States wool growers were "above the margin" then, and 7 per cent were in a similar position in 1910,[22] at least a like number may be assumed to produce at a loss now. The fact that when a new equilibrium is reached, a like proportion might still be found producing at a loss,[23] does not invalidate the conclusion that the output would be lessened by a decrease in price. The temporary depression would probably eliminate some producers who are "on the margin," as well as those now above the margin. It is because of these facts and in view of the history of the industry in 1894-97, 1912-14 and 1919-22, that the prediction is made that removal of the present duty would cause a decrease of 10 or 15 per cent from the present level of domestic production.

One other possibility remains—that is, a decrease in the duty rather than a complete abolition of it. A reduction of the rate from 31 cents per scoured pound to 22 cents per scoured pound, for example, probably would cause very little decrease in the domestic output. We have little to guide us here, in the history of the industry since the Civil War.

[22] See chart on p. 127.
[23] Cost studies generally have shown a number of producers operating at a loss.

Changes in the tariff, aside from those we have already considered, have been so slight as to have little significance. Obviously, however, reduction of the duty would not exert as strong an influence toward a reduction of the output as abolition of the duty. And complete removal, as we have seen, probably would not bring about a great change.

Even if free wool is adopted as a permanent policy, the United States will continue to have a large output of wool. The estimates which have been made above, concerning the effects of different rates of duty and of free wool, have dealt primarily with the immediate or short-run outcome. There are natural forces at work, however, which will continue to operate, in the long run, irrespective of tariff policy. Their effect may be partially neutralized for a time by a duty, but they influence production so strongly that in the end they will outweigh the tariff. It has been shown that there is an irresistible tendency in the western United States toward curtailment of the range sheep industry through the encroachment of agriculture. We have seen, also, that even in the absence of tariff assistance this country will continue to produce a large quantity of wool on the farm, where it is quite incidental. The continuance and increase of sheep raising on farms depends mainly on the profit in lamb production. The demand for mutton and lamb will increase with the growth in population, although probably not per capita. As the range industry declines, a larger proportion of the mutton and lamb, and incidentally wool, will be produced on farms. The limitation upon this form of sheep raising is found in the competition with crops and other livestock. The by-product character of sheep on the farm gives that branch of the industry a vitality which range sheep raising does not possess. It is, of course, impossible to predict the total production of wool in the United States for any long period, but it is safe to say that it will not be much greater with a duty than without one.

IV. CONCLUSIONS

The nature of the demand for wool makes it possible to raise the price by a duty, and if the domestic production is increased the grades grown in the United States may be used in place of much of the imported wool. The increase in the domestic output resulting from a duty on wool, however, will not be proportionate to the rise in price. The demand for mutton and lamb is so restricted that if flocks are increased to secure profits from the higher price of wool, the fall in the price of the meat will at least partially offset the gain to sheep owners. The nature of the demand for mutton and lamb is such, moreover, that duties on them would probably not raise the price greatly. This, however, is not a present problem because of the prejudice against the frozen product. Rising costs also militate against any considerable increase in the output of wool and lambs on the range, and, to a less extent, on the farms also.

Retention of the rate of 31 cents per scoured pound on wool may be expected to cause a slow growth in the wool output of the United States for several years. A duty of 50 cents per scoured pound would do scarcely more toward augmenting the domestic supply than the present rate, while lowering the tariff to 22 cents a pound would not exercise a very depressing effect on the industry. Abolition of the present duty probably would cause a 10 or 15 per cent reduction in the output, as an immediate result. The long-run development of the industry will depend, however, on factors other than the tariff. Nevertheless, the money receipts of sheep owners are augmented by a duty, and the prosperity of the industry is promoted thereby. The social aspects of this result will be considered in the following chapters.

CHAPTER X

COST OF THE WOOL DUTY

In determining the expediency of levying a duty on wool, attention in the United States has been directed in the main to the effect of the duty as a necessary stimulus to wool growing. Recent debates, however, have dealt in some measure with the incidence of the duty and the nature and amount of the burden entailed on manufacturers and consumers. This aspect of the wool tariff is obscured by many uncertainties. The amount by which a duty on wool raises the price that consumers must pay for articles made of wool can not be ascertained with complete accuracy. But the amount may be estimated with sufficient approach to exactness to indicate in a general way the nature of the burden. Its importance as a factor in determining tariff policy requires that it should here be given consideration.

There are usually five stages in the passage of wool from the producer to the ultimate consumer. Through the first it is conducted by the wool merchant. The large wool dealing firms, most of which are located in Boston and Philadelphia, send buyers all over the country. In the Far West these buyers commonly purchase directly from the growers, although in some sections, notably the Willamette Valley in Oregon, they have to deal with growers' co-operative associations. In the "farm states" the wool is usually collected by local traders and sold by them to buyers for the large wool dealers. The clip of the individual grower in these states is so small that it would not be worth while for the city wool merchant to deal directly with him. Co-operative associations have been increasing their activities in these states and they now handle a substantial though still the smaller part of the clip. In addition to buying and assembling wool an important function of the wool merchant is to assort and recombine it in varieties and grades to suit the needs of his customers. Occasionally also the merchant aids in financing growers and small manufacturers.

The larger manufacturing concerns sometimes evade the merchant intermediary and buy wool directly from the growers or from the co-operative associations representing them. Ordinarily, however, their purchases are made from the regular dealers, and the location of wool merchant firms in Boston and Philadelphia has been determined by the advantage of being near to the leading wool manufacturing districts. Thus by far the greater part of domestic wool must pass through the hands of the wool merchant.

Through the second stage the wool is conducted

by the manufacturer. Wool scouring, to be sure, might be regarded as an additional stage; but this is the principal business of but few concerns. The operation is usually performed by the cloth manufacturers themselves. Better results are usually secured with wool scoured in the plant where it is to undergo additional processes. In the United States the same manufacturer usually puts the wool through all the manufacturing processes and sells it as finished cloth. This stage is much less frequently subdivided into top making, spinning, and weaving and finishing than it is in England. There is, however, a considerable sale of surplus tops and yarn by large mills in the United States, and there are some spinning mills which do no weaving.

The third stage is the disposal of the wool fabric after it has been manufactured. The cloth is frequently sold for the mill by a commission house. Until within quite recent years this method was typical. The commission firm frequently performed also important financial functions such, for example, as indorsing the paper of the manufacturer and guaranteeing his accounts. Indeed, this practice even now is not uncommon. Many mills, however, now have selling departments of their own.[1] One selling agency often acts for several mills which manufacture different lines of goods. The commis-

---

[1] A selling department is an integral part of the mill organization, while an agency is not, although it may be financed by the mill.

sion house or selling agency sometimes sells to a cloth jobber or wholesale house but more frequently it sells directly to the clothing manufacturer.

The turning of wool cloth into clothing or some other article ready for consumption is the fourth stage. Beyond this there is usually only one more intermediary—the retailer—before the wool reaches the final consumer.

The typical passage of wool from producer to consumer is, therefore, through the hands of wool merchant, cloth manufacturer, commission agent, clothing manufacturer, and retailer. In addition a spinner and, infrequently, a top maker, sometimes intervene between wool merchant and cloth maker. Much more often, especially in the case of women's suits and cloaks, a jobber or wholesale house intervenes between the garment manufacturer and the retailer.

A duty which raises the price of wool necessarily adds to the expenses incurred in each stage of its passage to the consumer. For this reason the duty may be said to be "pyramided." A higher cost of wool to the wool dealer means that he must incur additional expenses for interest to carry his stock at the higher price, that his taxes and insurance charges will be greater, and that if he is to secure the customary rate of profit from his enterprise and investment he must take into account the higher annual value of stock turned over. His increased expenditures will, therefore, raise the price of the wool to the cloth manufacturer by something more than the amount of the duty. Similarly, the cloth maker and those who follow in subsequent stages, if they are to recoup themselves for their increased outlays, must raise their prices above the actual amount of the duty. The fact that this is necessarily done is often obscured by the operation of other forces which affect the prices of wool and wool manufactures more powerfully than does a duty. These forces frequently interrupt the normal course of trade and compel those engaged in it to accept prices much lower or to offer prices much higher than those which would be determined if the duty were the only disturbing factor in the market. Nevertheless a careful analysis shows not only that the incidence of the duty is normally on the consumer but that he must pay even more than the duty if those who prepare the wool for his use are to receive the current rate of remuneration for their enterprise or the customary return on capital invested.

Assuming normal trade conditions, the continuance of "business as usual," and no disturbing market factors, the operation of the existing duty may be described as follows. The duties placed by the Tariff Act of 1922 upon wool cloth, of the kind used in suits of the medium and better grades, are 45 cents per pound upon the wool content thereof and 50 per cent ad valorem. The specific duty of 45 cents is intended to compensate the manufacturer for the higher price of his raw material caused by the duty on wool, while the ad valorem rate is intended to protect him against the lower conversion costs of foreign competitors. These are the rates imposed upon all cloth valued at more than 80 cents per pound.[2] Suitings range from 10 to 14 ounces per square yard, and a good grade of cloth usually sells for $1.25 or more per square yard, so it is evident that this bracket of the law covers cloths of both medium and high quality. It is these cloths which have been chiefly imported. The compensation for the wool duty thus given to the domestic manufacturer makes no allowance for any "pyramiding" of the duty by the wool merchant; it may be regarded, however, as the actual equivalent of the specific duty.[3]

The amount of wool necessary to make one pound of cloth is increased in price, on account of the duty, therefore, by 45 cents. Upon this enhanced price the cloth manufacturer must calculate his overhead and profit. His insurance fees and taxes will be raised, and, as additional capital is necessary to carry the stock at a higher price, his interest charges will be increased. Since the imposition of the duty com-

[2] Tariff Act of 1922, Paragraph 1109.

[3] This compensatory duty is computed on the basis of figures given by the Tariff Board Report on Schedule K, made in 1912 (p. 619 ff.) In making a pound of tops, 1.1 pounds of wool is required. In the manufacture of a pound of yarn, 1.08 pounds of tops are used and in making a pound of cloth, 1.20 pounds of yarn. The duty upon scoured wool is fixed at 31 cents a pound by the Act of 1922. Compounding the duty by these three rates, 10 per cent, 8 per cent and 20 per cent respectively, gives approximately 45 cents, which is fixed as the compensatory duty on the cloth.

pels him to operate with more costly materials, he must either increase the capital in his business or must reduce the scale of his operations.

To illustrate how this pyramiding takes place, let us take the case of a hypothetical wool manufacturing concern which we will call Company X. This firm carries on the average a stock of 150,000 pounds of wool, which makes 100,000 pounds of cloth. Like many other wool manufacturing companies, this organization makes spring and fall patterns of goods. Its 150,000 pound stock of wool is used up every six months, therefore, and the length of time which elapses between the purchase of the wool and the receipt of payment for the finished cloth, we will assume to be no greater than half a year.

The wool which this factory uses is of various kinds, but on the average it is of equivalent value with Half-blood Territory Combing. This kind of wool increased in price from $1.00 per scoured pound to $1.31 between February, 1922, and February, 1923. We are not interested at this point in determining whether the Emergency Tariff Act and the Tariff Act of 1922 were responsible for this rise in price, but rather in finding out what increased charges would result from such a rise in price of the raw material; for, as we have seen, the duty may be fully effective in the long run.

The stock of 150,000 pounds of wool at the old price of $1.00 per scoured pound cost $150,000. At the new price of $1.31 per scoured pound, it cost

$196,500. The company must have, therefore, $46,500 greater capital upon which interest must be paid at 6 per cent per annum. It makes no difference whether the extra capital is borrowed or owned: if the former, interest will actually have to be paid out; if the latter, earnings of 6 per cent per annum must be imputed to it. Since the goods are sold in six months from the time the wool is purchased, however, interest at 3 per cent only should be reckoned upon the additional required capital of $46,500. This amount is $1,395, which is added to the overhead expense of Company X because of the higher price of wool.

The higher value of the stock also necessitates a greater outlay for fire insurance. The rate varies from 50 cents per $100 in fire resisting steel and concrete warehouses, and 90 cents or $1.00 per $100 in brick warehouses, to $1.50 per $100 in frame warehouses. At a fair average rate for wool risks of ¾ of 1 per cent per annum, the charge for insurance of a stock worth $150,000 was $562.50 for six months. After the duty was imposed and the value of the stock rose to $196,500, the charge for insurance became $736.88 for the same length of time. The increased cost of fire insurance to be ascribed to the rise in price of wool is, therefore, $174.38.

The higher value of the stock also augments the risk which the company bears in another way than through possible fire. Deterioration in the condition of the wool from various causes and spoilage in the process of manufacture are avenues of loss which are always open. A constant loss ratio of ½ of 1 per cent of the value of the raw material should be allowed to cover these items. On the previous value of the stock, this amounted to $750, while on the new value, it amounts to $982.50, an increase of $232.50.

The general property tax bears more severely on the stock of Company X, since the rise in the price of wool. It is evident that the firm must keep replenishing its stock of wool as it is used in the process of manufacture. It must keep on hand, on the average, a stock of 150,000 pounds, which was valued, at the old price, at $150,000, and at the new price is worth $196,500. If this stock should be assessed at 50 per cent of its true value and taxed at $18 per thousand on the assessed value, the tax to be paid by the company would equal $1,768.50 at the later as against $1,350 at the earlier date, an increase of $418.50.

From this stock of 150,000 pounds of wool, Company X will make, as we have seen, 100,000 pounds of cloth. Having manufactured this cloth, and having determined its cost, the managers of the business must fix its selling price. Now, it is understood that prices sometimes bear little relation to cost; certain fancy patterns may sell at a large surplus over cost, while staple goods yield only a small profit. Yet in the long run, the firm must sell its product at a clear margin over cost. The minimum excess of price over cost must be at least 6 per cent. If the raw material cost is raised by $46,500, as it is in this instance, the basis, upon which the 6 per cent profit is reckoned, becomes greater by that amount. The rise in price of wool consequently necessitates a return to the Company of $2,790 more in profit on sales.

We find, therefore, that the necessary increase in expense amounts to $5,010.38, divided into interest, $1,395.00; fire insurance, $174.38; miscellaneous risk, $232.50; general property tax, $418.50; profit at 6 per cent on the cost of the goods, $2,790. It is apparent, therefore, that while the actual rise in the price of the wool because of the duty is $46,500, the expenses caused by this higher price of wool, amount to at least 10 per cent more. It is for this reason that the wool duty is said to be "pyramided" at each step in the process of manufacture and sale of the goods. The additional cost of a pound of cloth is thus raised from 45 cents to 49.5 cents.[4]

---

[4] A similar line of reasoning was followed by the Committee of Congress which framed the original compensatory duty on wool in 1867, as shown by the following quotation from their report. See Tariff Board *Report on Schedule K*, p. 102. The committee says: "To determine the amount of reimbursing specific duties which the manufacturer should receive as an equivalent for the proposed increased duty on wool, we must, in the first place, apply the rule adopted in the present and preceding tariff bills, and multiply the proposed duty on the wool, 11½ cents, by four, the number of pounds of wool to a pound of finished cloth, which would give 46 cents. To this should be added the duties upon drugs, dyestuffs, and other imported materials, although these are provided for, in the present tariff (*i.e.* the act of 1864) under the ad valorem clause. The duties are estimated, from authentic data, at an average of 2½ cents to a

In the next stage the duty is pyramided by an additional 5 per cent, since at least this amount must be allowed for overhead expenses of the commission house or selling agency. From 2 to 5 per cent is charged as commission on sales, and the commission house frequently guarantees the accounts of the mills with its customers, for which it charges 2 to 2½ per cent additional. Expenses and commissions must be computed upon a new and higher scale of values. This 5 per cent or more added by the seller of the cloth increases the burden of the compensatory duty to 51.975 cents.

Fifteen per cent must next be allowed for the additional expense and the profit of the clothing manufacturer; [5] and finally, 50 per cent of the whole must be added for the retailer.[6] This makes the

pound of cloth, making the whole direct duty on the raw material 48½ cents. *But the manufacturers are subject not only to this duty directly, but to charges and expenses in consequence of the duty.* Six months at least must elapse from the time of paying the duty on the raw material before payment is received for his finished goods. He is therefore entitled to interest for six months upon the whole duty upon the raw material, which at 7 per cent, the average rate of interest, would be 3½ per cent. He is also subject to charges for commissions on sales and guarantees, which commissions are increased in amount in proportion to the amount of the duty. The average rate of these commissions, as determined by reliable statements, is 6½ per cent. *The two items of interest and commissions on sales and guarantees together amount to 10 per cent which, upon the whole duty, is 4.85 cents, which sum should be added to the direct duty on raw material to fully reimburse him.*" (The italics are ours.)

[5] U. S. Department of Commerce, *The Men's Factory Made Clothing Industry*, 1916.

[6] U. S. Tariff Board, *Report on Schedule K*, p. 884. Fifty per cent of the wholesale price is equivalent to 33⅓ per cent of the retail price.

total cost of a pound of cloth to the consumer approximately 90 cents (89.66 cents) higher than it would be without a duty on wool.

The effect upon the cost of clothing if the duty should be thus pyramided may be exhibited in tabular form.[7] It should be carefully borne in mind, however, that such a table can disclose only a tendency. Since it is based on the assumption that the duty is the sole disturbing influence in the market, an assumption that is never fully realized, the actual effect of the duty in terms of dollars and cents can not be shown with the exactness displayed in the table.

Garment	Weight of Cloth per Linear Yard (54-56 in. Wide)	Linear Yards Required	Weight of Cloth in Article	Cost of Duty per Article (Based on $0.90 per Pound of Cloth)
	Ounces		*Pounds*	
Suits .... {	10	3½	2 3/16	$1.97
	12	3½	2 5/8	2.36
	14	3½	3 1/16	2.76
Ordinary Style				
Lined	20	2¾	3 7/16	3.09
Unlined	20	3	3 ¾	3.38
Heavy Ulsters				
Lined	28	3¼	5 11/16	5.12
Unlined	28	3½	6 1/8	5.51

[7] *Congressional Record*, July 14, 1922, pp. 1105 and 1106, citing estimate of U. S. Tariff Commission. The same type of garments and same weights per yard have been used in the present estimate.

It has been often denied that a duty on wool burdens the American consumer in the manner and degree that have been described.[8] The grounds for denial have been numerous, and although they are not all consistent with each other they deserve careful consideration. In the first place, it is maintained, the price of wool is not always raised by the full amount of the duty. This is undoubtedly true. Conditions may well exist in the wool market of such a nature as to modify, or even altogether to nullify, the influence of a duty on the price of it. Thus when wool was removed from the free list by the Emergency Tariff Act of 1921 and subjected to a duty of 15 cents a grease pound the price of domestic wool did not go up. The failure of price to respond to so drastic a tax on imports was due to the previous accumulation within the country of surplus stocks temporarily greater than the pros-

---

[8] "It has been claimed by certain clothing manufacturers that compared with free wool, the present tariff will increase the consumers' clothing bill by from $4.00 on a summer suit to $7.50 on a heavy winter overcoat. The Tariff Commission checked up on their figures and found that, using the same methods, the estimated possible cost would be from $2.03 on a summer suit to $5.70 on a heavy winter overcoat, but indicated that because of various factors the real cost might amount to no more than from $1.62 on a summer suit to $4.56 on a heavy overcoat. The Manufacturers' Club, of Philadelphia, whose members are as much interested in cheap raw materials and high selling prices as the clothing manufacturers, takes exception to both the foregoing estimates and states that, compared with free wool, the true cost to the consumer properly attributable to the present tariff, should range from $1.14 on a summer suit to $2.78 on a heavy winter overcoat." "The Tariff on Wool and Its Cost to the Consumer," *The Manufacturer,* Philadelphia, November, 1922, Vol. 4, No. 11, p. 3.

pective demand.[9]   Again, in the summer of 1924 the domestic price was higher than the world price by less than half the amount of the duty.   The explanation, in this case, lay not on the supply side but on the demand side of the equation.   The mills were curtailing their takings of raw wool because of a prolonged agricultural depression and other causes [10] had made it impossible to dispose of wool manufactures at the established prices.[11]

To just the extent, however, that a duty fails to raise the price of wool it fails also to effect the purpose for which it is imposed, that is, to benefit domestic wool growing.   To admit, therefore, that a peculiar market conjuncture may render a duty temporarily nugatory by no means weakens the conclusion that normally a duty raises the price of wool in the United States, and that the higher price is further increased as the wool passes through the successive stages on its way to the consumer.

In the second place, it is urged, those who handle wool in the various stages of its progress do not estimate their costs and profits on the basis of the price paid for a pound of wool.   Thus yarn spinners compute their profit not per pound of wool consumed but per spindle; cloth makers figure profits per loom; and clothing manufacturers, per machine

[9] See p. 138.

[10] Other causes probably were abnormal seasons which discouraged buying, and the liberal purchases of wool made by dealers and mills, after the Tariff Act of 1922 went into effect, in anticipation of a rise in price.

[11] Special Report of Department of Agriculture, July 1, 1924.

or per worker.[12] Therefore when the cloth maker, for example, names the price he will take for his product he does not calculate that price as a certain percentage of the cost only of his wool; he fixes it so far as market conditions allow at an amount which will reimburse him for his *total* costs and in addition will yield him the current rate of profits per loom. In consequence it may well happen that reduced wage expenses, the operation of his mill at increased capacity, or a reduction of his total costs in some other way, would offset the higher cost of his raw material and enable him to secure the customary profit per loom without raising the price of his product so as to shift the enhanced price of wool on to the consumer.

Such reasoning is fallacious. It implies that the consumer can rely on a reduction in other costs keeping pace with the rise in cost of the raw material. This, of course, is an unfounded assumption. Moreover, if there should indeed occur a reduction in other costs the price to the consumer would normally go down; and the rise in the cost of raw material, by compelling manufacturers to maintain their prices at the old level, would affect the consumer adversely, because he would fail to get the benefit which otherwise would have inured to him. There is no system of accounting which simply by ignoring a rise in the cost of materials will enable

[12] *The Manufacturer*, November, 1922, Philadelphia, Vol. **IV**, No. 11, pp. 3-4.

manufacturers to evade it. Common sense refuses to admit that manufacturers can pay a price higher by 50 per cent or more for the wool they use and then, through the application of any conceivable system of bookkeeping, maintain their customary rate of net profits without reducing their other costs or raising their prices. When the cost of raw materials goes up it is clear that either prices must follow suit or else profits must come down.

A reduction of profits distributed among the several stages through which wool passes has been offered as a third ground for denying that a duty is burdensome to consumers. Granted that the producer and the importer sell wool at a higher price because of the duty, can not the various intermediaries "absorb" the increase instead of passing it along to the purchaser of clothing? Is it conceivable that a suit or an overcoat of such a sort as has been commonly sold for a standard price of, say, $30, would be marked up to $32.76 and $35.12 respectively in order exactly to recoup the merchants and manufacturers for the higher price of raw wool? Is it not rather inevitable that this comparatively small increase in cost will be distributed among the intermediaries between producer and consumer in such a way that the standard retail prices will remain undisturbed?

The opinion behind these questions gains plausibility from familiar practices in retail trade. Retail prices are usually expressed in round numbers.

Hats, suits, overcoats, blankets and the like are commonly sold over the counter at certain "set prices," and the price of a particular article does not change by small fractions so as to maintain an accurate adjustment of profits to costs. When it becomes necessary to raise or lower the amount asked, it is moved from one "set price" to another and the width of the spread between such prices is determined by custom for each branch of trade. Retail prices, therefore, do not move on an evenly sloping plane; they go up and down on a conventional stairway as it were, and the height of the rise between the treads is first fixed with a view to convenience in retail transactions and subsequently maintained with a view to business steadiness.

In accordance with this principle one may assume that a suit of standard grade was offered when wool was on the free list at a certain "set price." The imposition of a duty has made it necessary for the retailer to add $2.36 to that price if he is to maintain the customary rate of profit from his investment and his enterprise. The addition would result, however, in an amount that does not coincide with any of the "set prices" familiar in his branch of business. Such an irregular charge would be apt to impair the smoothness of retail trade, to stimulate captious questionings among his customers and to rouse a keener competition from other merchants in his vicinity.

To avoid the irregularity, the retailer may resort

to any one of three courses. In the first place, he may raise his charge for the suit to the "set price" next *above* the amount actually required by the addition to his cost. This would be the course of his natural preference, and he will follow it unless he fears that at the higher charge he will lose more through the falling away of his customers than he would gain through the better price received for the smaller number of suits sold. In the second place, he may by the threat of diminished sales induce the clothing manufacturer to assume all or a part of the increased cost and to let him have the suits on terms that will not compel him to alter the "set price" for retail. In that event the clothing manufacturer by the use of similar arguments will endeavor to shift back upon the cloth merchant and the cloth maker, and these in turn upon the wool merchant, the burden of the higher price of wool. Through such a process the effect of the duty would be "absorbed" in the various stages of the trade, and the "set price" of a suit to the consumer would remain the same. The third and last recourse of the retailer would be to take himself a reduction in his profits and thereby to maintain his customary retail price in spite of his greater costs.

If the retailer should follow the first of these possible courses it is clear that consumers would be burdened by reason of the duty even more heavily than is indicated in the table on page 244. But if he should follow either of the others, those are right who claim that the duty will not be felt by consumers of wool fabrics. What then, in the actual conduct of business as it is, does the retailer do? His practice varies. He has no stereotyped plan for meeting this emergency but must adjust his policy of purchase and resale to the actual conditions prevailing in the market.

In times of depression when employment is diminishing and the purchasing power of consumers is reduced he endeavors to keep his business going by taking smaller profits himself and by persuading those from whom he buys likewise to accept a lower return from their activities. A severe depression, indeed, sometimes results not only in a cessation of all profits but even in actual losses to the retailer, the manufacturer, and all others in related branches of business. They take the loss entailed by lowering the price of what they have to sell in order to maintain the organization of their business until a turn of the tide may enable them to re-establish prices on a profitable level.

But men do not long continue to carry on business that must be operated at a loss. They do not make investments and devote enterprise to a branch of industry which offers a rate of profit lower than the rate offered by other accessible industries. The merchants and manufacturers, therefore, who are engaged in any stage of the wool business must in the long run secure prices which afford them profits that compare favorably with the profits in other fields of enterprise; otherwise they will reduce their operations or even discontinue them altogether. Consequently they can not be expected to "absorb" the cost of wool when enhanced by a duty unless it can be shown that their profits, even after being reduced by the process of "absorption," will still offer a sufficient incentive to continue their operations.

So far as can be judged by the evidence available the profits in wool manufacturing and wool dealing have never been high in comparison with profits in other long established and highly developed American industries. Here and there, indeed, individuals of exceptional ability have accumulated substantial fortunes, but the number of these has been surprisingly small when compared with the number who have succeeded in cotton, silk, steel, and other industries that are comparable in the amount of capital invested and the number of laborers employed. Domestic competition has been strong enough, not indeed to reduce prices to the levels prevailing abroad, but at least to prevent exceptional rates of profit.

The conclusions must be reached then, first, that the enhancement in the price of wool is in fact sometimes distributed temporarily among the various stages of the woolen industry; but, second, that relatively low profits due to strong domestic competition in the long run compel those engaged in the industry to shift the burden, somewhat increased in every stage, to the shoulders of the consumers of woolen manufactures. These conclusions are no less inevitable by reason of the irregular and interrupted process of shifting as it occurs in actual market transactions.

It is vain to imagine that the price of wool can be raised by a duty or by any other cause without affecting the consumer. Those who use woolen goods must pay in the long run not only the increase in the price of wool but also the additional expenses entailed on those who deal in wool by the higher price of the material they handle.

There are indications that the burden imposed by the wool duty in the Act of 1922 has been shifted in the manner described. After the European War began in 1914 the prices of wool cloth and clothing, in the United States, in common with those of most other necessities of life, rose rapidly. They soared to unprecedented heights during the war and after its close continued at very high levels. In 1920-21 there was a temporary decrease, but during 1922, 1923, and 1924, the prices of woolens have been relatively higher than the prices of almost any other group of commodities. Since 1922 these high prices appear to have been due in considerable measure to the duty on raw wool, although the incidence and the nature of the burden have varied somewhat to accord with changes in the market conjuncture.

Soon after the passage of the Act the leading wool manufacturing company announced an increase of about 16 per cent in the price of worsteds and woolens to be produced for delivery in the following autumn. On March 14, 1923, six months after the Act took effect, the president of this company was quoted in the press as saying:

"We open our line for the spring of 1924 some time in the summer, and I can not see how we can avoid higher figures. In other words, raw wool having gone higher, the quotations on the fabrics must be raised. I can scarcely deny that it may be a little difficult to explain the reason for the higher prices to the multitude. You must not forget that the average man or woman is not quite familiar with the methods that are followed in the marketing of raw wool, and in the ultimate analysis the price of the raw commodity determines in a large measure the price of the cloth."

Commenting on this statement a well known New York financial newspaper said: [13]

"It is well known that the company, following a far sighted buying policy, bought wool when many others were afraid to buy: that stocks were therefore laid in at an advantage; and that part of this advantage was passed on to the consumer when the (company) announced price schedules for the coming fall. Consequently, many of its products have been selling below a parity with the replacement market. Such a condition can not last; such wool purchases naturally affected only the cloth going into fall goods."

[13] *Commerce and Finance*, March 14, 1923, Vol. XII, No. 11.

The actual course of wholesale prices of cloth in recent years is shown in the following table, which gives the annual quotations of the leading manufacturing company. It should be remembered in studying it that the announcements of this company strongly influence the price policies of others in the industry and may be taken as indicative of the general trend of manufacturers' prices of wool fabrics. It will be seen from the table that prices for the autumn of 1925 were substantially higher than for the fall of 1922 when the existing tariff law was passed.[14]

Further light is thrown on the effect of the wool duty by index numbers of the prices of wool and wool fabrics. Taking as a base the average price of representative grades of wool in 1911, 1912, and 1913 we find that the average price of domestic wool in 1923 was 113.16 per cent higher than the average before the war. There was a slight additional rise in the first six months of 1924. The average price at which imported wool, duty paid, was sold in

---

[14] Concerning prices for the heavyweight season of 1925 the manufacturers' bulletin said, "Average advances of more than 6 per cent on staple and semi-staple worsteds, of 10 to 12 per cent on some distinctive woolens, of 7 to 10 per cent on overcoatings and of 5 to 7½ per cent on semi-staple standard and fancy worsteds were reported. Those on high-grade specialties advanced from 5 to 10 per cent. For mills well provided with wool purchased at prices prevailing six months prior to the openings, these prices were satisfactory, but for those who purchased wool later, or needed a further supply, they were too low, being less than the replacement value at current wool quotations."—*Bulletin of National Association of Wool Manufacturers,* July, 1925, Vol. LV, No. 3, p. 411.

Prices of Woolen Cloth *

No.	Oz.	Fall 1925	Fall 1924	Fall 1923	Fall 1922	Fall 1921	Fall 1920	Fall 1919	Fall 1918	Fall 1917	Fall 1916	Fall 1915
Washington Standard Clays												
200	16	$3.47½	$3.35	$3.30	$2.77½	$2.85	$6.02½	$3.50	$4.15	$2.37½	$1.82½	$1.55
338	14	3.20	3.07½	3.02½	2.45	2.50	5.22½	3.05	3.60	2.05	1.65	1.30
Washington Serges												
209-2	9	.....	1.50	.....	1.17½	1.20	2.25	1.50	1.82½	1.20	.95	.....
209½-1	9½	1.70	1.55	.....	1.22½	1.25	2.32½	1.57	.....	1.32½	1.02½	.77½
340	11	1.97½	1.82½	1.77½	1.40	1.47½	2.67½	1.92½	.....	.....	.....	.....
Washington Cheviot												
12061x	18½-19	2.40	2.17½	2.12½	.....	1.50	.....	.....	3.22½	1.97½	1.00	1.27½
316-34	16	1.97½	1.75	1.45	1.15	1.20	2.57½	1.37	.....	.....	.....	.....
312-32	12	1.65	1.47½	1.22½	1.00	1.05	2.20	1.57½	.....	.....	.....	.....
Wool Serges AA												
9713-10	13	2.87½	2.70	2.60	2.15	2.25	4.35	2.75	3.22½	1.97½	1.62½	1.32½
9305	12	.....	2.62½	2.50	2.10	2.17½	4.15	2.62½	.....	.....	.....	.....
Fulton Serges												
3192	..	2.75	2.67½	2.67½	2.35	2.42½	4.50	2.62½	.....	.....	.....	.....
3194	..	3.27½	3.17½	3.20	2.80	2.85	5.50	3.20	3.77½	2.35	1.95	1.50
5048	15	3.30	3.20	3.12½	2.72½	2.77½	5.12½	3.17½	3.80	2.42½	1.95	1.62½
Ayer Mill Serges												
1814-44	..	.....	3.10	3.07½	2.67½	2.75	5.50	3.30	3.70	2.27½	1.77½	1.45

* Daily News Record.

256

Boston in 1923 was only 82.12 per cent higher than before the war; but it rose during the first half of 1924 to be higher than the pre-war average by 125.17 per cent.

For obvious reasons changes in the prices of fabrics are not exactly contemporaneous with changes in the price of wool. Owing to the time consumed in the processes of manufacture the price of the finished fabric responds to an alteration in the price of the raw material after the lapse of about a year. It should be expected, therefore, that a rise in the price of wool during 1923 would be reflected in the price of cloth in 1924 if not offset by a fall in wages or overhead costs.

Taking again as the base of its calculation the average prices of 1911, 1912, and 1913, fabric prices in 1924 were higher than before the war by the following percentages:

Piece goods	113.60 per cent
Woolen suitings	123.98 per cent
Worsted suitings	117.69 per cent
Woolen overcoatings	70.57 per cent
Cotton warp serges	82.11 per cent
Summer suitings	106.66 per cent

While in every instance the prices of these fabrics rose high above the average prevailing before the war the amount of the increase varied widely. So far as the rise was due to the higher price of the raw material such a variation was to be expected. For some fabrics the cost of wool is a much larger part of the total cost than it is for other fabrics on which there must be greater outlays for labor, dyestuffs, selling expenses, and the like. Naturally, therefore, the price asked for the finished product will be affected in different degree by a rise in the single item of cost of raw material.

Again, some fabrics admit more readily than do others the use of cheaper substitutes for wool. The heavier, coarser, and more roughly finished a fabric may be the easier it is to reduce the amount of new wool it contains and to use instead "reclaimed wool" or shoddy, and cotton. Indeed, the possibility of some substitution extends through the whole industry and the amount of it is difficult to detect. To the extent that the manufacturer ventures to use cheaper substitutes he is relieved of the necessity of raising the price of his fabric. Without doubt the higher the price of wool the further will he venture, and the consumer will feel the burden of a duty not so much in a higher price of what he buys as in a deterioration in the quality of it. The only practical limit to the manufacturer's shifting the duty by this method appears to be the worth to him of the reputation of his products. Whether his business will suffer more by lowering the quality than by raising the price of his output is a question which he will decide only after studying the various forces that at the time affect the market. Under the market conditions of recent years there is reason to believe that he has in many instances settled the question by a compromise.

For these reasons the figures quoted above show no close correspondence between the rise in the price of wool and the rise in the price of different varieties of cloth. They do show, however, that the price of cloth has gone up by an amount quite sufficient to cover the increased cost of wool, particularly when allowance is made for some substitution of cheaper fibres.

To attribute to the higher price of wool the whole rise in the price of cloth during the past decade would be absurd. Wages, taxes, and other necessary outlays of the manufacturer have likewise gone up, and these component elements of cost must be covered by the price of his product as well as the outlay he makes for raw material. Moreover, there have been wide fluctuations in the demand for wool manufactures, owing in part to changes in fashion, in part to the upsetting of personal habits and standards of living by the war and its consequences, and in part to violent changes in the employment and purchasing power of consumers. No investigator, therefore, can look back over a period of such unstable business, and disclose statistically or in any other wise just what part of the increase in cost of material was "absorbed" by the manufacturer and what part was shifted by raising the price of the finished product.

The rise in the cost of the raw material has certainly played a prominent part in the rise in the price of cloths since 1922. When cloth prices prevailing in the fall of 1925 are compared with prices in 1922 or with the average of prices before the war, and when a similar comparison is made of the prices of raw wool, it is clear that at the later date little of the effect of the duty was being "absorbed" by manufacturers.

There is evidence also that the price of clothing responded fully to the rise in the price of cloth. The evidence is furnished through an investigation made by one of the leading trade and textile journals of the operations of 15 large manufacturers of ready-to-wear garments. The investigation showed that the average price at wholesale of a man's suit during the years 1911, 1912, and 1913 was $11.42, and that in 1924 it was $25.54, an increase of 122.39 per cent. The average wholesale price of overcoats during the same period rose from $12.27 to $25.23.[16] For clothing, therefore, as for cloth, the rise of prices has been enough to recoup the manufacturer for the higher price of wool.

The conclusion from this private inquiry is borne out by the price investigations of the Bureau of Labor Statistics. For purposes of convenience, the detailed table showing the Bureau's index numbers and a chart based upon the table, are presented in Appendix B.

Unfortunately, retail prices are not available for the articles included in the wholesale price lists. During 1924 and 1925 there was a marked slackness

[16] *Daily News Record*, New York, Oct. 15, 1924.

in buying. This appears to have been met, however, chiefly by a curtailment of production by manufacturers, as the index of the Bureau of Labor Statistics shows a very slight fall in wholesale clothing prices. Retailers likewise handled smaller stocks, and there is no evidence of a reduction in the "set prices" previously established. "Mark-down" sales are common but goods are often first "marked up."

This brief survey shows that evidence in regard to the incidence of the tariff burden is fragmentary and is quite inadequate to justify naming a definite monetary sum as the share of that burden which is borne at any particular time by the consumer or by the various intermediaries between consumer and wool grower. But after all, when considered as a national instead of a class interest, does it matter where the monetary burden actually rests? What though the consumer evades any part of it, as protagonists for a high duty maintain that he may; will the burden then be simply dissipated? Assuredly it will not, for the consumer can evade the burden only by refusing to purchase woolen manufactures. This does not remove the burden, it merely changes the form of it. Instead of increased monetary outlays for clothing or other goods he must take up a burden of self-denial. It is true that temporarily merchants and manufacturers may meet the resulting fall of demand by distributing among themselves the higher cost of raw material and by so doing give relief to the consumer. This additional burden on them, however, would eventually weaken the power of industry to satisfy the consumer's needs; and therefore, in the long run, those who use woolen goods must either suffer deprivation or must pay the higher price caused by the higher cost of wool.

Whether in the form of money or of deprivation a duty on wool is a heavy burden on the country. In the fiscal year 1923 the imports of wool suitable for making clothing were 346,655,553 pounds. Re-exports, however, amounted to 24,187,994 pounds in the grease (about 12,000,000 pounds scoured wool). The duties collected on the balance amounted to $46,356,667.11, or 31 cents a scoured pound; and this sum was paid out by the importers in addition to what they would have paid if wool had been on the free list. In that year the domestic production of wool was 266,830,000 pounds in the grease, or 106,-732,000 clean pounds at 60 per cent shrinkage. It is reasonable to assume that the price per pound received for it by the growers was increased by an amount no smaller than was the price paid for imported wool, for there would be no object in buying wool abroad if it could be had on better terms at home. Wool merchants, therefore, paid out $33,-086,920 more for domestic wool than they would have paid had there been no duty. Of these two sums the first went into the U. S. Treasury, the second into the pockets of the wool growers. Taken together, this $79,443,587.11 represents the additional outlay made by merchants in order to get possession of the wool supplied to industry.

But it will be remembered that these two sums do not represent the total cost of the duty to the merchants. Upon them and upon all other intermediaries between producer and consumer additional expenses are imposed by the rise in value of the material they handle. Therefore to arrive at the full cost to the country in 1923 which was imposed by the wool duty, it is necessary to increase these sums by certain percentages which have been enumerated above, namely, 10 per cent for the wool merchant, 10 per cent for the cloth maker, 5 for the selling agency, 15 for the manufacturer of clothing, and 50 for the retailer. Thus calculated the cost of the duty in 1923 was approximately $174,109,558.55.

Now who paid this cost? It has been shown that the price of finished goods went up sufficiently to cover it. But following the rise there was a pronounced falling off of sales. While statistical evidence is far from complete, it suffices to show that the money spent by the public for cloths and clothing in 1924 and 1925 was not substantially greater than it had been in 1922. Old clothes were worn longer and fewer new clothes were purchased. What then became of the goods for which wool was bought in 1923? Many of them accumulated in the warehouses of manufacturers and merchants and were held there until the growing need of the public should permit sales at the prices asked for them. A part of the high priced wool, however, was not actually turned into finished products but was likewise held in warehouses. Manufacturing slowed down until existing stocks of goods could be disposed of. Factory owners, lacking orders for their products, stopped their machinery in part or sometimes altogether, reduced their output, and cut down their purchases of raw wool. Depression in the textile trades was severe throughout the greater part of 1924 and 1925.

This picture of the situation discloses that ultimately the consumer of wool fabrics was compelled to pay the whole amount of the costs arising from the duty levied on wool in 1923, but that by postponing purchases he was able to distribute the payment over a somewhat protracted period. Against such relief as he may have derived from this postponement of payment two things appear as offsets. The first is the deprivation he himself suffered in his supply of clothing, the second is the damage suffered by industry in reducing operations. Although the consumer ultimately paid the price demanded, the merchants and manufacturers saw their profits from investment and enterprise substantially cut down by the reduction in volume of their business. To construct an estimate of the monetary equivalent of this deprivation on the one hand and of the business depression on the other is obviously impossible. Their weight, however, as component parts of the national burden imposed by the duty is in no wise diminished by the fact that they can not be stated in terms of money.

To the extent that the wool grower is a purchaser of woolen manufactures he shares with others in bearing the cost of a duty. And since the price he pays for the wool in finished articles ready for consumption is increased by the duty much more than is the price for the raw wool which he sells, it must result that the small grower is actually a loser under the law. Thus, assuming the correctness of the calculation made above, the average gain per pound attributed to the duty in 1923 was 31 cents. But when the grower in 1924 bought back this wool in the form of clothing he had to pay 65.25 cents for a pound of it.

There is no means of ascertaining the average annual consumption of woolen goods by American farm families. Purchases of woolen clothing, blankets, and other manufactures depend on climate, on fashion, on taste and habit, on the standard of living, on purchasing power, and on other influences which vary widely not only from one region to another but also from one neighborhood or even one family to another. Any estimate, therefore, of the number of wool growers who lose under the duty more than they gain presents too many uncertainties to justify an attempt to make it.

The conclusion is inevitable that the duty imposes a burden upon the consumers. The burden may take different forms but it cannot be evaded. A

temporary assumption of part of it by the manufacturers or dealers only postpones the day when in-
jurious effects fall upon the general public. Through
the outworking of the forces of competition the
users of woolen goods must in the end pay a higher
money cost, put up with poorer goods, or go without. They may be affected in all three ways. The
history of the market for wool and woolens under
the Tariff Act of 1922 corroborates these assertions.
It is unnecessary, as well as impracticable, to compute exactly the cost of the duty. The fact remains that the people of the United States are not
as well or as cheaply supplied with clothing and
other wool manufactures as they would be if no wool
duty were levied.

CHAPTER XI

PUBLIC POLICY IN REGARD TO THE WOOL DUTIES

The effect of the wool duty upon the producers of wool and mutton was presented in Chapter IX and it was shown that, although the output of these commodities in the United States is not greatly stimulated, the price of wool is somewhat raised and the profits of sheep owners are augmented. The effect of this increase in price was examined in Chapter X and it was found that a burden is imposed upon the consumers of wool goods and clothing. Before deciding whether there is a net gain or loss to the country on account of the duty, there are questions of public policy which must be raised.

The answer to the question whether there should be a duty upon wool depends, in the last analysis, upon judgment regarding the national welfare. Now, there is no single test of public policy. The decision must be reached after weighing many factors. It is the purpose of this chapter to survey the relation of the sheep industry to various aspects of public welfare and thus to reach a decision upon the best course of action in regard to the wool tariff.

We shall make a critical examination of the rights and duties of the government with regard to the industry and the possible benefit or detriment to the people collectively.

Among the principal reasons advanced for the retention of a duty is the maintenance of the value of investments made under the implied promise of protection. Capital has been invested in the enterprise because of the policy of the government, and the investment might be impaired if that policy were abandoned. The value of the sheep in the United States on January 1, 1924, was $302,092,000;[1] of this total the value of sheep in the 12 Range States was $200,555,000. It is conservative to estimate the investment in land and capital, used for the sheep business in the Range States, at an equal amount. Even when part of the grazing is secured on the public ranges and in the National Forests some land must usually be owned.[2] Sheep wagons, lambing equipment, corrals, burros, dogs, stocks of provisions for herders and of feed for the sheep in wintry weather, all help to swell the total. The investment in sheep, equipment and accessories was therefore $502,647,000, even if only the value of the sheep in the farm states, with no allowance for other capital, is added. Obviously there is some additional investment in sheds, tools, and other necessaries for the sheep business in the other states, especially in

[1] Estimate of United States Department of Agriculture.
[2] See Chapter I.

the Ohio Region. The figure of half a billion dollars is, therefore, a low estimate.

It is difficult to say how much this investment would be reduced by removal of the duty. Little can be learned from experience with free wool under the Wilson Tariff. It is true that the price per head of sheep in the United States dropped from $2.66 on January 1, 1893, to $1.58 on January 1, 1895, and the total value from $125,909,000 to $66,686,000 at the same time.[3] This loss of value can be ascribed only in part to the removal of the duty, however, as it followed a financial crisis and was attended by general business depression. Nor is later experience more illuminating. At the time the duty was removed in 1913 a continuation of the already diminishing number of sheep was accompanied by an actual increase in price per head.[4] The fall in value from $495,660,000 on January 1, 1920, to $288,732,-000 on January 1, 1921,—a decline in price per head from $10.52 to $6.41,[5]—was in no way attributable to the tariff. It was part of a world-wide tendency, and was due simply to the existence of a large surplus of wool and mutton contemporaneous with slackening demand.

If the duty on wool were removed, no such collapse of sheep prices should be expected as occurred under the peculiar conditions prevailing either in 1894 or 1920. Some decrease might be expected,

[3] United States Department of Agriculture, *Yearbook,* 1920, p. 743.　　[4] Ibid.　　[5] Ibid.

however, for a duty of 31 cents per scoured pound, even if only half effective, as it has been for some of the time, adds about 50 cents a year, about 8 or 10 per cent, to the income from a sheep.[6] This could hardly be removed without impairing its capital value. The "vested rights" argument cannot, therefore, be altogether ignored.

On the other hand, it should be remembered that through the public land system, especially the provisions for the National Forests, the Government already contributes a great deal to the maintenance of the wool growing industry. It also aids the wool growers by carrying on scientific experiments and disseminating information. Through its assistance to the industry in these ways the Government has in some measure fulfilled any obligation it may have incurred by previous tariff encouragement of wool-growing. Whether aid through the tariff should be continued or not, is, therefore, a question of expediency rather than of justice.

An increase in sheep husbandry might direct more population and capital into agriculture, and thereby strengthen the relative importance of the latter in the national economy. Even if the industry is not expanded, at least its maintenance in present size and importance is considered imperative by many persons. Undoubtedly it should be the concern of

---

[6] Eight pounds of wool in a fleece equals, at 60 per cent shrinkage, 3.2 pounds of clean wool; 3.2 pounds times 15.5 cents equals 49.6 cents.

any country to promote favorable conditions in agriculture. There is much plausibility, at least, in the assertion that complete industrialization weakens the fiber of a people, in both physique and morale. If the wool duty adds to the profit in farming sufficiently to induce more people to take up agriculture, or even if it helps to keep people on the farm, there is some point in using it as part of a national policy, to prevent the decadence of country life. But there is little evidence that it exerts a strong influence in this direction. The wool duty has a more positive effect upon the range branch of the industry than upon the farm branch. But range sheep raising, from the very nature of the industry, cannot maintain a large population. Irrigated ranching or dry farming are both more desirable from that point of view. So far as the promotion of country life is concerned, the pastoral industry cannot be considered in the same class with farming, and when the interests of the two groups come into conflict, as, for example, in regard to the land laws,[7] the stockmen, as the representatives of a primitive economic stage, ought to give way, if true national interest were consulted.

It is argued that the stimulation of sheep husbandry keeps in use land otherwise waste. In the Far Western states there are large areas of semi-arid land, like the "Red Desert" in Wyoming, which cannot be utilized for anything but sheep raising at

[7] See Chapter I.

present. The feed is too sparse for cattle. Dry-farming has been tried in many of these regions and has failed. Irrigation is not yet, and may never be, technically or economically possible. But, when a wool duty is in force, this unpromising territory makes some contribution to the national wealth and affords a field of activity to some persons.

Obviously, however, a national loss is involved when the contribution from these waste lands is less than the cost to the nation of keeping them in cultivation. But while there is a loss to the country as a whole, in summing up the total effect of a duty upon the national welfare, it is only fair to point out that in maintaining the range industry the loss is partially offset by the profit from otherwise idle resources. The sheep raising localities of the western states, moreover, derive a positive benefit through keeping this land in use, even if the rest of the country loses. If perfect fluidity of capital and labor existed, it might be better to abandon these areas entirely, but at present the withdrawal of capital and labor devoted to sheep husbandry in those regions could not occur without some economic damage to the range localities.

The growth of sheep husbandry, it is said, not only keeps in use land which otherwise would lie idle but it also improves land for other purposes. In a previous chapter [8] the great value of sheep in connection with certain kinds of diversified agricul-

[8] See Chapter II.

SHEEP ON OPEN RANGE IN IDAHO

ture has been pointed out. Circumstances are forcing the American farmers toward more diversification in some regions and toward more intensive methods in others. Maintenance of the maximum productive power of the land should be a matter of deep national concern. It is, therefore, cited as an important purpose of the wool duty to help in promoting crop rotation and soil fertility. But we have seen that sheep will be used extensively for this purpose, even in the absence of a duty. The importance of this consideration, therefore, depends upon the actual degree of stimulation exerted upon the industry by a duty; and this, we have seen, is not great.

It is commonly regarded as one of the main purposes of the stimulation of sheep husbandry that it makes the United States less dependent on foreign sources for an important raw material which is needed in national defense. Wool is one of those raw materials which are almost as necessary to the prosecution of war as arms and ammunition. There is bound to be a prevalent feeling that judged in the light of events of the last decade, national self-sufficiency is an end much to be desired, and this feeling is perhaps bound to affect the policy of the United States toward the wool growing industry. Nothing yet discovered will take the place of wool clothing for wear by those who are exposed to the elements, as are soldiers in the field. Nothing else is comparable with it for protection from cold and moisture; and the value of the fabric for field wear diminishes sharply if the wool is adulterated by admixture of cotton, or any other substitute shoddy.

The quantity of wool needed to satisfy the requirements of a large army and navy is enormous. The soldiers of the United States Army in the late war were scheduled to consume more wool than the entire civilian population of the country, if the wants of the latter had been supplied at the normal peace-time rate. Stocks of uniforms were negligible when the war began, and this gave rise to an extraordinary demand for wool. In any future contest of arms the needs of the fighting men would probably not be less. On the contrary, the natural development would be toward a greater demand for this raw material because of the growing complexity of the war machine. During the recent war we were so situated that our need for wool was partially satisfied by an associated nation; and moreover, the South American market was accessible. How should we fare if we were cut off from these sources of supply?

It is to be noted in this connection that the Departmental Committee on the Textile Trade appointed by the British Board of Trade treated this question of the supply of textile fibers very thoroughly. The Committee found that: Of the world's production of wool for export the British Empire contributes 68 per cent and South America 32 per cent.[9] The supply of the two types of wool is as follows: Of the Merino, the British Empire has 85 per cent of the world's exportable surplus, and South America 15 per cent; of crossbred, the British Empire has 46 per cent, and South America 54 per cent.

It may be admitted that in any crisis of similar magnitude to that experienced in 1917-18 this country would suffer a serious shortage of wool if cut off from the foregoing sources of supply. Three methods of procedure are open to us in preparing to meet such an eventuality: 1. Accumulation of stocks of wool; 2. Dependence upon substitutes; 3. Direction of production so that there will be a constant supply sufficient to cover all military, and the greater part of civilian, needs.

The first method may be dismissed as impracticable. It is entirely contrary to the policy of this country. It would create misunderstanding as well as tying up capital in a commodity which is likely to deteriorate somewhat with age. The sec-

[9] The British Government has given much consideration, since the war, to the question of raw material supply. In its summary of the subject of cotton the Committee says:

"a. The cotton trade of the United Kingdom is at present mainly dependent on the United States for its supply of raw material.

"b. It is eminently unsatisfactory that one of the principal industries of the United Kingdom should be so largely dependent on one source of supply and that a source entirely beyond its control.

"c. If proper steps are taken, it is reasonably certain that all the cotton required by the British Empire can in time be grown within its own territories."—British Blue Book, Cd 9070, 1918.

ond method, however, could be depended upon to a considerable extent. It should be remembered that if our export, as well as import, trade were cut off we should have a great over-supply of cotton, and it is conceivable that the domestic output of wool could all be turned to military uses and the civilian population be clothed in cotton and re-worked wool products.

The stimulation of production so that we should constantly have an adequate supply may be considered, however, the only sure way to provide for an emergency. How can we so direct production that we shall have a supply which is sufficient for our military needs? It is to be emphasized that a shortage of Merino wool would not affect us very adversely.[10] We have seen that one great development of the war was the enormous demand for crossbred wool for use in making khaki. It has been pointed out in previous chapters that the crossbreds and mutton sheep are the ones best suited to American purposes. They are adapted to farm conditions; and it is to sheep raising as a

---

[10] The British Empire has had practically a monopoly of the exportable fine Merino wool. The report on the textile trades cited above says, however (p. 25): "There has been, of late years a serious decline in the production of Merino wools owing to:

"a. Serious droughts in Australia and a consequent reduction in the number of sheep.

"b. The fact that crossbred sheep are gradually supplanting Merinos owing to the requirements of the frozen meat trade.

"c. The gradual encroachment of arable upon pastoral lands in South America."

part of diversified agriculture that we must look for the maintenance of our supplies of wool and mutton. Consequently, the kind of wool which may be but little affected by the tariff is the kind most important from a military point of view. Moreover, the supply of wool is quite rapidly extensible. If no sheep or lambs were slaughtered, the rate of increase of the flocks would be about 70 per cent a year. Since we have other meat producing animals, we probably could enforce a measure of this kind without great hardship; in fact, action of the sort was suggested during the war, although it was not necessary to regard the proposal seriously. However, if the small additional amount of wool produced because of the duty is necessary to enable the country to meet sudden emergencies then the wool tariff is valuable in the scheme of national defence.

A further consideration which exerts some influence in favor of a wool duty is that it furnishes revenue for the Government. Practically throughout the history of the United States, a substantial part of its revenue has been raised by the imposition of customs duties. The amount now raised in this way is a much smaller proportion of the total revenue than it was before the Federal income tax was levied. Nevertheless, the average amount coming from ths source is an important item. In 1923 the sum collected was $566,663,978. The sum raised by taxing imports of wool at 31 cents per scoured pound was $50,076,667 in 1923, or 8-⅘ per cent of the total revenue from customs duties. Although the wool duty is, therefore, a source of substantial receipts by the Treasury yet its industrial effects so far outweigh its fiscal effects that tariff discussions both in Congress and elsewhere have not attached great importance to it as a source of revenue.

We turn now to a review of some of the undesirable consequences of the duty which have been mentioned previously,[11] and to an estimate of other reasons advanced for its abolition. They may be arranged under three headings, according to the groups upon which they fall, namely, the consumers of woolen products, the wool manufacturing industry, and the sheep husbandmen themselves.

The wool duty has effects which are burdensome to the consumers of woolen goods. The amount of wool necessary to make one pound of cloth will probably be enhanced in price, in the long run, 45 cents by the duty of 31 cents per scoured pound on the wool. Computing the increase in price to each producer and distributor in the chain between the wool-growers and the ultimate consumer, it appears that the duty will be pyramided to 90 cents. At each step in the process, interest, taxes, insurance, and profits must be charged against a higher capital value because of the greater initial cost of wool. No matter upon what basis the manufacturer figures his profit—whether it be per spindle,

[11] See Chapter X.

per loom, or in any other way—this additional cost must enter into the final price of the goods.

The burden on the consumer may not be expressed altogether in dollars and cents, however, but may at times take the form of lowering the quality of goods. The only way in which the consumer can avoid the burden of higher prices or a poorer quality of clothing is to refrain from purchasing, and in that case his burden becomes one of deprivation.

The duty has an adverse influence upon the wool manufacturing industry. Developments in each branch of industry—the production of the raw material and of the finished goods—in this country are likely to have an influence on the other branch. The countries which lead in wool manufacture are the United Kingdom, the United States, France, Germany, and Belgium.[12] Of these countries the only ones which have important sheep raising industries are the first two, and the wool output of the United States is more than twice as large as that of the United Kingdom. This country occupies, therefore, a different position, with respect to the relation of its pastoral industry to manufacturing, from that of any of the other countries.

[12] Competition in the manufactured fabrics has come principally from England, but to some extent also from Belgium, France and Germany. Goods of fine material or fancy weave, or specialties, have been the classes most largely imported. The conditions of manufacture in this country have been such as to enable the domestic industry to compete more successfully in the staple varieties.

The wool grower supplies a greater proportion of the raw material for the manufacturer than in any other country. If the wool growing industry suffers an increasing disadvantage in its competition with foreigners, and if this results in high duties on wool and correspondingly high compensatory duties on woolen goods, it will have serious results for the wool manufacturing industry, which may have to bear part of the burden, at least temporarily. It will compel an addition to the investment and increase the risk. An influence will be exercised on the varieties and blends of wool which can be used by the domestic industry. The consumption of wool products may be lessened by the higher price and poorer quality of the goods, and such slackening in demand for the products of the industry will affect its organization and its technical progress and reduce employment.

While the domestic manufacturers of woolen goods were restricted to the home market, as they were almost altogether before the war, the question of free raw materials was less important for them. Their principal concern was to secure an adequate compensating duty to offset the wool duty. Our exports of woolen goods increased greatly during the war, however, and we have exported large quantities since the signing of the Armistice. This trade might not continue even in the absence of a wool duty, but it is much more unlikely to continue with the duty in force.

EXPORTS OF MANUFACTURES OF WOOL *

Year	Wearing Apparel	All Other	Total
1914	$2,148,235	$1,668,199	$3,816,434
1915	9,108,900	16,829,617	25,938,517
1916	19,368,501	33,331,873	52,700,374
1917	4,452,258	12,342,168	16,794,426
1918 ª	7,283,457	9,454,014	16,737,471
1919	14,665,069	33,167,699	47,832,768
1920	8,160,416	36,410,586	44,571,002
1921	3,296,490	6,600,711	9,897,201
1922	2,637,703	3,971,492	6,609,195
1923	2,844,934	5,032,612	7,877,546
1924	2,776,060	2,962,690	5,738,750

* U. S. Department of Commerce, *Foreign Commerce and Navigation Reports*, 1916-23.
ª Fiscal years to 1918; calendar years since.

The "drawback" granted to the exporter of woolen goods manufactured from imported wool does not neutralize the disadvantage of the wool duty.[13] Those who advocate a duty on wool must

[13] The drawback amounts to 99 per cent of the duty. This payment is approximate reimbursement for the duty paid on the wool, the intention being to place the exporter on the same basis, so far as the procurement of raw material is concerned, as his foreign competitor. The equalization of raw material cost alone is not sufficient to stimulate exports to any great extent, however, because of the conditions attendant upon the trade. In order to secure the drawback, proof must be given of the foreign origin of the wool. This is difficult unless the business is organized with special reference to the export trade. Sporadic sales abroad of surplus merchandise or of goods for which the foreign demand is especially active, are often the means of building up an export business. The exporter is usually not in a position to claim the drawback on such sales because they were not originally intended. Thus he is handicapped in extending his trade to the foreign market. Comparatively few American firms have found it worth while to organize especially for the foreign trade even in those branches of the woolen business which at times dispose of large quantities of goods abroad. Especially when domestic and foreign

believe that the interests of the wool manufacturers lie exclusively in home trade, for the wool duty penalizes them to such an extent that they can not hope to develop foreign trade while under that handicap.[14]

The maintenance of a duty may even possess dangers for the sheep husbandmen themselves. Artificial price stimulation almost invariably has a weakening effect upon the producers of a commodity. The adoption of new methods is delayed, and those in the industry come to feel that a subsidy is indispensable. Depending upon tariff help they compete no more effectively, and their profits

---

wools are mixed, the cost and trouble of keeping the record are great. Free raw material would furnish a greater incentive than dutiable raw material with a drawback.

[14] In 1914, the woolen and worsted manufacturing industry ranked seventeenth, in value of product, among the industries of this country. It stood second among the textile industries, with a total value of output of $379,484,000; cotton manufacturing ranking first, with a value of product amounting to $676,569,000; and silk manufacturing third, with a product valued at $254,011,-000. In 1919, woolen and worsted manufacturing ranked fifteenth (second among textile industries) with a total value of $1,234,-657,000, while the value of cotton manufactures was $2,195,566,000, and of silk goods $688,470,000. In 1921, woolen goods reverted to the same relative position, seventeenth, which it held in 1914. Among the 16 industries which ranked ahead of the wool manufacturing industry were several which should be classified rather as groups of industries than as single industries, because their products are so diverse; for example, "Foundry and Machine Shop Products," "Lumber and Timber Products," "Cars and General Shop Construction and Repairs of Steam Railroad Companies," and "Printing and Publishing Newspapers and Periodicals." There are also "Smelting and Refining of Copper" and "Petroleum Refining," which rank very much lower in "value added by manufacture" than in "value of products." Among the industries which rank ahead of the woolen manufacture, there are very few which import a large share of their raw materials.

are often no greater, than before the duty was levied. If the margin of production were fixed at a natural instead of an artificial point, the wool-growing industry might be given a strength which it does not now possess.[15]

It also leads to the practice of political bargaining, through which the interests of some classes

[15]That the dangers of prosperity are recognized by some wool growers may be seen from the following quotation from column entitled "Affairs of Wool and Sheep," in *The National Wool Grower*, January, 1923, Vol. XIII, No. 1.

"It is now time for sheepmen to get back at work upon some of the internal problems of their business that were discussed but not solved prior to the war. Conspicuous among these are wool marketing, range control, and settled plans of more intelligent and economical production.

"Accomplishment of post-war years include fair tariff legislation and improvement in transportation rates. A better credit system will soon be added to the list. These things may be termed as external affairs. They are not questions of production, but they do, largely, and sometimes altogether, determine the success of the business. Organized work will always be needed along such lines but right now the first call is for advance in internal matters.

"There seems to be a promise of reasonably good markets for two or three seasons. No business can see further ahead than that. And prosperity always brings new problems. To the wool grower these may be over-stocking of the open range, and production of a supply of lamb greater than can be disposed of at the present level of prices. The wool outlet is broad and the exporting countries are not in a position materially to expand the volume of their production. But with both wool and lamb high, values work against volume of consumption and contribute to the raising of wages and other expense, thereby adding to production cost and taking away from profits.

"*It is therefore the duty and problem of the producers to put into their business such American efficiency as will continue production at a price that will allow the largest consumption.*" (Italics ours.)

Professor W. C. Coffey is quoted as having said: (*Annual Wool Review,* 1922, p. 140) "I hope the recent tariff legislation will not lead any sheepman to feel that it is not as necessary now to be as careful in the management of his business as it has been in the past."

are sacrificed, and through which the wool industry itself may be the loser in the end. To be specific, if the wool-growers purchase protection for wool, the benefits of which are dubious, at the cost of other duties clearly detrimental to them, they drive but a poor bargain.

One must conclude that as a permanent policy imports of wool should be admitted to the United States free of duty. The maintenance of a duty does not markedly stimulate wool growing in this country. On the other hand, this particular raw material is a prime necessity, and a duty upon it augments the cost of living. In the passage of wool through the processes of manufacture and distribution, the duty is multiplied until in its final incidence it is much greater than the sums gained by the producers in higher prices and by the government in revenue. The national balance of gain and loss thus falls distinctly on the wrong side of the ledger.

None of the familiar arguments relating to public policy is conclusive in favor of the duty. It is not necessary to national defence. Wool-growing is certainly not an "infant industry"—a type of enterprise sometimes entitled to extra consideration. And the government has extended to the industry so much assistance and guidance, in other ways than through the tariff, that the "vested rights" argument for protection is not strong. Furthermore, little can be said for it on the ground that it "diversifies production."

Even under a system of protection, duties are not levied upon all products. It is significant to note that the Tariff Act of 1922 left upon the free list the following articles: long staple cotton, potash, agricultural implements, binding twine, brick, cement, coal, hides, wood, wood-pulp, phosphates, and turpentine. When it is shown that a particular duty does not greatly assist agriculture, is distinctly to the disadvantage of a domestic manufacturing industry, and materially burdens consumers, free admission of the commodity is clearly indicated.

Nevertheless the fact must be faced that at present there is a duty; and it cannot be removed without reducing in some measure the price of wool. The reduction would bring loss to all engaged in sheep raising, and to some it would doubtless bring bankruptcy. When the duty was enacted the industry was in the throes of a depression against which human foresight had been unable to make provision. The tariff is the means that was in fact applied to administer relief, and it did afford some aid in the acute emergency. Certain adjustments were made under the shelter of protection which, whatever the cost may have been to the rest of the country, saved many sheep owners from ruin. These adjustments have now had five years to effect consolidation, and there is no prospect that the shelter will be removed in the immediate future. Should the insecure position of the industry continue until the next general revision of the tariff is undertaken, it would be deeply regrettable, but it could no longer be designated an emergency. When the time comes for revision, therefore, continuance of protection to wool-growing must be determined from consideration, not of emergency or temporary conditions, but of the permanent position of the industry in the general economic system of the United States.

CHAPTER XII

SUMMARY

The Tariff Act of 1922, through the inclusion of a higher rate on wool, has brought to the fore the issues of present and future policy toward an important industry. The new law also changed the classification of wool, the method of levying the duty, and the treatment accorded carpet wools. A perusal of the technical matter relating to these difficult subjects may have left the reader in the frame of mind of John Randolph who, so the story goes, declared he "would go a mile out of his way, at any time, to kick a sheep." To his relief, the reader will find this summary short. The conclusions of the study are contained in the answers to the eight questions which were presented in the Introduction.

Can the American sheep industry hold its present position without tariff aid? A careful study of the effects of tariff change, especially of the removal of the duty in 1913, shows that some of the domestic producers would be eliminated by a transition from protection to free wool. This is true in spite of the fact that the tariff has not been of predominant

importance in the development of the industry in
the United States. World economic conditions,
wars, droughts, changes in fashion, and developments in the use of machinery have controlled the
rise and fall of wool prices to a greater degree than
has the tariff. Nevertheless, the tariff has created
a differential of several cents a pound between the
domestic and foreign prices of wool, and to wipe
out this differential would eliminate some of those
now in the business.

*If the American sheep industry, or a part of it,
as at present organized and conducted, can not
compete on even terms with the sheep industry of
foreign countries, what is the nature of its disadvantage?* The increased cost of production of wool,
due to the competition of other industries with
wool-growing for the use of land, labor, and capital
can hardly fail to constitute a permanent handicap
to the American sheep industry. The land situation, particularly, has created a difficult situation
for many range wool-growers of the United States.
The severity of the competition with the countries of the Southern Hemisphere will be mitigated,
however, by the halt in the increase (since the war
an actual decrease) in the world output of wool.
The slackening of production tends to keep up the
world price of wool, and thus to improve the position of the American wool-grower. Furthermore,
the prevalent tendency toward crossbreds will help
to keep up the price of fine wool through deficiency

in the supply, and will make it possible for American growers to secure a better price for their product by breeding for a finer clip.

The farm sheep industry occupies a more favorable position, in competition with foreign producers, than the range industry because it depends mainly on the production of meat rather than wool.[1] In the farm states sheep-raising has come to occupy an assured though minor place in diversified agriculture. Competition with other crops and farm animals prevents a large increase in numbers of farm sheep, however; and the industry is further limited by the nature of the domestic demand for mutton and lamb, which is not large nor readily extensible.

Can the disadvantage of the range and farm branches of the domestic industry, respectively, or of the unfavorably situated individual producers, be measured by any exact criterion? The mere determination of the fact that some domestic producers suffer under a disadvantage is not sufficient for purposes of tariff-making. It is desirable to go further and measure the disadvantage in some way, whether the duty be designed to offset it fully or only partially. This part of the investigation relates chiefly to the range industry, because it is more

[1] To the extent to which the American sheep raisers depend on meat production they are independent of foreign competition. Because of the prejudice of American consumers against frozen mutton and lamb the importation of foreign supplies of this kind of meat is negligible.

decidedly influenced by a duty on wool than farm sheep husbandry.

The most widely discussed method of measuring the disadvantage is by the difference in cost of production of a commodity at home and in the principal competing countries. It is clear from previous attempts to apply this rule, that such difference in cost can not be determined with exactitude, although it has been shown that domestic costs are higher than foreign. Moreover, it has been shown that if "marginal advantage" can be equalized at all, it may be done at any one of several points, and that choice of the correct point is a matter of judgment, not of mathematical certainty.

The Tariff Commission, in its latest investigation, did not secure figures for the cost of production in Australia, the principal competitor, and the costs secured in Argentina were not full enough to be entirely dependable. The outcome of this attempt of the Tariff Commission to supply figures suitable for the basis of a duty is not, however, different from the result of similar efforts. It is difficult, if not impossible, to measure relative competitive strength in this way.

Is there any scientific method for the determination of a correct rate of duty? If difference in cost of production is not a satisfactory basis for a duty, the next question is whether there is any other inflexible rule which may be followed. A prohibitory duty is not advocated even by the majority of the advocates of protection. It is not possible to enact a duty which will secure a fixed proportion of the home market for the domestic producers. A tariff which produces the most revenue for the government admits imports in such quantity that it is not usually satisfactory to domestic producers. "Equality of competitive conditions" may be established if wide latitude is given for the exercise of judgment in naming the rate; but it begs the question to assume that such a duty is the one which should be imposed. We are disappointed in our search for any unvarying rule. Demonstration of the fact that there is no scientific method of determining a correct rate does not show, however, that no duty should be levied. The conclusion is inescapable that the imposition of a duty does raise the price of wool and help the domestic growers. Therefore, the next problem which arises, is in regard to the results of any duty even if it has no scientific basis.

What would be the effect upon sheep husbandry in the United States of different rates of duty on wool? The industry has so far adjusted itself to the present duty that the maintenance of a rate of 31 cents per scoured pound would keep the margin of production at about the present, or a slightly rising, level for several years, in the absence of noticeably disturbing factors. The adoption of even a higher rate—say 50 cents per scoured pound—

would not raise the margin a great deal, on account of the competition of other crops and the necessary increase in costs.

Free wool might reduce the output 15 per cent, temporarily. However, the price of wool bids fair to continue high; and, further, an increased demand from American consumers would tend to raise the world price. For these reasons, and because much of the American output is grown as a by-product, the wool production of this country would not decrease greatly, in the long run. A reduction to 22 cents per scoured pound probably would keep the domestic price substantially above the foreign price and would not greatly lower the domestic output.

Is it possible to measure the burden imposed on consumers by the duty and, if so, how great is it? Because of the duty, the consumers must inevitably pay higher prices for woolen goods, use goods of poorer quality, or suffer deprivation. The burden may fall upon them to some extent in all three ways: the wool manufacturers may temporarily share the cost, but, since competition prevails in the wool manufacturing industry, the burden of the duty must fall finally on the consumers. And the higher price of wool is pyramided in the course of manufacture and sale of the goods, to an amount much greater than the total of both the enhanced receipts of the wool growers and the revenues obtained by the government from the wool duty.

Should changes be made in the wool schedule ir-

respective of any change in the duty? The new classification of wool which was established under the Tariff Act of 1922 conforms to trade practice and should be retained so long as a duty is retained. The present method of levying the duty on the scoured content is also an improvement, for it removes the discrimination which formerly existed between heavy-shrinking and light-shrinking wool, and will tend, in the long run, to give the growers the full benefit of the duty. The change in the compensatory duty largely removes the "concealed" protection of former laws. The new method bears more heavily on wools of low value, however, as the ad valorem rate on such wool sometimes amounts to more than 100 per cent. These wools are necessary to the domestic wool manufacturing industry, and the discrimination should be corrected by the enactment of a maximum ad valorem rate, if the duty remains in force. The present discrimination would be partially offset by the completely free admission of carpet wool, the duty on which is now refunded if it is shown that the wool is actually used in the manufacture of carpets. The competition between imported carpet wool and domestic wool is so slight that the American wool-growers could hardly be affected by the change.

What is the desirable public policy in regard to a duty on wool? It is not advisable permanently to maintain a duty on wool. The burden on consumers of wool goods more than counterbalances the gain to producers. Moreover, there is no element of public policy which dictates the indefinite retention of a duty. It is not necessary for national defence, nor because of "vested rights" of wool-growers. Sheep raising is not an "infant industry," nor can the duty be said to aid materially in the diversification of industry. In maintaining a duty we are, in the words of the old adage, "paying too much for our whistle."

Although the present duty has helped American wool-growers to extricate themselves from the difficult position in which they were placed by post-war depression, the emergency is passing away and doubtless will have disappeared altogether by the time the next general tariff revision occurs. The industry should then be dealt with on grounds of permanent rather than temporary policy. Therefore, when a comprehensive readjustment of tariff rates is made, wool should be placed upon the free list.

APPENDICES

APPENDIX A

WOOL PRICES AND THE TARIFF, 1860-1924

The price of wool in the United States is dependent on world-wide conditions in the wool growing industry as much as on domestic conditions of supply and demand. The "world price" may have wide fluctuations, according to basic conditions in the great wool growing regions and the demand for wool in the wool manufacturing centers. There may be, it is true, a differential between domestic and foreign wool prices, created by a tariff on wool. There has been such a differential during much of the time when a duty on wool has been levied in this country, particularly since 1867. Other factors than the tariff are, however, constantly causing wide variations between the prices in different countries. Therefore, while the tariff may influence the proportion of the domestic wool production to domestic consumption, that proportion is governed largely by other factors.

The six diagrams on pp. 301-6 show, by index numbers, the trend of general commodity prices and of wool prices in the United States and England from 1860 to the end of the Great War. Figures I, III, and V give a comparison of the index number of general prices in the United States with the index number of wool prices. The base of the index number is shifted twice. Figures II, IV, and VI give the comparison for England.

Inspection of the charts shows that at the times of

tariff revision in the United States—1883, 1890, 1894, 1897, 1909, and 1913—the changes which might have been expected if the tariff had exerted a strong influence, did not take place. The market tendencies and their relation to the tariff during this period are summarized in the following paragraphs:

1860-1870. The price of wool in the United States fell at the beginning of the Civil War, but before the war was over it had risen very high. There was a severe postwar depression in the industry from 1868 until 1870, in spite of the high duties on wool and woolens which were enacted in 1867. The price of wool in England was not enhanced particularly by the Civil War demand in the United States, and during the entire period 1860-70 the index number for wool was considerably lower than that for all commodities.

1870-1890. The price of wool rose in both England and the United States in 1871 and 1872 on account of the demands occasioned by the Franco-Prussian War. Then began a long decline in the price of wool in common with the prices of other commodities, especially farm products. In spite of the high tariff on wool which was in force in the United States during these years, the price was lower relative to the price of other commodities than it was in England. For example, from 1881 to 1889 the index number for wool was about 15 points below the index number for all commodities in the United States, while in England it did not fall more than 5 points below the general commodity index. A reduction of 10 per cent in the rate on wool was made in 1872, but the original rate was restored in 1875. A re-arrangement of duties (with elimination of the ad valorem part of the duty) took place in 1883. These changes in duty were slight, however, and any effect they may have had was obscured by the downward trend of prices which extended over the whole period. The Tariff Act of 1890 contained practically the same wool rates as the Act of 1867.

1890-1896. The price decline of general commodities in both England and the United States continued until 1896. The price of wool in the United States took an even sharper turn downward upon its free admission in 1894; while in England the price began to recover in 1894. This may be ascribed partly to the larger demand from the United States, for imports increased greatly when the duty was removed. The tariff change had a much more pronounced effect because it came at the end of a long period of declining prices.

1897-1912. By the Tariff Act of 1897 the wool duty was restored. The rate was the same as that of 1890 and substantially the same as that first enacted in 1867. The price rose in the United States after the enactment of the duty and fell slightly in England. The Spanish-American War in 1898 and the Boer War in 1899 exercised some influence in the direction of higher prices. During these years the price of wool was higher, relatively, than the prices of general commodities. The drought in Australia from 1895 to 1902 reduced the wool supply and stimulated prices. There was a temporary reaction in the wool price in the United States in 1901 and 1902, and in England in 1901; but this was followed by a rise in both countries lasting until 1905, due partly to the demand caused by the Russo-Japanese War. There were only minor fluctuations in both countries from that time until 1912. The re-enactment of the wool duty in 1909 was followed by a slight decline in the price of wool in the United States. From 1905 to 1912 the price of wool was higher, relative to the price of all commodities, in England than in the United States.

1913-1924. Soon after the outbreak of the World War an unprecedented rise in wool prices began. Throughout the entire war period the index number of wool prices in both England and the United States was higher than the index number for all commodities. There was a rapid decline in the price of wool in the United States in 1920 and 1921, followed by a recovery in the latter part of 1922, and in 1923, which is partly explained by the Emergency Tariff of 1921 and the Tariff Act of 1922, and partly by the upward swing of the business cycle which came at this time, bringing better conditions and a rise in general commodity prices. Industrial activity and prices underwent similar fluctuations in England during these years. The price of wool in the United States in 1924 was high relative to that of "all commodities," despite the slackening of business activity and a decreased consumption of woolens.

The following conclusions stand out clearly from the facts reviewed above:

1. Wool prices have fluctuated, for the greater part of the time, in close harmony with general commodity prices.

2. Although the tariff has exerted some influence on the price of wool it has usually been secondary to other factors.

3. Wars have had a much more pronounced effect on wool prices than the tariff.

I. Index Numbers of Wholesale Prices of All Commodities
and of Wool (Fine Washed Clothing, Ohio Fleece)
in the United States, 1860-89 (1860 = 100)

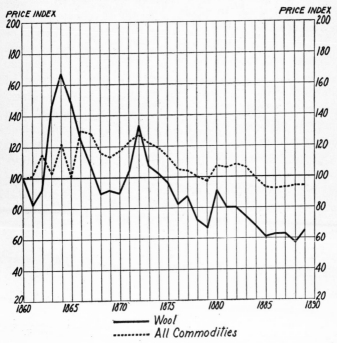

Index Number of Prices of All Commodities in the United States from U. S. Senate Report, No. 1394 ("The Aldrich Report") 52d Congress, 2d Session.

Index Number of Wool Prices based on quotations in Statistical Abstract of the U. S.

II. Index Numbers of Wholesale Prices of All Commodities and of Wool (Port Phillip Good Greasy Average) in England, 1860-89. (1860 = 100)

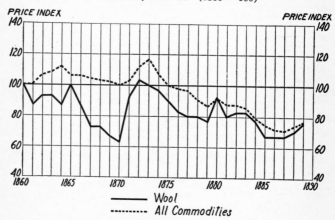

— Wool
---------- All Commodities

Index Number of Prices of All Commodities in England from Bulletin of U. S. Bureau of Labor Statistics, No. 284, p. 85.

Index Number of Price of Port Phillip Good Greasy Average in the London Market constructed from prices in C. W. Wright's "Wool-Growing and the Tariff," pp. 352-3.

III. Index Numbers of Wholesale Prices of All Commodities
and of Wool (Fine Washed Clothing, Ohio Fleece) in
the United States, 1890-1910.   (1890-99 = 100)

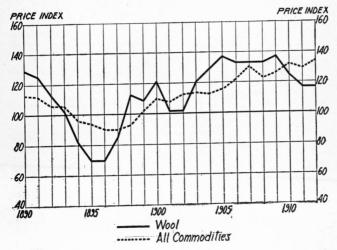

——— Wool
------- All Commodities

Index Number of Prices of All Commodities in the United
States from Bulletin of U. S. Bureau of Labor Statistics, No. 173,
p. 126.

Index Number of Wool Prices based on quotations in Statistical
Abstract of the U. S.

IV. Index Numbers of Wholesale Prices of All Commodities
and of Wool (Port Phillip Good Greasy Average)
in England, 1890-1910. (1890-99 = 100)

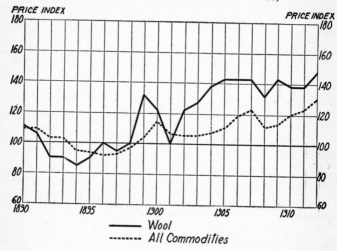

Index Number of Prices of All Commodities in England from
Bulletin of U. S. Bureau of Labor Statistics, No. 284, p. 85.

Index Number of Price of Port Phillip Good Greasy Average
in the London Market constructed from prices in C. W. Wright's
"Wool-Growing and the Tariff," pp. 352-3 (from 1890-1902) and
from "Statistics Relating to the Worsted and Woollen Trades of
the United Kingdom," published by the Bradford Chamber of
Commerce (1902-1910).

V. Index Numbers of Wholesale Prices of All Commodities
and of Wool (Fine Washed Clothing, Ohio Fleece)
in the United States, 1913-24. (1913 = 100)

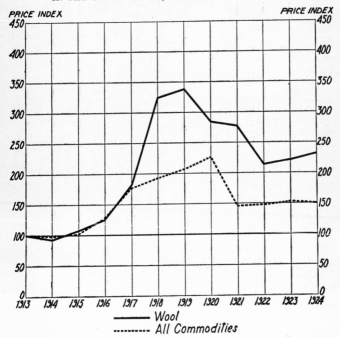

————— Wool
·········· All Commodities

Index Number of Prices of All Commodities in the United
States from Bulletin of U. S. Bureau of Labor Statistics, No. 335,
p. 9, and from U. S. Department of Commerce, Survey of Current
Business. Index Number of Wool Prices based on quotations in
Statistical Abstract of the U. S.

VI. INDEX NUMBERS OF WHOLESALE PRICES OF ALL COMMODITIES
AND OF WOOL (PORT PHILLIP GOOD GREASY AVERAGE)
IN ENGLAND, 1913-24.   (1913 = 100)

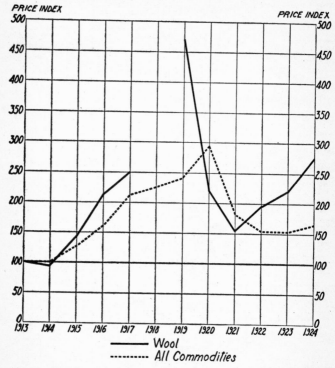

——— Wool
--------- All Commodities

Index Number of Prices of All Commodities from Harvard
Review of Economic Statistics, June, 1923, p. 159. 1923 and 1924
from London Statist.

Index Number of Price of Port Phillip Good Greasy Average,
London market, from "Statistics Relating to the Worsted and
Woollen Trades of the United Kingdom," published by the Brad-
ford Chamber of Commerce, and from Annual Wool Review of
the "Bulletin of the National Association of Wool Manufacturers"
(U. S.), 1924.

APPENDIX B

PRICE TRENDS

The following tables of index numbers indicate (1) the movements of commodity prices in the United States in recent years, and (2) the changes in the relative prices of woolen goods during the last decade and a half. The figures are taken from the U. S. Bureau of Labor Statistics.

INDEX NUMBERS OF WHOLESALE PRICES, BY GROUPS OF COMMODITIES *

(1913 = 100)

Year and Month	Farm Products	Food	Cloths and Clothing	Fuel and Lighting	Metals and Metal Products	Building Materials	Chemicals and Drugs	House Furnishing Goods	All Commodities
1921									
Average for year.....	124	144	180	199	129	165	136	195	147
January	143	162	196	247	153	192	153	217	170
February	133	151	188	225	147	180	149	217	160
March	127	151	183	212	140	173	143	216	155
April	117	144	176	205	138	167	135	216	148
May	118	139	173	200	138	165	134	209	145
June	114	137	172	191	133	163	133	196	142
July	119	141	172	186	124	160	129	180	141
August	123	146	171	184	117	156	129	179	142
September	124	142	178	181	116	156	131	179	141
October	124	140	180	189	116	159	131	180	142
November	121	139	180	197	114	163	129	178	141
December	120	136	180	199	113	158	127	178	140
1922									
Average for year.....	133	138	181	218	122	168	124	176	149
January	122	131	176	195	112	157	124	178	138
February	131	135	174	191	110	156	123	177	141
March	130	137	172	191	109	155	125	175	142
April	129	137	171	194	113	156	124	175	143
May	132	138	175	216	119	160	122	176	148

* Source: United States Department of Labor, Bureau of Labor Statistics, Bulletin No. 390, *Wholesale Prices, 1890 to 1924,* pages 16-23.

INDEX NUMBERS OF WHOLESALE PRICES, BY GROUPS OF COMMODITIES—*Continued*

Year and Month	Farm Products	Food	Cloths and Clothing	Fuel and Lighting	Metals and Metal Products	Building Materials	Chemicals and Drugs	House Furnishing Goods	All Commodities
June	131	140	179	225	120	167	122	176	150
July	135	142	180	254	121	170	121	173	155
August	131	138	181	271	126	172	122	173	155
September	133	138	183	244	134	180	124	173	153
October	138	140	188	226	135	183	124	176	154
November	143	143	192	218	133	185	127	179	156
December	145	144	194	216	131	185	130	182	156
1923									
Average for year.....	141	144	200	185	144	189	131	183	154
January	143	141	196	218	133	188	131	184	156
February	142	141	199	212	139	192	132	184	157
March	143	143	201	206	149	198	135	185	159
April	141	144	205	200	154	204	136	187	159
May	139	144	201	190	152	202	134	187	156
June	138	142	198	186	148	194	131	187	153
July	135	141	193	183	145	190	128	187	151
August	139	142	193	178	145	186	127	183	150
September	144	147	202	176	144	182	128	183	154
October	144	148	199	172	142	182	129	183	153
November	146	148	201	167	141	181	130	176	152
December	145	147	203	163	142	178	130	176	151
1924									
Average for year.....	143	144	191	170	135	175	130	173	150
January	144	143	200	169	142	181	132	176	151
February	143	143	196	180	143	182	131	176	152
March	137	141	191	181	144	182	130	175	150
April	139	137	189	179	139	182	128	175	148
May	136	137	187	177	135	180	127	173	147
June	134	136	187	175	132	173	127	171	145
July	141	139	188	173	130	169	127	171	147
August	145	144	190	170	130	169	130	171	150
September	143	148	187	168	128	171	131	171	149
October	149	152	188	162	127	171	132	171	152
November	150	154	190	163	129	172	134	172	153
December	157	158	191	165	133	175	135	172	157
1925									
Average for year	158	158	190	175	130	175	134	169	159
January	163	160	191	168	136	179	135	173	160
February	162	157	191	178	136	183	135	173	161
March	161	159	191	174	134	180	134	170	161
April	153	154	190	169	129	174	134	171	156
May	152	153	188	168	127	174	133	171	155
June	155	155	188	173	126	171	133	170	157
July	162	157	189	172	126	170	133	169	160
August	163	159	190	170	127	172	135	169	160
September	160	160	189	169	127	174	136	168	160
October	155	158	190	172	128	174	135	168	158
November	154	160	188	175	130	176	135	166	158
December	152	157	187	175	130	177	135	166	156

INDEX NUMBERS OF RELATIVE WHOLESALE PRICES OF WOOLEN GOODS
1910 TO JUNE 1924 *
(1913 = 100; Based on Average Price per Yard)

Year	Flannels White, 4-4 Ballard Vale No. 3	Suiting- Clay Worsted; Diagonal, 16-oz.	Women's Dress Goods— French Serge 35- 36 in.	Men's Union Suits: 33% Worsted
1910................	100.4	105.6	106.8	100.00
1911................	92.8	92.1	102.7	100.0
1912................	97.5	101.8	100.5	100.0
1913................	100.0	100.0	100.0	100.0
1914................	98.1	92.8	92.5	100.0
1915................	102.4	107.1	95.3	100.0
1916................	111.2	144.4	129.2	110.7
1917................	157.1	226.1	216.3	163.8
1918................	190.2	308.4	271.8	239.6
1919................	187.1	227.9	273.3	239.6
1920................	223.6	361.5	328.1	470.8
1921................	176.9	192.2	219.9	274.6
1922................	202.0	196.5	200.9	284.4
1923................	219.4	232.7	228.2	299.5
1924................	215.8	219.2	234.9	306.9
1925................	222.9	217.4	242.1	309.6
1921				
Jan.	176.9	243.3	286.6	289.4
Feb.	176.9	206.8	219.7	289.4
Mar.	176.9	186.3	219.7	289.4
Apr.	176.9	185.6	219.7	269.6
May	176.9	185.6	219.7	269.6
June	176.9	185.6	219.7	269.6
July	176.9	185.6	219.7	269.6
Aug.	176.9	185.6	219.7	269.6
Sept.	176.9	185.6	219.7	269.6
Oct.	176.9	185.6	200.0	269.6
Nov.	176.9	185.6	197.0	269.6
Dec.	176.9	185.6	197.0	269.6
1922				
Jan.	176.9	184.2	197.0	269.6
Feb.	176.9	180.7	197.0	269.6
Mar.	176.9	180.7	197.0	269.6
Apr.	194.2	180.7	197.0	269.6
May	200.1	180.7	197.0	269.6
June	205.0	201.4	197.0	269.6
July	215.8	204.6	197.0	299.5
Aug.	215.8	195.4	197.0	299.5

* For data, 1910-1922, see *Bulletin* 335, U. S. Department of Labor, Bureau of Labor Statistics. Since 1922, see *Wholesale Prices of Commodities*, monthly bulletin published by U. S. Bureau of Labor Statistics.

Year	Flannels White, 4-4 Ballard Vale No. 3	Suiting- Clay Worsted; Diagonal, 16-oz.	Women's Dress Goods— French Serge 35- 36 in.	Men's Union Suits: 33% Worsted
1922 (*continued*)				
Sept.	215.8	195.4	197.0	299.5
Oct.	215.8	214.0	198.4	299.5
Nov.	215.8	219.8	219.7	299.5
Dec.	215.8	219.8	219.7	299.5
1923				
Jan.	215.8	218.2	219.7	299.5
Feb.	215.8	214.9	223.5	299.5
Mar.	215.8	214.9	227.3	299.5
Apr.	224.4	247.5	227.3	299.5
May	224.4	247.5	227.3	299.5
June	224.4	....	227.3	299.5
July	224.4	236.1	227.3	299.5
Aug.	224.4	236.1	227.3	299.5
Sept.	215.8	236.1	227.3	299.5
Oct.	215.8	236.1	234.9	299.5
Nov.	215.8	236.1	234.9	299.5
Dec.	215.8	236.1	234.9	299.5
1924				
Jan.	215.8	218.2	234.9	299.5
Feb.	215.8	218.2	234.9	299.5
Mar.	215.8	218.2	234.9	299.5
Apr.	215.8	218.2	234.9	309.6
May	215.8	218.2	234.9	309.6
June	215.8	218.2	234.9	309.6
July	215.8	218.2	234.9	309.6
Aug.	215.8	215.2	234.9	309.6
Sept.	215.8	211.7	234.9	309.6
Oct.	215.8	223.7	234.9	309.6
Nov.	215.8	226.3	234.9	309.6
Dec.	215.8	226.3	234.9	309.6
1925				
Jan.	215.8	226.3	237.5	309.6
Feb.	215.8	226.3	242.4	309.6
Mar.	224.4	226.3	242.4	309.6
Apr.	224.4	226.3	242.4	309.6
May	224.4	226.3	242.4	309.6
June	224.4	226.3	242.4	309.6
July	224.4	226.3	242.4	309.6
Aug.	224.4	226.3	242.4	309.6
Sept.	224.4	198.2	242.4	309.6
Oct.	224.4	197.0	242.4	309.6
Nov.	224.4	201.7	242.4	309.6
Dec.	224.4	201.9	242.4	309.6

INDEX NUMBERS OF WHOLESALE PRICES OF SELECTED FABRICS AND APPAREL COMPARED WITH ALL COMMODITIES
(U. S. BUREAU OF LABOR STATISTICS INDEX, 1913 = 100)

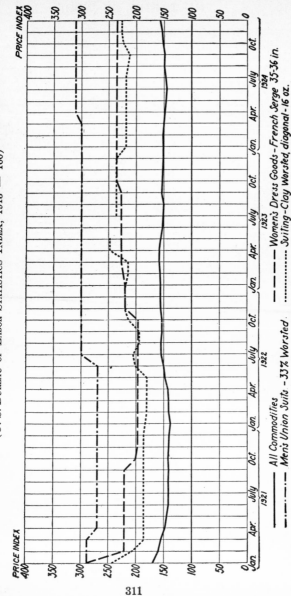

APPENDIX C

CARPET WOOLS: THEIR PRODUCTION, MARKETING, AND USES

A brief review of the conditions under which the various kinds of carpet wool are grown, prepared, and marketed, and a consideration of their uses, will bring out their non-competitive character. Much of this kind of wool does not enter into the world's commerce, but is woven on hand looms into garments by the natives of the countries where it is grown. Of that which enters into the United States, 90 to 95 per cent is used for making carpets or miscellaneous articles like felt boots, horse blankets, coarse upholstery goods, paper-makers' felt aprons, and wadding for gun cartridges.[1] Some varieties are scarcely better than animal hair, and are so mixed with all kinds of impurities that they scarcely deserve the name of wool.

Almost all of the countries of western Europe produce at least small quantities of the carpet wool used in the United States. Pyrenean wool comes from both the French and Spanish sides of the Pyrenees Mountains. The French variety is coarser and longer in staple, and more uniform than the Spanish. The Balearic Islands and Corsica also furnish some carpet wool. The former is similar to the Pyrenean; the latter is gray, brown and black, and of long staple. Scottish "black-face," grown

[1] U. S. Tariff Board, *Report on Schedule K,* p. 413.

in the highlands north of the Firth of Clyde and in the western highlands of Scotland, is one of the most important kinds. Very little is utilized by local manufacturers or spinners in Scotland, most of it being sent to the larger markets for sale. Some is of sufficiently high quality so that it is used in the manufacture of braids, or mixed with finer wools in the manufacture of homespun cloth or of other goods having a rough finish. The "heide," or heath wool, which is similar to Scotch "blackface," comes from Germany, Iceland, Norway, Finland, the Faroe Islands, and Russia. Some "pulled wool" comes from the tanneries of Naples. The island of Sardinia supplies wool of a carpet grade, small quantities of which are used in the United States.

Russia has always been one of the largest producers of carpet wool. In southern Russia most of the wool is of the Merino type, but the proportion of Merino grown in the country as a whole is small. The grades of Russian cahpet wool most familiar to American users, Douskoi and Savolga, come principally from the market at Rostov on the Don and from the region beyond the Volga. The Georgian wools called Toucha, Nouka, and Tartar or Tarakama, are also used in the United States. All these are strictly carpet wools and are coarse and harsh. In the Transcaspian region sheep raising is carried on by Turkomen, who are nomads of the steppes and sandy plains. The wool, which is harsh, colored, and dirty, was purchased in small amounts before the war by United States importers. Other varieties of Russian wool are the Merv, Bockhara, Afghan, Turkestan, Fergana, and Semirechi, all of which are similar in nature to the kinds described above.

Considerable wool is raised in Southeastern Europe and

in Asia Minor. Sheep raising is the chief occupation of Macedonian and Albanian peasants, who are mountaineers living under primitive conditions. Three kinds of wool are produced in Bulgaria: first, the Karnobat wool, soft and lustrous, which is used in making fine carpets; second, an average grade of wool having no special characteristics; and third, a coarse variety produced by the sheep belonging to Roumanian nomads. There are no special trade names for the two latter varieties. The wool which comes from Hungary, Bosnia, and Herzegovina is known as Zackel wool. Some of it is long-staple, but it is all coarse and is used for low-grade carpets.

Asiatic wools are all strictly carpet wools, with three exceptions: China lambs' wool, China ball wool, and Bagdad wool. The finest imported rugs and carpets come from Asia Minor, and from that region also are imported some of the best varieties of carpet wools. Three classes of wool are produced in Turkey,—namely, the Roumelian, Anatolian, and the Syrian. Under the first class the varieties best known in America are the Adrianople (placed in Class I in 1897), and the Kassapbatchi, a pulled wool which comes from the tanneries of Constantinople; under the second class the best known are the Smyrna and the Angora wools, which are of good length and quality but shrink heavily; under the third class, the Aleppo, and Damascus varieties, which are excellent carpet wools, and are usually imported in the washed state. The wool known as "Bagdad" is used at times in making cloth. It comes from lower Mesopotamia, a fertile country where the sheep are well cared for. The proportion of gray hairs and colored fibre in it is, however, sometimes as high as 40 per cent, so that it is supplemental to, rather than competitive with, American wool, although it also was placed in Class I in 1897.

Most of India has too hot a climate for successful sheep raising, but in the mountains and in the northern part of India, notably that region known as the Punjab, there is considerable sheep raising. There are more than 20,000,000 sheep in the whole country; but the average weight of fleece is only between two and three pounds. A large part of the Indian wool, which is exported to England and marketed in Liverpool, is taken from improved sheep rather than from the native sheep; yet it must be classed as carpet wool. It appears to be a mass of tufts, which look as though they had been pulled from the animal. Practically all Indian wool is marketed in a partially washed condition. The wool is bought up by native merchants at fairs and bazaars in the large towns, and is sold by them to the British importers. The principal varieties received from Bombay are the Joria, which is sometimes used in the manufacture of cloth and blankets, and the Vicanere, which is not quite as high in grade but is sometimes used in rough cheviots and "homespun." Wools from Afghanistan and Baluchistan are received in Bombay and Karachi, reassorted and exported. The Kandahar, from Afghanistan, is a high-grade carpet wool used in Wiltons, Brussels, and Axminsters while the Kelat Baluchistan is shorter and of poorer quality. Jesulmere is used only for filling, while Marwar is little better than goat hair. Although the number of sheep in the Madras Presidency is greater than in other sections of India, the wool is principally black or gray and of a hairy nature, and little of it is exported.

From one-third to one-half of the carpet wools used in this country come from China. The leading wool-growing provinces of China are Shantung, Mongolia, Manchuria, Kansu, and Szechwan. Wool is the leading item of export from Tientsin to the United States, and that port and Shanghai export practically all the wool coming out of China. Over 40,000,000 pounds of wool are exported each year. The amount used in China is also large although no statistics of production are available. The Chinese use lambskins and sheepskins for lining garments, but the principal product of the industry is mutton, rather than wool.

Most of the carpet wool which comes from Africa is grown in the northern part of the continent. Wool from Egypt and the Anglo-Egyptian Sudan is usually a by-product of sheep raising for mutton production. Bedouin sheep find pasturage on the cultivated borders of the desert. The industry is carried on under primitive conditions, and the wool is of low grade. Most of the Egyptian wool is exported to England. There are nomadic tribes in Algeria which have large flocks of sheep. It is said that the prototype of the Spanish Merino came originally from the plateaus of the Atlas Mountains. Algerian wools are classified into Arab wools, and Kabyle wools. The former are soft and elastic, while the latter, from open fleece sheep, are hard and glossy. The classification of native wools and colonists' wools is also sometimes used. Adulteration of the fleece by fine sand is common, and has given the Algerian wools a bad reputation. Poor wools have often been indiscriminately mixed with better wools, also. Some wool is raised in Tunisia by European settlers, but most of it is grown by native farmers. The Merino, crossbred, and fine Tunisia wools are used for textile purposes, but the coarse Tunisia is used only for stuffing mattresses. Most of the wool is used in the domestic industries, and some is sent to France; but the Tunisian wools are little used in the United States.

The only other source of carpet wool used in the United States is South America. This is designated in the tariff as "native South America," "Cordova," "Valparaiso," or "other wool of like character or description." [2] The native South American sheep are known as the Criollo breed. Their numbers are decreasing as improvement of the flocks progresses, but enough are still found in Chile, and in the provinces of Cordova and San Luis in Argentina, so that a considerable amount of this wool is available. Most of the Valparaiso and Cordova wool is of excellent quality for carpet making.

It is evident that by far the greater part of the carpet wool produced throughout the world is not adapted to the manufacture of fine goods. It comes from nondescript sheep which receive little attention. The methods of shearing and sacking the wool often cause it to deteriorate still further. Now and then small lots are adapted to the manufacture of cloth, and certain grades are regularly used in the manufacture of tweeds, homespuns, and other rough goods. But it offers little direct competition with American wool.

The changes in the sources of supply of carpet wool in late years are not striking. The most noteworthy difference is the absence of Russia from the list. The increase in the total amount of carpet wool imported into the United States is considerable.

[2] The Tariff Act of 1922, Paragraph 1101.

APPENDIX D

INQUIRY AS TO THE BEST METHOD OF CALCU-LATING COSTS IN CASES OF JOINT PRODUCTION

The following charts illustrate the difficulty of determining the cost of production of a commodity produced jointly with another. The conclusion reached by this study is that when two commodities produced jointly are of nearly the same importance it is best to allocate joint costs on the basis of the receipts which accrue to each product respectively. When, on the other hand, one commodity is clearly of major and the other distinctly of minor importance, it is best to subtract receipts from the sale of the by-product from total expenses of production, and to regard the balance as the cost of production of the major product.

The following charts show that both the foregoing methods are open to objection; that they both encounter logical difficulties. It is a question of expediency as to which method should be used. Expediency plainly dictates the use of the former method in the case of wool; and it was that method which was used by the U. S. Tariff Commission in its investigation of the cost of production of wool in 1918-21. The latter method was used by the U. S. Tariff Board in 1910-11.

So many commodities are produced jointly that the question as to which method is preferable frequently recurs. The conclusion reached in this instance is one which seems to have general applicability, and it is herewith presented not only for its bearing upon the question of wool costs but also for its wider significance.

The diagrams which illustrate this cost analysis are numbered from I to X, and are shown on pages 322-332. Figure I gives the results of the Tariff Board method of finding the cost of production of wool: from the total expense per head, deduct the returns from mutton; the balance is the "cost of production" of the wool. This diagram uses, first, the figures for expenses and receipts obtained by the Tariff Board in 1910-11, and second, the figures of the Tariff Commission obtained in 1918.

Figures II and III portray the fact that the cost of production of wool and the profits made in the sheep industry are just as dependent upon the returns from mutton as on the returns from wool; that the expense per head may remain the same, yet the cost of production of wool may go up or down as the returns from the sale of mutton and lamb fluctuate; and that the influence of this *joint product,* mutton, upon the cost of wool is much greater than would be the influence of a genuine *by-product*. The letter fact is further illustrated by figure IV. The total receipts from cottonseed, linters, and other by-products are about 12½ per cent of the total receipts for the cotton crop. A pronounced fluctuation in these receipts affects the costs and profits in the industry much less than a fluctuation in mutton receipts affects the sheep industry.

Figure V shows that the receipts from molasses would have to be multiplied several times in order to reduce appreciably the net cost of sugar production. It is interesting to note that the "Tariff Board method" was followed by the Tariff Commission in computing the cost of production of sugar, and that the method was criticized by some sugar producers on the ground that in some instances molasses becomes a very important product of the industry. In such cases, they maintained, the costs should be apportioned. Such instances are sufficiently rare, however, so that the method followed was satisfactory in application.

In figure VI mutton is regarded as the main product, and its "cost" is ascertained by the Tariff Board method; that is, receipts from wool are set off against the total expenses and the balance is designated the "cost" of the mutton. This method is applied to the figures for receipts and expenses obtained by the Tariff Board in 1910-11, and by the Tariff Commission in 1918. It is shown that the profit on mutton and net returns per head increased greatly. This diagram VI and figures VII and VIII illustrate the fact that when mutton is considered the main product and wool the by-product, and the Tariff Board method of finding cost is employed, the "cost" of mutton depends as directly on the returns from wool, as did the cost of wool on returns from mutton when we used the converse method. Compare figures II and III with figures VII and VIII.

In figure IX a new method is applied: expenses are apportioned between wool and mutton in the same ratio as the receipts from each. By this method, an increase or decrease in the receipts from one of the joint products does not affect the cost of the other product in such a pronounced manner.

In figure X a third method is applied,—that of the Tariff Commission in 1918. Expenses which can be directly traced to wool are charged to it, while the remaining expenses are apportioned between wool and mutton. This method reflects the true state of affairs even more closely than Method 2 shown in figure IX. The cost of wool decreases from 18 cents a pound to 15.4 cents a pound, while the profit per pound increases from 2 cents a pound to 4.6 cents a pound.

Under the third, or Tariff Commission method, the cost of wool appears somewhat higher. By this method, wool is made to bear an increased share of the cost because of the increasing proportion of the returns which come from that source. Both Method 2 and Method 3 give results which are less capricious than Method 1. They afford the means of finding the cost of production of joint products at one and the same time, without duplication in the figures; and they do not err in ascribing all the profit of the industry to one product. They are predicated on an assumption, which may or may not be true, that the increase in receipts for one of the joint products is an index of a corresponding increase in costs for that product. But the Tariff Board method, on the other hand, assumes that an increase in the returns from one of the joint-products is an indication of a decrease in costs for the other joint-product, which may or may not be true. Since none of the methods is free from logical weakness, the most expedient method should be adopted; and this appears to be the third or Tariff Commission method.

1. Cost Method Used By Tariff Board

I. Cost of Wool in 1910 and 1918

From the total expense per head, deduct the returns from mutton; the balance is the "cost of production" of the wool.

Item	A. (1910)	B. (1918)
Returns from wool	$1.15	$4.32
"　　" 　　mutton	1.40	4.50
Receipts per head	$2.55	$8.82
Expense per head	2.11	6.64
Net profit	$ .44	$2.18
Total expense minus receipts from mutton equals "cost" of wool............	.71	2.14
"Cost" of mutton equals receipts from mutton	1.40	4.50

From 1910 to 1918 the price of wool went up; returns from mutton increased (number of pounds of each remaining the same); expense per head and "cost of production" of wool both went up; profit per pound on wool and net returns per head both increased greatly.

II. COST OF WOOL, WITH MUTTON RETURNS INCREASING AND WOOL RETURNS DECREASING

Total Receipts $2.80

A.

| MUTTON COST = RECEIPTS FROM MUTTON $1.40 | WOOL COST $.70 | NET PROFIT $.70 |

Receipts from Wool $1.40

Total Expense $2.10

Total Receipts $2.85

B.

| MUTTON COST = RECEIPTS FROM MUTTON $1.80 | WOOL COST $.30 | NET PROFIT $.75 |

Wool Receipts $1.05

Total Expense $2.10

From the total expense per head, deduct the returns from mutton; the balance is the "cost of production" of the wool.

Item	A.	B.
Returns from wool (7 lbs. at 20¢)..........	$1.40	$1.05 (7 lbs. at 15¢)
Returns from mutton	1.40	1.80
Receipts per head	$2.80	$2.85
Expense per head	2.10	2.10
Net Profit	$0.70	$0.75
Total expense minus receipts from mutton equals "Cost of Wool"	.70	.30
Cost of wool per pound....................	.10	.043
Cost of mutton equals receipts from mutton..	1.40	1.80

In this hypothetical case, price of wool goes down (from A. to B.); returns from mutton go up; expense per head remains the same; "cost of production" of wool goes down; profit per pound on wool and net returns per head both increase.

III. Cost of Wool, with Mutton Returns Decreasing and Wool Returns Increasing

Total Receipts $2.80

A.

MUTTON COST= RECEIPTS FROM MUTTON $ 1.40	WOOL COST $.70	NET PROFIT $.70

Receipts from Wool $1.40
Total Expense $2.10

Total Receipts $2.75

B.

MUTTON COST= RECEIPTS FROM MUTTON $ 1.00	WOOL COST $1.10	NET PROFIT $.65

Receipts from Wool $1.75
Total Expense $2.10

From the total expense per head, deduct returns from mutton; the balance is the "cost of production" of the wool.

Item	A.	B.
Returns from wool, 7 lbs. at 20¢ lb...........	$1.40	$1.75 (7 lbs. at 25¢ lb.)
Returns from mutton	1.40	1.00
Receipts per head	$2.80	$2.75
Expense per head	2.10	2.10
Net Profit	$0.70	.65
Total expense minus receipts from mutton equals "cost" of wool	.70	1.10
"Cost" of mutton equals receipts from mutton	$1.40	$1.00

In this hypothetical case the price of wool goes up (from A. to B.); returns from mutton go down; expense per head remains the same; cost of production of wool goes up; profit per pound on wool and net returns per head both decrease.

IV. COST OF COTTON, WITH BY-PRODUCT RETURNS DECREASING

Total Receipts $.30

NET COST OF COTTON. 16.25¢	RECEIPTS FROM BY-PRODUCTS 3.75¢	**NET PROFIT** 10¢

A.

├──── Total Expense, $.20 ────┤

Total Receipts $.28

NET COST OF COTTON 18.25¢	BY-PRODUCT RECEIPTS 1.75¢	**NET PROFIT** 8¢

B.

├──── Total Expense $.20 ────┤

From the total expense per pound, deduct receipts for by-products; the balance is the "cost of production" of the cotton.

A. Total Receipts .... 30¢ per lb.
    Cotton, 26.25 cents
    Seed and Linters 3.75 cents
  Total Expense .... 20¢ per lb.

    Net Profit .... 10¢ per lb.

B. Total Receipts .... 28¢ per lb.
    Cotton 26.25 cents
    Seed and Linters 1.75 cents
  Total Expense .... 20¢ per lb.

    Net Profit .... 8¢ per lb.

A reduction of over 50% in the returns from by-products reduces the net profit only 20%.

V. Cost of Sugar, with Molasses Returns Increasing

Total Receipts 5.06

A. | NET COST OF SUGAR 3.88¢ | NET RECEIPTS MOLASSES | NET PROFIT 2¢ |

Total Expense 5.04

Total Receipts 6.48

B. | NET COST OF SUGAR 3.4¢ | RECEIPTS FROM MOLASSES .6¢ | NET PROFIT 2.48¢ |

Total Expense 5.04

From the total expense per pound, deduct receipts for by-products; the balance is the "cost of production" of the sugar.

A. Total Receipts .... 6¢   per lb.
    Sugar 5.88 cents
    Molasses .12 cents
    Total Expense .... 4¢   per lb.

    Net Profit .... 2¢   per lb.

B. Total Receipts .... 6.48¢ per lb.
    Sugar 5.88 cents
    Molasses .60 cents
    Total Expense .... 4¢   per lb.

    Net Profit .... 2.48¢ per lb.

A 400 per cent increase in receipts from molasses only increases the net profit by 24%.

VI. Cost of Mutton in 1910 and 1918

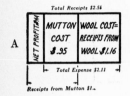

A

Total Receipts $2.55

| NET PROFIT | MUTTON COST $.95 | WOOL COST= RECEIPTS FROM WOOL $1.16 |

Total Expense $2.11

Receipts from Mutton $1.~

B.

Total Receipts $8.82

| NET PROFIT $2.18 | MUTTON COST $2.32 | WOOL COST= RECEIPTS FROM WOOL $ 4.32 |

Total Expense $6.64

Receipts from Mutton $4.50

Mutton considered principal product.

Returns from wool set off as a credit against expenses and balance considered as "cost of production" of mutton.

Item	A. (1910)	B. (1918)
Returns from mutton	$1.39	$4.50
Returns from wool	1.16	4.32
Receipts per head	$2.55	$8.82
Expense per head	2.11	6.64
Net Profit	$0.44	$2.18
Total expense minus receipts from wool equals "cost" of mutton	.95	2.32
Cost of wool equals receipts from wool......	1.16	4.32

From 1910 to 1918 the price of mutton went up; the price of wool increased; expense per head also increased; "cost of production" of mutton increased but the profit on mutton and net returns per head increased greatly.

VII. Cost of Mutton, with Mutton Returns Constant and
Wool Returns Increasing

Total Receipts $2.80

A.

| NET PROFIT $.70 | MUTTON COST $.70 | WOOL COST = RECEIPTS FROM WOOL $1.40 |

Receipts from Mutton $1.40

Total Expense $2.10

Total Receipts $3.50

Γ.

| NET PROFIT $1.40 | WOOL COST = RECEIPTS FROM WOOL $2.10 |

Receipts from Mutton $1.40

Total Expense $2.10

Mutton considered principal product.

Returns from wool set off as a credit against expenses
and balance considered as "cost of production" of mutton.

Item	A.	B.
Returns from mutton	$1.40	$1.40
"　　" 　wool	1.40	2.10
Receipts per head	$2.80	$3.50
Expense per head	2.10	2.10
Net Profit	$0.70	$1.40
Total expense minus receipts from wool equals "cost" of mutton	.70	0
"Cost" of wool equals receipts from wool.....	1.40	2.10

In this hypothetical case returns from mutton remain
the same; expense per head remains the same; returns
from wool increase by 50%; "cost" of mutton goes down
to zero; profit on mutton increases from 70¢ a head to
$1.40 a head; net returns per head are doubled.

VIII. Cost of Mutton, with Mutton Returns Constant and
Wool Returns Decreasing

Total Receipts $2.80

A.

| NET PROFIT $.70 | MUTTON COST $.70 | WOOL COST= RECEIPTS FROM WOOL $1.40 |

Receipts from Mutton $1.40

Total Expense $2.10

Total Receipts $2.40

B.

| NET PROFIT $.30 | MUTTON COST $1.10 | WOOL COST= RECEIPTS FROM WOOL $1.00 |

Receipts from Mutton $1.40

Total Expense $2.10

Mutton considered principal product.

Returns from wool set off as a credit against expenses and balance considered as "cost of production" of mutton.

Item	A.	B.
Returns from mutton	$1.40	$1.40
" " wool	1.40	1.00
Receipts per head	$2.80	$2.40
Expense per head	2.10	2.10
Net Profit	$0.70	$0.30
Total expense minus receipts from wool equals "cost" of mutton	.70	1.10
"Cost" of wool equals receipts from wool.....	1.40	1.00

In this hypothetical case returns from mutton remain the same; expense per head remains the same; returns from wool decrease; "cost" of mutton increases; profit on mutton decreases; net returns per head decrease.

2. Apportionment Method of Determining Cost

IX. Cost of Wool, with Mutton Returns Increasing and Wool Returns Constant

Total Receipts $2.80

A.

MUTTON EXPENSE $1.05	WOOL EXPENSE $1.05	MUTTON PROFIT $.35	WOOL PROFIT $.35

←— Net Profit $.70 —→

←———————— Total Expense $2.10 ————————→

Total Receipts $3.50

B.

MUTTON EXPENSE $1.26	WOOL EXPENSE $.84	MUTTON PROFIT $.84	WOOL PROFIT $.56

←——— Net Profit $1.40 ———→

←———————— Total Expense $2.10 ————————→

Expenses apportioned between wool and mutton in the same ratio as the receipts from each.

Item	A.	B.
Returns from wool, 7 lbs. at 20¢.............	$1.40	$1.40 (7 lbs. at 20¢)
"　　"　　mutton	1.40	2.10
Receipts per head	$2.80	$3.50
Expense per head	2.10	2.10
Net Profit	$0.70	$1.40
Returns from wool	50%	40%
"　　"　　mutton	50%	60%

Expense charged vs. wool (in A) = $1.05 ÷ 7 lbs. = 15¢ lb.; (in B) = 84¢ ÷ 7 = 12¢ lb.

Expense charged vs. mutton (in A) = $1.05; (in B) = $1.26.

Profit per lb. on wool (in A) = 5¢; (in B) = 8¢.

Total profit on wool (in A) = 35¢; (in B) = 56¢.

Total profit on mutton (in A) = 35¢; (in B) = 84¢.

In this hypothetical case the price of wool remains the same; expense per head remains the same; returns from mutton increase by 50%; profit on mutton increases from 35¢ to 84¢; cost of wool decreases from 15¢ to 12¢ lb.; profit on wool increases from 5¢ lb. to 8¢ lb.; net returns per head doubled.

3. Modified Apportionment or Tariff Commission Method

X. Cost of Wool, with Mutton Returns Increasing and Wool Returns Constant

Total Receipts $2.80

A.

| MUTTON EXPENSE $.85 | WOOL EXPENSE $1.25 | MUTTON PROFIT $.55 | WOOL PROFIT $.15 |

Net Profit $.70

Total Expense $2.10

Total Receipts $3.50

B.

| MUTTON EXPENSE $1.02 | WOOL EXPENSE $1.08 | MUTTON PROFIT $1.08 | WOOL PROFIT $.32 |

Net Profit $1.40

Total Expense $2.10

Expenses which can be directly traced to wool are charged to it; shearing, dipping, wool twine and sacks, packing and marketing wool. The remaining expenses are apportioned between wool and mutton in the same way as in Method No. 2; that is, in the same ratio as receipts from each.

Item	A.	B.
Returns from wool, 7 lbs. at 20¢............	$1.40	$1.40 (7 lbs. at 20¢)
Returns from mutton	1.40	2.10
Receipts per head	$2.80	$3.50
Expense per head	2.10	2.10
Net Profit	$0.70	$1.40
Expenses for shearing, etc., are charged to wool, per head	.40	.40

$2.10 — .40 = $1.70 (balance to be apportioned).

This remainder ($1.70) apportioned 50% to each; share borne by wool $0.85

Total expense charged vs. wool $1.25
Total expense charged vs. mutton .... .85

$2.10 — .40 = $1.70 (balance to be apportioned).

Remainder ($1.70) apportioned 60% and 40%; share borne by wool $0.68

Total expense charged vs. wool $1.08
Total expense charged vs. mutton 1.02

Cost of wool (in A) 18¢ lb.; Profit on wool (in A) 2¢ lb. Cost of wool (in B) 15.45¢ lb.; Profit on wool (in B) 4.55¢ lb.

In this hypothetical case the price of wool remains the same; expense per head remains the same; returns from mutton increase by 50%; profit on mutton increases from 55¢ to $1.08; cost of wool decreases from 18¢ lb. to 15.45¢ lb.; profit on wool increases from 2¢ lb. to 4.55¢ lb.

BIBLIOGRAPHY

A. **Official Publications**:

1. United States

   Congressional Documents

   Tariff Acts of the United States, 1789-1909, 61st Congress, 2nd session, H.D. No. 671, 1909.

   Report of the Tariff Board on Schedule K, 62nd Congress, 2nd session, H.D., No. 342, 1911.

   Senate Document No. 458, 61st Congress, 2nd session, reprint of an extract from Report No. 13, made in May, 1866, by U. S. Revenue Commission on Wool and Manufactures of Wool, 1910.

   Hearings on Tariff before Ways and Means Committee of the House, and Finance Committee of the Senate, 1890, 1894, 1897, 1909, 1913, and 1922.

   Tariff Act of 1922, 67th Congress, 2nd session, H.R. 7456, to provide revenue, to regulate commerce with foreign countries, to encourage the industries of the United States, and for other purposes, passed September 20, 1922.

   Department of Commerce

   Commerce and Navigation Reports; monthly bulletins and annual reports; statistics of imports and exports.

   Weekly Reports; notes on industry and trade in the United States and foreign countries.

Survey of Current Business; published monthly.

Monthly Bulletin on wool consumption in the United States.

Monthly Bulletin on activity of wool machinery in the United States.

U. S. Department of Commerce and Labor, *Manufacture of Woolen, Worsted and Shoddy in France and England and Jute in Scotland,* W. A. Graham Clark, Special Agent, 1908.

Special Agents Series, No. 146, by Juan Homs, Commercial Agent, Bureau of Foreign and Domestic Commerce, 1917.

Bureau of Foreign and Domestic Commerce, *Statistical Abstract of the United States,* Published annually.

Bureau of the Census, *Decennial Reports; Special Reports.*

Department of Agriculture

Yearbooks; statistics of numbers of sheep, and wool production; Marshall, F. R., *Sheep and Intensive Farming,* 1917, pp. 311-20.

Crops and Markets, weekly bulletin published by the Bureau of Agricultural Economics.

Monthly Wool Stock *Report,* published jointly by the Bureau of Agricultural Economics, Bureau of the Census, and the Department of Commerce.

Report of American Agricultural Commission to Europe, Jan. 16, 1919; observations made by American agriculturists in Great Britain, France, and Italy.

Department *Bulletin* 206, "The Wool Grower and the Wool Trade," Marshall, F. R., and

Heller, L. L., 1915; includes glossary of terms used in the wool trade.

Bureau of Markets, *Government Control of the Wool Crop of 1918-19.*

Bureau of Animal Industry, *Special Report* on the history and present condition of the sheep industry of the United States, prepared under the direction of Dr. D. E. Salmon, chief of the Bureau of Animal Industry, by Ezra A. Carman, H. A. Heath, and John Minto, 1892 (about 1,000 pages).

Department *Bulletin* No. 1214, January, 1924, "Family Living in Farm Homes, an Economic Study of 402 Farm Families in Livingston County, New York," by E. L. Kirkpatrick, Helen W. Atwater, and Ilena M. Baily, in co-operation with the New York State College of Agriculture.

Statistical *Bulletin* No. 3, "Sheep, Lamb, Mutton and Wool Statistics, year ended March 31, 1923, with comparable data for earlier years," prepared by the Bureau of Agricultural Economics, May 9, 1924.

State Department

Consular Reports, Special, Volume 9, 1892.

Special Report of Consul General Robertson of Buenos Aires, Aug. 8, 1918.

Department of Labor

Bureau of Labor Statistics, *Bulletin* No. 335, "Wholesale Prices 1890-1922."

Department of the Interior

Reclamation Service, 21st *Annual Report,* 1921-22.

Report of the Commissioner of the General Land Office to the Secretary of the Interior for the fiscal year ended June 30, 1922.

Treasury Department

U. S. Bureau of Statistics, *Special Report* relating to the imports and exports of wool and its manufactures in the United States and the principal foreign countries; also its production, consumption, and manufacture; also the tariff duties imposed on the imports of wool and the manufactures of wool from 1789 to the present time. (50th Congress, 1st session, House miscellaneous documents, No. 550.)

Federal Reserve Board, *Monthly Bulletins.*

Tariff Commission

Report on the Wool Growing Industry, 1921; "In the preparation of this report the Tariff Commission had the special and equally helpful service of Mr. Mark A. Smith, Mr. George P. Comer, and Mr. Louis G. Connor of the Commission's staff. In addition, assistance was rendered in field investigations and in the preparation of the text by Mr. J. S. Cotton and Mr. Harry Petrie in the United States, and of Mr. and Mrs. Albert Schofield in South Africa; Mr. W. I. Carney and Consul General Alfred A. Winslow in New Zealand; Mr. A. W. Ferrin, Trade Commissioner of the Department of Commerce, in Australia; and Consul General W. Henry Robertson in Argentina."

A Survey of the British Wool Manufacturing Industry, 1920; "In the preparation of this report the Commission has had the services of Dr. Arthur H. Cole."

Summary of Tariff Information, 1920, and revised edition, 1921.

"Operation of Rates in the Emergency Tariff Act," Letter from the Tariff Commission transmitting in response to Senate Resolution No. 284 of April 28, 1922, a *Report* of the operation and results of the rates carried in the Emergency Tariff Act approved May 27, 1921.

War Industries Board

"Government Regulations for handling the wool clip of 1918," as established by War Industries Board, Wool Division, May 21, 1918.

State Reports

State of Massachusetts, *Report* of the Special Committee on the Sheep Industry, Agriculture, and Related Matters, Senate Document No. 293, 1919.

2. Great Britain

Tariff Commission

Report, *The Textile Trades,* Volume 2, Part 2, London, 1905.

Report of the Agricultural Committee, with appendices, Volume 3, London, 1906.

Diplomatic and Consular Reports, Annual Series.

Special War Reports

The War and British Economic Policy, 1915.

Memorandum on War Office Contracts, paper by command 8447, London, 1917.

Report of the Departmental Committee appointed by the Board of Trade to consider the position of the textile trades after the war, British Blue Book, 1918, paper by command 9070.

3. Australia

   The Pastoral Industry of Australia, published by the Commonwealth Government, October, 1914.

   Report of the Royal Commission on the Meat Export Trade of Australia, paper by command 7896, Commonwealth of Australia, 1915.

   Statistical Bulletin No. 1, Commonwealth of Australia, Central Wool Committee, 1917-18.

   Queensland Sheep and Wool Industry, compiled and issued by the Government Intelligence and Tourist Bureau, Brisbane, 1918.

4. Canada

   Canadian Department of Agriculture, Livestock Commissioner's Branch, *The Sheep Industry in Canada, Great Britain, and the United States,* by W. A. Dryden and W. T. Ritch, Ottawa, 1911.

   Department of Trade and Commerce, *Weekly Bulletin.*

5. South Africa

   The Preparation of Wool for the Market, by Charles Mallinson, published by Union of South Africa, Department of Agriculture, Pretoria, 1912.

   South Africa as a Sheep Country, by Charles Mallinson, published by Union of South Africa, Department of Agriculture, Pretoria, 1913.

   Report by the Central Wool Committee, Union of South Africa, Department of Agriculture, on the Government purchase scheme of wool and sheep skins, up to the 31st of July, 1918.

Report by the Central Wool Committee dealing with the trade in wool, mohair, skins and hides, in South Africa, and recommendations to effect improvements in the present system, Port Elizabeth, Sept. 4, 1918.

6. Other Foreign

Argentina, *Publications* of Department of Agriculture, 1914.

Argentine International Trade, published for the Panama-Pacific Exposition.

B. **Unofficial Publications:**

1. Books

On Tariff History and Economic Position of Wool Growing

Taussig, F. W., *Tariff History of the United States* (7th edition, revised with additional material including consideration of the tariff of 1922), 1923.

Taussig, F. W., *Some Aspects of the Tariff Question* (Harvard Economic Studies, XII), 1915.

Wright, C. W., *Wool Growing and the Tariff* (Harvard Economic Studies, V.), 1910.

Connor, L. G., *A Brief History of the Sheep Industry in the United States*, Washington, Government Printing Office, 1920; (Reprinted from the Annual Report of the American Historical Association for 1918, pp. 89-197).

Bishop, James Leander, *A History of American Manufactures from 1608 to 1860:* Comprising annals of the industry of the United States in machinery, manufactures and useful arts, with a notice of the important inventions, tariffs and the results of each decennial census, 1866.

State Papers and Speeches on the Tariff, with an introduction by F. W. Taussig, published by Harvard University, 1893.

On Finance

Dewey, Davis R., *Financial History of the United States,* (8th edition), 1922.

On Technical Information Concerning Sheep and Wool

Coffey, W. C., *Productive Sheep Husbandry* (Lippincott's Farm Manuals, Edited by Kary C. Davis), 1918.

Hart, Stanley H., *Wool; The Raw Material of the Woolen and Worsted Industries,* Published by Philadelphia Textile School of the Philadelphia Museum and School of Industrial Art; edited by E. W. France, 1917.

Kleinheinz, Frank, *Sheep Management, Breeds and Judging for Schools:* A textbook for the Shepherd and Student (4th edition), 1918.

Ormerod, Frank, *Wool* (Staple Trades and Industries Series; edited by Gordon D. Knox), 1919.

Bowman, F. H., *The Structure of the Wool Fiber,* London, 1908.

Hunter, J. A., *Wool* (Pitman's' Series on Common Commodities and Industries), London, 1917.

On The Wool Growing Industry in Foreign Countries

Smith, Henry B., *The Sheep and Wool Industry of Australia:* A practical handbook for sheep farmers and wool classers with chapters on wool-buying and selling, sheep skins, and kindred products, London, 1914.

Hawkesworth, Alfred, *Australasian Sheep and Wool,* Sydney, 1911.

On Wool and the War

Gray, Howard L., *War Time Control of Industry: The Experience of England,* New York, 1918.

Hall, A. D., *Agriculture after the War,* London, 1916.

On Woolen and Worsted Manufacturing

Clapham, John Harold, *The Woolen and Worsted Industries,* London, 1907.

Barker, A. F., and Priestly, E., *Wool Carding and Combing:* with notes on sheep breeding and wool-growing, 1912.

Lipson, E., *History of the English Woolen and Worsted Industries,* London, 1921.

Lister, John, *The Manufacturing Processes of Wool and Worsted, Manchester* (England), 1911.

Customs Tariffs of the World, 1923 (annual publication by Kelly's Directories, Ltd., London).

2. Special Articles

Page, T. W., "Our Wool Duties," *North American Review,* April, 1913, Vol. 197, p. 445.

Page, T. W., "The Tariff and the Woolen Industry," *Quarterly Bulletin* of the National Association of Wool Manufacturers, June, 1913.

Taussig, F. W., "The Tariff Board Report on

Wool and Woolens," *American Economic Review*, June, 1912.

Arkell, J. Reginald, "The Present State of Sheep Breeding in Canada," *International Review of the Science and Practice of Agriculture*, October, 1917, Vol. VIII., No. 10, pp. 1333-8.

Zimmern, Dorothy, "The Wool Trade in War Time," *The Economic Journal*, March, 1918.

3. Publications of Scientific Societies and Educational Institutions

International Institute of Agriculture (Rome), April, 1913, pp. 616-7; May, 1913, pp. 680-8.

Royal Agricultural Society of England, *Journal*.

Harvard Economic Service, *The Review of Economic Statistics*, Cambridge, Mass.

Bulletin of the Imperial Institute, London, Vol. XVI, No. 4.

South Dakota College of Agriculture and the Mechanic Arts, Holmes, J. C., *Co-operative Wool Marketing*, 1921.

4. Periodicals

a. United States

The National Wool Grower, official organ of the National Association of Wool Growers, Salt Lake City, Utah, monthly.

The Breeders' Gazette, Chicago, weekly.

The American Sheep Breeder and Wool Grower, (In which is incorporated The Sheep Farmer, The Chicago Wool Journal, and the Shepherd's Guide), Chicago, Monthly.

The Monthly Bulletin, the National Association of Wool Manufacturers, Boston.

The Commercial Bulletin, Boston, weekly.

The Daily News Record, New York, daily.

The Journal of Commerce, New York, daily.

Textile Review, Boston, monthly.

b. Great Britain

The Board of Trade Journal, London, weekly.

The Statist, London, weekly.

The London *Times*, Imperial and Foreign Trade Supplement, weekly.

The British Trade Review, London, monthly.

The Economist, London, weekly.

The Wool Record and Textile World, Bradford, weekly.

The Textile Manufacturer, Manchester, monthly.

The Financial Review of Reviews, London, quarterly.

The African World and Cape Cairo Express, London, weekly.

c. Australia

The Pastoral Review, Melbourne, monthly.

d. South Africa

The Cape Times, Cape Town, daily.

The Cape Argus, Cape Town, daily.

e. South America

The South American Journal and Brazil and River Plate Mail, London, weekly.

The Buenos Aires Herald, Buenos Aires, daily.

5. Reports and Bulletins of Business Organizations

Dalgety's *Annual Wool Review*, London (The most comprehensive annual report on world production and consumption of wool).

Schwartz Buchanan and Company, *Wool Report*, London.

W. Weddell and Company, *Annual Review of the Frozen Meat Trade*, London.

Commerce, Official organ of the Sydney Chamber of Commerce, Sydney, N.S.W.

Australasian Shipping *Bulletin*, issued by S. W. Birt and Company, Ltd., Sydney, N. S. Wales.

Helmuth, Schwarze and Company, *Wool Circulars*, London.

INDEX